209

INSIDE IPOs

THE SECRETS TO INVESTING IN TODAY'S NEWEST COMPANIES

RICHARD J. PETERSON

McGraw-Hill

NEW YORK • SAN FRANCISCO • WASHINGTON, D.C. • AUCKLAND • BOGOTÁ
CARACAS • LISBON • LONDON • MADRID • MEXICO CITY • MILAN
MONTREAL • NEW DELHI • SAN JUAN • SINGAPORE
SYDNEY • TOKYO • TORONTO

Library of Congress Cataloging-in-Publication Data

Peterson, Richard J., 1955-
    Inside IPOs : the secrets to investing in today's newest companies / by Richard J. Peterson.
        p.   cm.
    ISBN 0-07-135885-4
    1. Going public (Securities) 2. Investments. I. Title
HG4028.S7 P477 2000
332.63'22—dc21   00-042390

McGraw-Hill

A Division of The McGraw·Hill Companies

1 2 3 4 5 6 7 8 9 0 AGM/AGM 0 9 8 7 6 5 4 3 2 1 0

ISBN 0-07-135885-4

The sponsoring editor for this book was Kelli Christiansen, the editing supervisor was Maureen B. Walker, and the production supervisor was Maureen Harper. It was typeset in New Century Schoolbook and Copperplate by Patricia Caruso of the Hightstown McGraw-Hill Desktop Publishing Unit.

Printed and bound by Quebecor/Martinsburg.

McGraw-Hill books are available at special quantity discounts to use as premiums and sales promotions, or for use in corporate training programs. For more information, please write to the Director of Special Sales, Professional Publishing, McGraw-Hill, Two Penn Plaza, New York, NY 10121-2298. Or contact your local bookstore.

This publication is designed to provide accurate and authoritative information in regard to the subject matter covered. It is sold with the understanding that neither the author nor the publisher is engaged in rendering legal, accounting, or other professional service. If legal advice or other expert assistance is required, the services of a competent professional person should be sought.
—*From a Declaration of Principles jointly adopted by a Committee of the American Bar Association and a Committee of Publishers.*

 This book is printed on recycled, acid-free paper containing a minimum of 50% recycled, de-inked fiber.

Contents

When television was introduced to many American families in the 1950s, it was common for youngsters to dream of being cowboys or cops. In the 1960s, when the Beatles captured our imagination, the fantasy of the moment was to be a rock star. Fast-forward to the 1990s, and instead of television cowboy Hopalong Cassidy commanding the early morning airwaves, it's now CNBC stock commentator Joe Kernan and company. Where once teenagers screamed as John Lennon sang "Money," today the under-20 venture capitalists are taking a Pete Townsend–like view of currency as they see it, feel it, and touch it. Yet, perhaps the ultimate sign of the times was when the television child actress who was featured on the 1980s situation comedy "Punky Brewster" announced that she was completing an initial public offering (IPO) to raise capital to explore a new media venture. Indeed, the times they are a-changing.

In no small part, a major contributor to these moves has been the publicity, and perhaps some puffery, associated with the explosive growth in IPOs. If, perhaps 20 years ago, a pollster had asked a random sample of individuals "What is an IPO?" it's likely that the response would have been many blank faces. However, today's investing public, fast fed on cable TV shows, Internet chat rooms, and investment newsletters, as well as blanketed with advertising on billboards, in mailboxes, and over airwaves, if confronted with the same question, would likely have a strong and seemingly keenly knowledgeable opinion of the IPO marketplace. Perhaps by chance, some may even have invested in one or two IPOs.

This ballyhoo is chiefly the result of the incredible fortunes that many have amassed by means of IPOs. Individuals who, in the opinion of some, may be no brighter than their peers, nor have the same work ethic of their contemporaries, suddenly become billionaires. Likewise, the appearance of the relative ease by which such fortunes are made seems to the common eye a much easier route to easy street than standing in line to purchase a lottery ticket or enduring rush-hour traffic in one's SUV.

Yet, just as only a select few families across America are monitored by Nielsen to determine broadcasting ratings, or a handful of individuals are chosen as a sample for an opinion poll to access a politician's popularity, so, too, within the IPO marketplace is the expression "Many are called, but few chosen" most appropriate. Furthermore, the straight line that many perceive occurs with IPOs all too often heads in a downward direction: For every successful IPO, such as Cisco Systems, America Online, or Dell Computer, there are so many more whose corporate remains litter the financial landscape—Peoples Express, Discovery Zone, and nearly every "business to consumer" Internet issue completed in the late 1990s.

However, opportunities exist in the IPO marketplace for investors if they understand how such investments operate, as well as if they learn of various alternative passages to gain entrance. The mission of this book is to serve as a primer for individuals to learn of such matters. In that regard, no secrets are unmasked, nor are any mysteries unearthed; rather, the explanations are intended to be straightforward and honest. For example, to some, the lofty gains many IPOs achieve on their first trading day may appear as actions taken by unbridled and greedy speculators to profit at all expense. Yet, the simple fact is that such strong gains are, in large part, due to the fact that many IPOs begin trading on the NASDAQ, which is a specialist-free market of buyers and sellers driving prices by raw supply and demand, rather than on the New York Stock Exchange, where each stock is assigned a specialist to control an orderly market for buying and selling and whose rules demand that, before any stock opens the day $2 above or below its previous day's close, approval must be granted by an exchange governor.

If, in my effort to shed some light on the IPO process, some individuals shy away from an investment that subsequently loses money, then I will have accomplished my objective. If, on the other hand, some readers follow the insight afforded with respect to alternative IPO objectives and wind up beating the major market averages, then my success would be that the more greater. Hopefully, such mastery of the IPO process will in some small portion be the result of this work.

Acknowledgments

It's been said that today's innovators and thinkers stand on the shoulders of yesteryear's giants. While, over time, my effort would be considered neither innovative nor thought provoking, but rather a modest attempt to shed some light on a specific investment topic, my gratitude is extended to many individuals without whose unwavering support, understanding, and faith this work would not have been possible.

Credit must be extended to Alexandra Reed Lajoux, an accomplished author and expert in the area of mergers and acquisitions, whose initial support was key in the development of this proposal and its subsequent acceptance. Kelli Christiansen of McGraw-Hill earns my thanks and gratitude as well, for her steadfast commitment to the book. Kelli's dedication and guidance have made my first efforts as an author an enjoyable experience.

I must also express my gratitude to my colleagues at Thomson Financial Securities Data for their patience and assistance as I completed the project. In particular, I am indebted to Fran Falchook for her insightful comments and guidance, as well as to Carrie Smith, who shouldered many tasks and projects during the period the book was being written.

In addition, I thank my daughters, Julia and Vivienne, whose patience and tolerance were boundless as I was composing this work and whose pride in their dad is matched only by his love of them. Finally, I pay special appreciation and deep thanks to my wife, Madeline. Her tolerance of my less-than-orderly work habits in particular, as well as her stamina in dealing with me in general, earns her a special place in my heart. Without her love and kindness, and an occasional kick for motivation, this work would still be in progress rather than completed as it is before you.

1

IPOs 101

I F ONE PHENOMENON CAN BEST CHARACTERIZE THE FINANCIAL MARKETS OF THE 1990S, IT IS THE SEEMINGLY WILDFIRE SPREAD OF COMPANIES ISSU- ING COMMON STOCK THROUGH INITIAL PUBLIC OFFERINGS (IPOS) AND THE CORRESPONDING WINDFALL THAT OFTEN IS BESTOWED UPON THE LUCKY INDI- VIDUALS WHO HAD THE OPPORTUNITY TO BUY SHARES AT THE OPENING PRICE. IF AMERICA WAS CAPTIVATED BY THE GAME SHOW "WHO WANTS TO BE A MILLIONAIRE," SO, TOO, IT WAS SPELLBOUND BY THE IPO GAME. UNLIKE THE 1980S, WHEN SOME OF THAT DECADE'S BEST GAINERS, SUCH AS THE HOME SHOPPING NETWORK OR ADOBE SYSTEMS, SAW THEIR STOCK PRICE GROW BY SEVERAL HUNDRED PERCENT OVER THE COURSE OF SEVERAL YEARS, THE ROARING NINETIES SAW NO LESS THAN 152 IPOS DOUBLE IN VALUE OR DO EVEN BETTER ON THEIR VERY FIRST DAY OF TRADING. MOREOVER, NEARLY THREE-QUARTERS, OR 110, OF THOSE IPOS THAT CAN BE CALLED "DAILY DOUBLERS" APPEARED JUST IN 1999 ALONE.[1] NOR WAS IPO FEVER SOLELY AN AMERICAN PHENOMENON: IN THE EARLY 2000S, AS MANY AS 300,000 INDI- VIDUALS LINED UP AT BANKS IN HONG KONG TO TRY TO PURCHASE SHARES IN TOM.COM'S 42.8-MILLION-SHARE IPO; AND IN AN ATTEMPT TO GAIN ENTRY

When future generations study the economic history of the final years of the 20th century, they may very well marvel at the incredible fortunes that were made by those who invested in such companies as Cisco Systems, Dell Computer, or America Online when those concerns were in their infancy. For example, Cisco Systems, which first sold common stock to the public in February 1990, has seen its shares soar nearly 70,000 percent; and Microsoft, which went public four years earlier, has enjoyed a better than 61,000 percent increase in its stock price. As such recognizable names as cosmetic giant Estee Lauder, luxury retailer Gucci, and posh department store Saks Fifth Avenue went public in recent years, so, too, have such once obscure or regional firms as Starbucks and Outback Steakhouse, which subsequently went on to transform the consumption habits (not to mention the wealth) of many. To paraphrase an oft-used quote, never have so many been so enriched by so few stocks.

Yet, IPOs are not a new development in the financial world. Each year, hundreds of companies opt to remove themselves from the shadows of being a private enterprise and embark on the path of being a publicly traded company. As shown in Figure 1-1, IPO proceeds soared in the 1990s whereby in 1999 over $68 billion was raised from such offerings. Throughout the modern history of organized stock exchanges, there have always been new entrants. Furthermore, such businesses are not exclusively start-up operations. For example, International Business Machines Corp. (IBM) technically debuted as an IPO in the early years of the 20th century, when it first issued publicly traded common stock. Similarly, Ford Motor Company's evolution from a private newly formed company in June 1903 owned by Henry

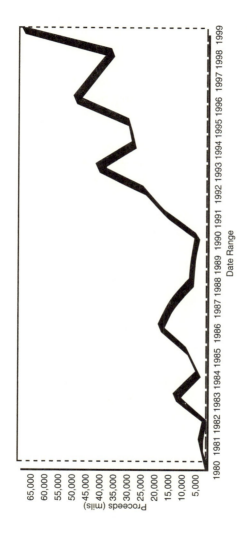

Figure 1-1 IPO Proceeds

Ford and a handful of individuals to a public corporation was realized on January 18, 1956, when the automotive giant, through the Ford Foundation, offered shares to the investing public at a price of $64.50 each.[2] In the following 40-plus years, an investor who purchased just 10 shares for $645 at the offering would, after stock splits, own 225 shares at a value of nearly $12,000, excluding dividend reinvestments and other distributions. However, it wasn't until recently that new stock offerings began to capture the general public's fascination as the velocity, as well as the valuation, of deals reached once unattainable levels. Nearly every day, a story appears in a financial magazine or on some Internet chat site discussing how some entry-level employee at a new high-tech company suddenly became a millionaire through his or her IPO stock options. Adding to the fascination is the fact that there has been a rise in the so-called first-day pop: During 1999, a typical IPO climbed an unprecedented 66 percent in its first day of trading, compared with about 18 percent for IPOs completed in 1998 and just 12 percent for those coming to market in 1997. For many investors, the appeal of such potential returns is indeed compelling and led, among other things, to the terms "day trading" and "IPO mania," which became part of the lexicon as advertisements and magazine covers heralded the new path to prosperity.

And who could blame individuals if they acted upon what the economist John Maynard Keynes called "animal spirits" in their pecuniary pursuit as they prowled Web sites for information on IPOs or clicked away at night in the hope that their "interest of indication" in an upcoming deal would be approved. During the first half of 1999, when 226 companies went public, nearly 50 IPOs more than doubled in value on their first day of trading. That figure compares with only 42 previous instances out of more than 4800 new issues that were priced in the entire preceding nine years in which IPOs displayed such a monumental jump. Yet even that pace was surpassed in the first three months of 2000, when, of the 140 IPOs completed, no less than 46 gained 100 percent or more in value from their offering price on the first day of trading. Furthermore, as mentioned later, nearly all of the strongest first-day price gains by IPOs of all time occurred in recent months, and many were technology related. For stock handicappers, the IPO market seemingly was giving odds better than a sure thing.

Yet, on the other hand, critics of IPOs were quick to argue that such stock offerings are perilous investments that should be considered only by those individuals most comfortable with risk.[3] Although many IPOs often enjoy good reviews and receive accolades from members of the financial media, the fact is that, over time, a fair number fail to live up to their expectations. For example, consider how some recent IPOs performed after one year. Of the 872 IPOs completed in 1996, 334, or about 38 percent, were below their offer price after one year of trading history. The next year was even worse: After one year, 285, or 45 percent, of the IPOs that came to market in 1997 were showing losses to investors. Finally, among those IPOs priced through August 1998, more than half were trading under the price at which they became public.

One negative factor, claim IPO opponents, is that many companies issuing such stock usually are suffering from a string of losses with limited prospects of earnings. All too often a company's balance sheet is riddled with debt, while its income statement is virtually nonexistent. Also, IPO naysayers charge that too many companies go public for the wrong reasons, be it seeking to pay down debt or pursuing overvalued acquisitions, and that many times the early promises of management and dreams of shareholders are dashed by the realities of the marketplace. Whether it is a celebrity-endorsed restaurant or a beverage supposedly made with "the best stuff on Earth," many companies that jump on the IPO bandwagon are left stranded once it becomes clear that the promise of ever-expanding earnings gives way to eroding margins and analysts' downgrades. In sum, for every IPO such as The Cheesecake Factory, which has risen some 245 percent from its debut in September 1992, there are dozens of deals like Arthur Treacher's Fish & Chips, which left investors with a bitter aftertaste.

For IPO critics, the near-textbook example of an IPO that soared on its debut, only to leave its early shareholders, if in fact any still remain, with just a fraction of their initial investment, is Boston Chicken. The company, which marketed itself as a provider of the "home-meal replacement," completed its IPO in November 1993 at a price of $20 a share, with Merrill Lynch as its underwriter. At the time of its underwriting, Boston Chicken was one of the hottest IPOs ever. Within days following the offering, the stock was trading at about $40 and was the darling of Wall Street. Boston Chicken, later renamed Boston Market, opened stores across strip malls and downtowns throughout America, and customers flocked to feast on its offerings. Yet, it soon became apparent that Boston Market was, as skillfully detailed by the noted restaurant analyst Roger Lipton,[4] less a fast-food company than a fast-finance company. Due to its funding arrangements with its franchisees, the firm saw its stock price begin to decline, and by October 1998 Boston Market could no longer pay its bills. That month, the company filed for protection from its creditors under Chapter 11 of the Uniform Commercial Code. By mid-1999, Boston Market's stock, which at one point crossed hands at over $50 a share, was now being valued at about 50 cents per share. The announcement in late 1999 that restaurant leader McDonald's, Inc. had entered into an agreement to purchase Boston Market's remaining assets—primarily real estate leases—was the final blow, as the terms of the transactions called for neither common-equity holders nor secured creditors to receive any payment in the deal.

Between the collapse of Boston Market and the surge of the latest Internet deal lie other stories of both reward and ruin that intrigue the potential IPO investor. Consider, for instance, the following situation: In November 1997, Todd Krizelman and Stephan Paternot, the under-30 co–chief executive officers of a then three-year-old operation named theglobe.com, formerly known as WebGenesis, were still giddy from a recent $20 million infusion of capital into their efforts to build an on-line community targeting 18- to 35-year-olds. The investment, by former Alamo Rent-A-Car chairman Michael Egan, who had recently sold his business to Republic Industries for $625 million, was, in part, representative of mainstream business buying—a stake in an emerging Internet operation. In return for his investment, Egan gained approximately 45 percent of the business. Hence, in the fall of 1997, theglobe.com, which would end that year with revenues of under $1 million and losses from operation of nearly $4 million, was being valued by its largest investor at about $45 million. Yet, beyond merely betting on the outcome of a business model or seeking entry into a promising and exciting enterprise, the investment was part of a larger and grander plan.

On July 24, 1998, theglobe.com[5] filed a registration statement with the United States Securities and Exchange Commission (SEC) to issue 3.1 million of its common shares to the public in an IPO at an expected price between $11 and $13 per share. If events ran their normal course, by late September theglobe.com would have raised about $37 million before underwriting fees of about $2.5 million. However, the summer of 1998 was not a particularly friendly period for the financial markets. Fears that the Russian government would default on loans by Western banks and worries that the collapse of the Thai currency would lead to a domino effect whereby, instead of nations falling to Communism, currencies of developing nations would unravel, leading to social unrest and economic panic that would send markets into a tailspin worldwide.

Bear Stearns, the New York–based investment firm that was the managing underwriter of theglobe.com's deal, responded to the unfavorable financial conditions by postponing theglobe.com's offering. In total, more than three dozen IPO's filings were withdrawn from registration between June and September of 1998, including brand name deals such as Tropicana Products and Goldman Sachs. For Egan, Krizelman, and Paternot, the possibility of getting the deal done, let alone getting it at the price they wanted, seemed remote. By August 1998, financial conditions were such that only 19 IPOs were completed that month, compared with 49 a year earlier and 60 during August 1996.

However, as it became apparent that the developing nations would not vanish, nor would Russia be swallowed in turmoil, and as loan workouts were embraced and conditions improved, the likelihood of such delayed deals as theglobe.com's getting their IPOs done was becoming brighter. Yet, from the perspective of Bear Stearns, theglobe.com's deal was in need of change. Instead of an anticipated price of as much as $13 a share, Bear Stearns was now proposing that the company issue its shares at between $8 and $10. As a result, a deal that was once expected to fetch nearly $40 million for the firm now would likely generate as little as $24 million. Apparently, something unexpected and unimaginable had happened to the investing environment prior to theglobe.com's IPO being priced.

Essentially, like a wanderer in the desert who comes upon an oasis and begins consuming nearly everything in sight, so, too, IPO investors acted in the fall of 1998. Between August 28 and September 24 of that year, just one IPO was completed. For the IPO market, the period represented one of the longest droughts on record. However, the deal ended that underwriting void, on-line auctioneer eBay,

Inc. (www.ebay.com)[6] set the stage for the current Internet IPO boom. In part, eBay's role in the IPO rebound wasn't due to its being a consistent strong performer in its early days as a public company. In fact, in the week after its deal was completed on September 24, 1998, the stock saw a big dip. On the first day of trading, eBay gained 163 percent, but in the days that followed, the advance eroded. After a week of trading, the gain had slipped to 121 percent, and then it fell to just 61 percent after two weeks of trading. But soon thereafter, a turnaround occurred: By the end of the fourth week of trading, eBay's stock had gained 186 percent from its offer price, and it continued to surge to the point where, after two months of trading, the IPO had gained nearly 1000 percent from its offer price. In the opinion of some, this was a signal as to what type of industries and companies Wall Street underwriters saw as having the strength and ability to restore investors' confidence in the markets after the currency crisis of the summer of 1998. In sum, Wall Street wanted a winner, and in eBay, it got one.

By late November 1998, eBay's stock price had climbed to over $190, or better than a ninefold increase from its offer price. Investors clamoring for another eBay were poised to pounce on the next Internet IPO, which, in this case, was theglobe.com. On November 12, 1998, theglobe.com's IPO was priced at $9 a share. By the time the imbalance in ordering was cleared, the first trade crossed hands at over $80, whereupon it reached a high of $97 and then an intraday low of $59. By the end of the day, theglobe.com's stock was at $63.50, for a gain of over 600 percent, as more than 15 million shares, or five times the original number issued, crossed hands. That translated into the largest gain by an IPO in its first day of trading, a record that stood for more than a year, until VA Linux's deal soared more than 700 percent in its first day of trading in December 1999.

For the founders and early investors in theglobe.com, it was a windfall. Krizelman and Paternot were the media darlings of the moment, heralded as whiz kids. Egan saw his initial investment skyrocket. Investors scrambled to get on board theglobe.com's runaway train. But something happened. The stock, which ended the year trading at under $32, managed to rally by the spring of 1999, when it reached $55. But by early summer, after a two-for-one stock split in May, the price was under $15, and subsequently, in early August 1999, it hit a low of under $12. For some investors who purchased 100 shares of theglobe.com in late November 1998, the aftermath was a swift and costly lesson: They saw their investment of over $6000 fall to just under $2400, a loss of more than 60 percent. Such was the stuff of IPO dreams. By the fall of 1999, Egan had already filed an SEC Form 4, indicating that he had sold about one-quarter of his stake in theglobe.com. In the *Silicon Alley Reporter*'s[7] 2000 survey of the top 100 executives, Paternot and Krizelman came up as number 96, and theglobe.com earned the distinction of likely being the first major Internet company to file for bankruptcy. By late January 2000, the two wunderkinds had resigned their positions, although each left with about a 7 percent stake in the company (which was still valued at several million dollars), and operations were taken over by the chief operating officer, Dean Daniels. In the eyes of many, the two left a legacy, not of being the architects of one of the fastest-growing Internet IPOs, but rather, of having impoverished many shareholders, since the stock had lost more than 80 percent of its value from its first day of trading to their departure. At the same time theglobe.com revealed its managerial changes, it also announced that it was awash in red ink for 1999: On a pro forma basis, the company claimed revenues of $18.6 million, but its losses were really over $30 million. Registered users totaled just 3.6 million. Welcome to IPOs 101!

FINANCING NEW COMPANIES : THE IPO CHOICE

But aren't all IPOs destined to rise? Why would a company allow its stock price to fall? What was management's obligation to the shareholders? Aren't IPOs a "sure thing," given such lofty performance statistics? Those who often rush to invest in a deal only to see their initial stake nosedive ask questions like these. So it is important for investors to know what an IPO is and how it operates. Yet, all too often, many individuals, as well as company executives, haven't the slightest notion of either concept. The multitude of issues involved in the IPO process, from the selection of a banker, to how a deal is priced and under what conditions the terms of the deal are to be amended, to determining what the proceeds are to be used for—issues that will be addressed in the chapters that follow—are often passed over by average investors. Similarly, company owners who could brush aside questions from a curious public when their companies were private now are obligated to disclose the most intricate financial aspects of their operations. Avoiding this obligation would be as foolhardy as attempting to navigate a plane without the aid of instruments or hiking in uncharted woods without the use of a compass.

Simply stated, an IPO can be described as just another means for a company to raise money to meet its business objectives. In the world of corporate finance, there are dozens, if not hundreds, of specific types of securities or financing methods for generating capital for businesses. From issuing subordinated convertible debt to privately placing collateralized mortgage instruments, companies have a multitude of weapons in their financial arsenal to fund their operations. Furthermore, different types of financing affect a company's capital statements in different ways: Some involve tax consequences, others affect the company's capacity for borrowing, and still others influence the company's ability to call for cash payments to third parties.

In the case of the IPO, investors are dealing with but a tiny sliver of the overall corporate financing picture. Of the $2.26 trillion in capital raised by corporations, public agencies, and other entities during 1998, more than $2 trillion was through debt-related issues.[8] Furthermore, it is not unusual for companies such as General Motors, AT&T, or International Business Machines to issue several billion dollars in bonds each year.[9] But, unlike outside funding or debt deals, the IPO is unique.

First, by definition, an IPO is the initial, or debut, offering by a company. Thus, a company can have only one IPO. Second, an IPO is "public." This means that, whereas once a company, as a private concern, was not mandated to reveal its revenues, earnings, or corporate activities, as a publicly traded entity it is now usually required to disclose such facts, not only to its shareholders, but for all the world to see. From an IPO registration statement—a document that will be discussed in detail in a later chapter—a prospective investor could learn specific details of a company's financial history, its relationship with management, and the existence of any legal matters that may adversely affect the company's performance. For example, the World Wrestling Federation (WWF) Entertainment, Inc.'s decision to issue an IPO made the public aware of the fact that the company's revenues nearly tripled to $251 million in the year ending April 30, 1999, from a period two years earlier. Furthermore, pretax profits for the WWF climbed to $56 million from a loss of over $6 million in the year ending April 30, 1997. In addition, prospective shareholders were informed of litigation regarding ownership of the stage names of some of the WWF's characters, such as "Ultimate Warrior" and "Sable," as well as of the company's intention to create a theme restaurant.[10]

Furthermore, an IPO comes in different varieties. Besides the traditional IPO, wherein the company issues publicly traded common stock for the first time, there is the tracking-stock IPO, whereby an already public company issues shares for one of its divisions, and the performance of those shares "track" those of the company as a whole. Examples of companies that have issued tracking stocks include CarMax, which was originally a unit of Circuit City Stores, and ZDNet, formerly a division of the publishing concern Ziff-Davis. Another variety of IPO is the so-called unit offering, which typically comprises one or two common shares and several warrants (i.e., rights to purchase a fixed number of common shares at a particular price by a specific date). Usually, this kind of IPO is offered by a small company that is underwritten by the so-called penny stock brokerage firms. Although there have been exceptions, the track record for unit offerings has been very poor, with many of the companies offering such IPOs often failing and the issues themselves frequently no longer trading once their underwriter stops "making a market" in the shares. For instance, based on available data, of the 94 unit IPO offerings that came to market in the peak year for this type of deal (1994), only less than a dozen are currently trading on a regular basis. Finally, as will be discussed in detail in a later chapter, there is the spin-off IPO. Unlike the tracking stock, a spin-off is a share in a parent company's operation or division that is generally considered to be no longer essential to the parent's fundamental corporate mission. Among the more notable spin-off offerings are Lucent Technologies, formerly a unit of AT&T, Conoco, once part of Du Pont, and Allstate, previously operating under Sears, Roebuck's ownership.

Yet, each type of financing, whether debt issuance or stock offering, has its risks and rewards. On the one hand, debt financing is often viewed as an inexpensive means of raising money, because the underwriting fee on most investment-grade corporate bonds is generally under 1 percent. But for companies that rely on high-yield bonds—mostly companies that are valued not on earnings, but on cash flow (e.g., cable television operators)—a downturn in economic conditions may make it more difficult for them to service their debt. On the other hand, private equity deals may be inappropriate for some companies, since these deals are designed, in most cases, for a single institutional holder, such as a commercial bank or an insurance company, as an investment to generate an income stream. Finally, the issuance of asset- or mortgage-backed securities obviously would be inappropriate for a business that did not possess such collateral. When it comes to financing new businesses, the choices are few.

LAWS GOVERNING THE UNDERWRITING OF IPOs

Like all securities underwriting, the process of arranging and completing an IPO is an extremely regulated procedure. In the absence of oversight, unscrupulous individuals may seek to exploit an uninformed public. The various securities laws enacted by the federal government include the Securities Act of 1933, the Securities Exchange Act of 1934, and the Investment Company Act of 1940.[11] The Securities Act of 1933 governs the offering and selling of securities. According to the act, prior to a security being sold, a registration statement must be filed with the SEC. The statement is also referred to as Form S-1. The Securities Exchange Act of 1934 oversees the activities of securities exchanges, securities firms, and those employed within the securities industry. Among the sections that are of note, especially with regard to IPOs, are those which mandate the registration of securities when a certain threshold of shareholders (at least 500) or assets (in excess of $5 million) is crossed.

Companies that file with the SEC are not burdened with paperwork; instead, the reports are filed electronically through the Commission's EDGAR system. "EDGAR" stands for "Electronic Data Gathering and Retrieval," and its information may be viewed at www.sec.gov.

With respect to Form S-1, specific standards and guidelines must be adhered to. For example, on the front cover of the document, among the items that must be printed are the exact name of the company registering the securities, the state in which the company is incorporated, the primary standard industrial classification (SIC) code of the company, the company's IRS employer ID number, and the address and phone number of the company's executive offices. (There is no requirement as of yet for an E-mail address.)

Aside from filling out an S-1 registration, companies that meet the definitional requirements of being a "small-business issuer" may seek to issue up to $10 million in common stock through a public offering and may file an SB-1 registration, which, unlike Regulation A offerings (described in a later chapter), requires three years of audited financial statements. Regulations define a small-business issuer as a U.S. or Canadian enterprise with less than $25 million in revenue in the previous fiscal year and whose outstanding publicly held common shares do not exceed $25 million in value. Small-business issuers may issue an unlimited amount in common stock by filing Form SB-2. In doing so, the issuer must provide at least two years of audited financial statements.

SB-1 and SB-2 differ in other ways, not just in the number of years of audited financial statements that are needed to be submitted by the company applying for an IPO. First, the SB-2 requires a less extensive disclosure of company information than does the SB-1. Second, the financial statements provided by SB-2 issuers need only conform to generally accepted accounting practices, whereas the SB-1 issuer must overcome the hurdle of preparing the statement in accordance with detailed SEC regulations. According to Thomson Financial Securities Data, more than 800 IPOs in the 1990s used Form SB-2 in their debut offering.[12] Among these IPOs were CNET's July 1996 offering, which was managed by Morgan Stanley, and Yahoo!'s April 1996 IPO, underwritten by The Goldman Sachs Group, Inc.

Yet, the appeal of SB-2 filings is fading, at least among underwriters who specialize in offerings that require firm commitments. In 1995, of the 580 companies that completed IPOs, approximately 25 percent filed SB-2 forms, compared with about 64 percent of those companies which used form S-1. By 1998, those proportions changed modestly, as nearly 18 percent of the 374 companies that offered IPOs which came to market that year used Form SB-2, while two-thirds of the firms filed Form S-1. By 1999, less than 10 percent of companies completing IPOs filed Form SB-2, versus over 80 percent that filed Form S-1. Furthermore, the actual number of SB-2 filings has steadily declined from its peak year of 1996, when 207 SB-2 IPOs were completed.[13] In 1997 there were just 113 small-business IPOs and in 1998 only 68. This information, which is derived from Thomson, whose database does not track best efforts deals, indicates that when it comes to investment banks that risk their own capital in completing IPOs, SB-2 deals have lost much of their appeal. Thus, the fact the some IPOs were not even considered worthy of being supported, at least in terms of their own money, by their underwriters gave some investors sufficient reason to pause.

Investors should note that there are two key exemptions whereby companies seeking to sell securities do *not* need to register with federal regulators. First, a company seeking to raise under $5 million in a 12-month period can, instead of electronically filing a registration statement, simply file a hard copy of an "offering circular" with the SEC. Offerings filed in this manner are commonly referred to as Regulation A, or "Reg A," offerings. Second, companies can offer to sell IPOs under a Regulation D, or "Reg D," offering exemption, whereby the offering is limited to $1 million in a 12-month period, or up to $5 million over the same period as long as the offering is sold to 35 or fewer individuals or an equal number of "accredited investors." Besides federal laws governing stock and bond offerings, certain state laws oversee the selling of securities to residents within their borders. Often, start-up companies seek to sell common stock to individuals who reside in the state in which the company is doing business or is incorporated. Usually, these offerings will carry a disclaimer that the offering is valid only for residents of, for example, Pennsylvania or California, should the company issuing the offer be conducting business there.

TYPES OF IPOs: FIRM COMMITMENT VERSUS BEST EFFORTS

IPOs come with specific terms and conditions. When a company opts to raise funds through an IPO, many choices are presented to the company's management. One involves what type of arrangement should be made with the prospective underwriter. Some investment banks offer so-called firm-commitment terms wherein the underwriter essentially will put up a specific dollar amount of its own capital for the company that is going public, in order to guarantee that the deal goes through. For example, in the case of specialty retailer Yankee Candle's $225 million IPO, Morgan Stanley Dean Witter, the investment bank managing the deal, assures that it will deliver to the company that amount, less its expenses or underwriting fees (in this case, 6.5 percent of the total proceeds). Accordingly, although Yankee Candle's stock was offered at $18 a share to the underwriter's clients, the company received net proceeds of approximately $213.3 million, which was based upon a net price per share of $16.83. The difference of $11.7 million is called the "gross spread" and is composed of a management fee, an underwriter's fee, and a selling concession. The management fee is the portion of the gross spread allocated to the lead manager of the IPO in deals in which a group of underwriters, commonly referred to as a syndicate, assists in underwriting the deal. The underwriting fee is the portion of the gross spread paid to lead managers and co–lead managers who were part of the purchasing group involved in the IPO. Finally, the selling concession is that share of the gross spread allocated to the selling group, defined as the lead, co–lead, and syndicate members, equal to the discount at which the IPO is allocated to the selling group for resale to investors, less the offer price. In the case of Yankee Candle's IPO, in percentage terms, the management fee was 1.306 percent, the underwriting fee totaled 0.972 percent, and the selling concession was 4.222 percent, for an aggregate gross spread of 6.5 percent.

Thus, the firm-commitment deal is a deal in which the investment bank buys the company's offering with its own capital and then resells it to institutional and retail investors. If, for any reason, the underwriter is unable to sell the necessary shares to meet the firm-commitment level for its client, the underwriter is still obligated to make the company whole by paying it the amount agreed to.

Alternatively, there is the best efforts offering, wherein the underwriter makes no commitment as to how much the company can expect from the IPO, but only the promise that the investment bank will seek to sell as many shares as possible (i.e., that the bank will exert its "best efforts" to complete the offering). In this case, the underwriters are not risking their own capital. Often, smaller or regional investment banks typically arrange best efforts deals, since they do not wish to risk their own capital. In this regard, some market observers believe as a general rule that best efforts IPOs should be avoided on the grounds that if the bank arranging the offering would not commit its own capital, neither should the average retail investor.

However, the decision-making process of launching an IPO often goes beyond just determining whether the investment bank will commit its own capital to the deal. Among the issues a company must address are what the proceeds of the IPO will be used for, how much of the company should be sold to the public, and where the shares should be traded once the deal is complete. For example, where once new high-growth companies would opt to list their shares on the National Association of Security Dealers Automatic Quotation (NASDAQ) National Market system, now some high-tech companies are listing their stock on the emerging Brussels-based European Association of Security Dealers Automatic Quotation (EASDAQ).

Beyond the mere definitions, it is also critical to understand for what purpose the deal is being done. If the IPO is proposed merely to raise cash to pay down debt, then that should serve as a clue that perhaps the company was overextended to begin with. Conversely, if the company's motivation to go public is to generate capital to fund acquisitions, then potential shareholders may be seeing a glimpse of management's strategic plans to grow the business. Surprisingly, when most investors think of IPO financings, the first thoughts that often come to mind are firms using proceeds to build plant and equipment, expand operations, hire employees, and increase their market share. Yet, nothing could be farther from the truth. According to information compiled from company prospectuses, among the more frequent use of IPO proceeds are paying off bank debt, refinancing existing loans, and providing capital to the firm's original investors. A case in point is the crop of deals issued during 1998. Of the nearly $37 billion raised by companies that year through IPO financings, no less than $17.7 billion was used for refinancing bank debt or paying off debts. Further down the list, one may find that a company will use its newfound bounty to acquire another company, fund present acquisitions, or perhaps embark on a marketing and advertising campaign. Similarly, more than one-third of the $43.4 billion in IPO proceeds amassed during 1997 was used to pay off debts or restructure loans.

Another reason a company may decide to issue an IPO may be simply to rid itself of an unwanted minority investor. For example, purveyor of style and entertainment Martha Stewart made a decision to sell stock in her company, Martha Stewart Living Omnimedia, Inc. The sale was supposedly motivated not only by Stewart's desire to find extra capital to expand her media and retailing empire, but also to buy out her original investor, media giant Time Warner. Over time, the most frequent reasons a company decides to go public have ranged from desiring to pay off long-term debts, to wishing to repurchase stock, to pursuing general corporate objectives. The desire to finance acquisitions is another key motive companies have in issuing public stock. Throughout the 1990s, as merger activity escalated, swapping stocks was one of the most frequent techniques used to acquire companies. For example, Company A would offer some combination of its outstanding shares for taking over Company B. What makes the method attractive is that if the acquiring company's stock is trading at a higher price relative to the target company's shares, then the former can often offer a premium bid. Furthermore, as some industries (in the past, telecommunications and media in particular) consolidate, considering the company's equity becomes popular. Therefore, to some analysts, it is imperative that a company quickly become public in order to compete in the merger and acquisitions (M&A) "game."

In this regard, it is impressive to note the proportion of newly minted IPOs that quickly plunge into the M&A field. For example, of the 374 companies issuing IPOs during 1998, many were actively acquiring businesses in the 12 months following the completion of their deal. Among the larger deals were the purchase of Global TeleSystems Group, which went public at $20 in February 1998, the acquisition of British telecommunications service firm Esprit Telecom Group PLC for $917 million in December 1998, the acquisition of L-3 Communications Holdings, Inc., a firm that raised $105.6 million in May 1998 in an IPO priced at $22 per share, and the purchase of SPD Technologies, a unit of MidMark Capital LP, for $230 million in July 1998.

Finally, one other reason that a company may decide to go public is to recruit and to retain key personnel. With the availability of a publicly traded stock, a company may be able to attract talented staff members to its organization, as well prevent key personnel from leaving. Often, the attraction of a compensation package loaded with stock options and the corresponding gains that may transpire if an IPO takes off turn the most loyal employee into a former toiler for his or her current company.

WHO GOES PUBLIC?

If one thought that technology IPOs were the most frequent type of offerings prior to 1999, one would be dead wrong. Just as it was revealed in a recent study that the typical millionaire in the United States was usually someone who operated a small business such as a dry cleaner, pest control company, or plumbing business, so, too, until recently, a typical IPO was likely to be issued by an oil service manufacturer, a restaurant chain, or a commercial bank—hardly the stuff of high-tech dreams. Surprisingly, 1999 marked the first year in which there were more technology-related IPOs than nontech deals. While it would be difficult to pinpoint the precise reason that technology issues began to flourish at the close of the 1990s, two explanations have merit. One is that the IPOs which dominated the classes of 1998 and 1999 were funded by venture-capital groups in the preceding years and now were poised to enter the public market. A second explanation is that individuals at such established technology giants as IBM, Hewlett-Packard, and Cisco Systems were branching out to begin companies of their own.

Before 1999, leading firms that completed IPOs were a hodgepodge of corporate America. In 1982, for example, when the bull market in equities commenced, among the leading firms issuing IPOs were manufacturing companies and personal-service businesses. Among these companies and businesses were firms that assembled switching components (InteCom, Inc.), plastic coolers (Gott Corp.), and measuring instruments (AMI Systems). In 1990, although a minirecession took hold in the United States, an eclectic group of manufacturing concerns still headlined the IPO market, with outfits such as a footwear manufacturer (K Swiss Inc.), a producer of respiratory care products (Bird Medical Technologies), and a maker of fans and air conditioners (Crest Industries) all issued IPOs. Following on their heels were several oil and gas concerns, including companies such as BJ Services International, Santa Fe Energy Resources, and Chiles Offshore. It is noteworthy that of the 14 natural-resources related IPOs that came to market in 1990, only 4 are trading today, while 1, Curragh Resources, subsequently went bankrupt. All things being equal, the "mortality" rate for many IPOs, which will be discussed in a subsequent chapter, is high.

Within a few years, the IPO map began to show a change of face. Gone were the start-ups from the Rust Belt. Though much had been said of the rise of the South in business matters with major banking and media operations run out of Charlotte, North Carolina, and Atlanta, Georgia, only a small fraction of IPOs was coming from the Southeast. In some cases, certain states often experienced a precipitous decline in IPO activity. For example, consider what occurred in Minnesota. In 1994, 24 IPOs were completed by Minnesota-based companies. However, within three years, that figure was more than halved to 11, and it dropped further in 1998, when Minnesota companies finalized just 5 IPOs. The pace was only slightly better in 1999, with 8 deals making it to market, marking the second-worst year for IPO activity in the state during the 1990s.

Increasingly, the profile of an IPO was a West Coast tech operation from a town such as Santa Clara, San Jose, or Palo Alto or an East Coast venture such as Stamford, Connecticut–based Priceline.com or New York City's Silicon Alley–headquarted ivillage.com. In fact, of the more than 4300 domestic IPOs priced between 1990 and 1999, no less than 38 percent came from three states: California, Texas, and New York, as shown in Figure 1-2. During the same period, a dozen states managed to generate nine or fewer IPOs, with Wyoming coming in dead last with a single IPO, Tri-County Bancorp, completed in September 1993.

HOW MUCH OF THE COMPANY IS BEING OFFERED?

A major factor in structuring IPOs is determining how much of the company should be sold to the public. Relinquishing ownership is often a complex and burdensome decision that

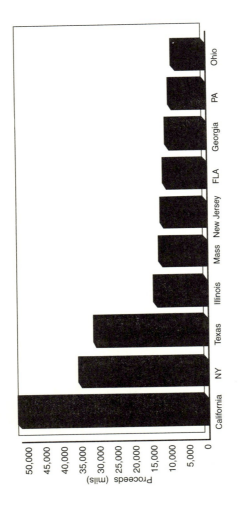

Figure 1-2 Leading Locations for IPOs in 1990s

affects the future of the company, impinging on such matters as the composition of the board of directors to executive compensation. Ideally, the owner(s) of a company would seek to offer only a small portion of the company to the general public. Yet, that often is not the case. For example, of the more than 200 IPOs that came to market in 1990, nearly one-third of them saw more than 50 percent of their outstanding common shares offered to the public.

However, such a high proportion of stock being offered in an IPO typically can be considered a red flag. Of those IPOs that came to market in 1990 with a greater than 50 percent diminution of their ownership, only a handful managed to double in value in the subsequent nine years. Conversely, of those IPOs in the class of 1990 which offered the public an opportunity to own less than a majority of the company, one-fifth either were subsequently acquired or doubled in value. In 1999, just 13 percent of the deals offered more than 50 percent of their stock. And as was the case earlier, a high proportion of those deals soon declined in value from their initial offering price. On the other hand, those IPOs which were stingy with respect to the number of shares offered to the public performed considerably better in terms of their subsequent price. Thus, as a general rule, it may be stated that those IPOs which offer more than a 50 percent stake to the public typically underperform those deals which limit the number of shares offered to the public to below that percentage.

IPO Insight: The IPO market has both strong advocates and zealous opponents. Yet, why do companies go public in the first place, what types of offerings are available, and how should investors review financial information related to an offering? The next chapter seeks to lay out some guidelines.

2

THE RED HERRING

A TRAVELER SETTING OUT TO VENTURE IN A NEW LAND WOULD BE FOOL-
ISH TO BEGIN HIS OR HER JOURNEY WITHOUT THE AID OF A MAP OR
GUIDE. WITHOUT THE TOOLS TO POINT THE WAY, ONE MAY BECOME DISORI-
ENTED AND WANDER AIMLESSLY, NEVER REACHING ONE'S DESTINATION. SO,
TOO, IS THE CASE WITH THOSE INVESTORS WHO WOULD RISK THEIR MONEY
WITHOUT READING THE VARIOUS DOCUMENTS A COMPANY MUST FILE WITH
REGULATORS PRIOR TO ISSUING AN IPO. INVESTORS' EYES MAY GLAZE OVER
AT THE PROSPECT OF READING ABOUT WHAT LED A COMPANY'S MANAGEMENT
TO OFFER SHARES OF THE FIRM TO THE PUBLIC. INVESTORS MAY BALK AT HAV-
ING TO PLOW OVER TECHNICAL JARGON EXPLAINING EVERY NUANCE OF SILI-
CON PROCESSORS IN THE HOPE THAT THE LANGUAGE CLEARLY EXPLAINS THE
COMPANY'S PRODUCT LINE, ITS PROSPECTS FOR FUTURE GROWTH, AND THE
LIMITED COMPETITION IT FORESEES. BUT THE FACT REMAINS THAT THE PRE-
LIMINARY PROSPECTUS, WHICH SERVES BOTH TO INFORM INVESTORS AND AS
A MARKETING PIECE FOR THE UNDERWRITER, IS PERHAPS THE FASTEST, IF

NOT THE ONLY, WAY A POTENTIAL SHAREHOLDER IN A COMPANY CAN LEARN KEY FACTS PERTAINING TO ITS OPERATIONS, FINANCES, AND MANAGEMENT AND THUS MAKE AN INTELLIGENT DECISION ABOUT WHETHER TO INVEST.

Yet, individuals often toss tens of thousands of dollars at an IPO merely on the opinion of a glib picker of stocks, a newsletter, or a soothsayer, rather than commit themselves to reading what is often the only available information revealing the operation, management, and business objective of the company issuing the IPO: the company's preliminary offering prospectus, commonly referred to as the red herring. This chapter examines the preliminary prospectus, what key section investors should focus on, and, finally, where investors can readily obtain copies of the red herring.

First, a quick history lesson about how the "red herring" got its name. Supposedly, the legend comes from a ruse used by criminals who, when pursued by bloodhounds, would rub a herring or some other pungent product along their escape path to cover their scent and ward off the dogs. As time went on, the term "red herring" was used to refer to an act that misled people away from the truth. By the early part of this century, "red herring" was the label associated with documents for the investing public, but with the caveat that the information contained therein was neither final nor complete. In fact, the current language used on the cover[14] of the red herring almost takes on the appearance of a warning label on a pack of cigarettes or a bottle of medicine. Typically, the language is as follows:

Neither the Securities and Exchange Commission nor any state securities commission has approved or disapproved of these securities or determined if the prospectus is truthful or complete. Any representation to the contrary is a criminal offense.

Similar words of caution, printed in red type (thus giving further insight into why the preliminary prospectus is referred to as a red herring) are placed along the borders of the document. These words usually read as follows:

> The information in this prospectus is not complete and may be changed. We may not sell these securities until the registration statement filed with the Securities and Exchange Commission is effective. This prospectus is not an offer to sell these securities and it is not soliciting an offer to buy these securities in any state where the offer or sale is not permitted.

Just these few words from the red herring's "warning label" enable individuals to learn some basic facts about the deal they are interested in. First, the clause stating that the sale of the security may not occur "until the registration statement filed with the Securities and Exchange Commission is effective" indicates some facts as well as raises some questions, including the following: What information is required in the registration statement? How is the document filed? What is defined as "effective"?

The preliminary prospectus comes in varying lengths. A red herring for an IPO for a company in a regulated industry, such as cable television broadcasting, may total several hundred pages, with page after page of jargon on operating frequencies, market penetration, and pending regulatory issues. On the other hand, a start-up software company's preliminary prospectus may total about a dozen pages or so, with the briefest of commentary on management, market conditions, and risk factors. Typically, however, a red herring runs over 100 pages or more.[15]

DISSECTING A HERRING: HOW TO TELL IF AN IPO IS FISHY

When examining a preliminary prospectus, an investor will find that the information contained therein covers various topics pertaining to both the company and its management. For example, consider some of the information provided in Breakaway Solutions' prospectus[16], in which the provider of e-business solutions addresses the following standard topics:

Risk Factors   This is a disclosure section informing potential investors of the inherent uncertainties that may exist in the company's operations and forecast.

Use of Proceeds   This section tells what the money raised in the offering will ultimately be used for.

Dividend Policy   A dividend option gives stockholders current income that they can spend immediately. The policy states the offering company's rules and regulations regarding the policyholders' dividends. (Nearly all growth-oriented IPOs will state that there is no prospect of receiving dividends. Hence, if you're looking for income, this type of IPO is not for you.)

Capitalization   Here, the company lists its financial position before and after the offering.

Selected Financial Data   In this section, the company may elaborate on any financial matters not found in its financial statements.

Management's Discussion and Analysis of the Financial Condition and Results of Operation of the Business   This section reveals what the IPO's management believes to be the ultimate aim of the offering and where the company is headed.

Management   This section informs investors as to who is filling management positions, as well as about the age, experience, compensation, and education of key personnel.

Certain Transactions Here, investors are informed of whether there exist any transactions or relationships between such interested parties as the company principals, the issuing company or related companies, or any other party that may give the appearance of impropriety or that may lead to a conflict of interest.

Principal Stockholders This section discusses those who own a controlling or significant interest in the company. (There may be no principal stockholders.)

Description of Capital Stock This section describes the different classes of stock the company has with respect to the voting rights they confer on the shareholders (e.g., "A" shares, which are owned by the general public, but which lack voting rights on such matters as determining who is on the board of directors and authorizing stock splits, and "B" shares, which are owned by management and insiders and which confer on their owners the right to vote on the aforementioned topics).

Shares Eligible for Future Sale In this section, the actual outstanding supply of stock and its ultimate price are described.

Underwriters This section describes who controls the "books" on the deal and presents the underwriter's track record with respect to supporting the stock once trading begins. Also stated in this section are the underwriter's fees and other compensation.

Validity of Common Stock This is essentially a statement by legal counsel sanctioning the transaction.

Interests of Counsel This section indicates who is the legal advisor to the issuer and what interests, if any, counsel will receive in the offering. For example, in the case of Breakaway Solutions' IPO, a partnership composed of partners and senior executives of the Boston-based firm of Hale and Dorr LLP owned 7695 shares of the company's Series B preferred stock.

Experts Here, other professionals (e.g., auditors associated with the offering) are described.

Changes in Independent Auditors This section indicates whether the company has changed auditors during its operating history, as well as whether any past reporting of financial results was classified as "qualified" or "modified" by accountants.

Index to Financial Statements In this section may be found income statements, the company's balance sheet, consolidated financial statements involving any subsidiary, and other financial reports.

Note: Much of the language used to highlight the preceding areas is crafted carefully in order to avoid the impression of exaggeration or misrepresentation.

WHAT MATTERS MOST?

Opinions vary as to what is the most important section of the red herring. One money manager may consider the "Other Transactions" to be a clue to discovering whether management is conducting activities outside the business at hand that may detract from the company's primary business. Another manager may target the "Financial Summary" section of the prospectus in order to determine whether inventories are rising, sales are declining, or some other aberration is present which may indicate that management is not doing its job. Still others will scout the "Business Summary" in order to determine whether the company depends too much on one or a handful of customers and thus may be vulnerable financially if any of its key accounts were to defect. In any event, investors will be well served if they focus on a handful of factors, such as the following:

- What does the company do?
- Who is the management?
- What is the appearance of company finances?
- Who is the underwriter?
- What are the risk factors associated with the IPO?

WHAT DOES THE COMPANY DO?

Although it may appear simplistic, perhaps the most critical section of the red herring is the one that describes the company's business. In this section, a company usually spells out what its primary business is, describes its products or services, and perhaps attempts to spell out how it differs from its competitors or how its products differ from its competitors' with respect to quality, pricing, service, and market share. But what may be a straightforward explanation of a company's operations all too often leaves many questions and uncertainties about the IPO. For example, consider the following paragraph from Red Hat's August 1999 offering:

> We are a leading developer and provider of open source software and services; including the Red Hat operating system. Unlike proprietary software, open source software has publicly available source code and can be copied, modified and distributed with minimal restrictions. Our web site, REDHAT.COM, is a leading online source of information and news about open source software and one of the largest online communities of open source software users and developers. In addition to offering extensive content for the open source community, REDHAT.COM serves as an impor-

tant forum for open source software development and offers software downloads and a shopping site. Our broad range of professional services includes technical support, training and education, custom development, consulting and hardware certification. We are committed to serving the interests and needs of open source software users and developers and to sharing all of our product developments with the open source community.

By putting on his or her "detective cap," a potential investor may deduce certain aspects of the deal. First, based upon the fact that the term "open source" is mentioned no fewer than eight times in the paragraph, that term must denote a critical aspect of Red Hat's business. The statement that Red Hat is "one of the largest communities of open source software users" suggests that there are other, possibly larger, communities of open source software users. The reference that the redhat.com Website will serve as a shopping place puts forth the questions: What will be sold? Who will be the competitors? To what extent, if any, will such a use of the site be a loss leader? Finally, the statement that the company is committed "to sharing all our product developments with the open source community" may be taken to mean that the company might not share its developments with those who are not members of the open source community. Furthermore, potential investors may have to weigh the degree to which such sharing comes at the expense of profits.

In drafting a description of the company's business, it is necessary to be factual in all aspects of the firm's past and present performance. The document should contain an overview of the company's operations and should provide background information on the industry in which the company operates. In addition, the unique service or product that the company provides should be highlighted, and the company's strategy for success should be discussed.

WHO IS RUNNING THE COMPANY'S OPERATIONS?

Company management is the lifeblood of many IPOs. Often, managers contribute substantial capital, time, and personal sacrifice to get a concept or service off the ground and sustain it in a competitive marketplace. The individual who sees a company go public has every reason to be exuberant and to be rewarded for his or her efforts toward that end. Within the red herring, there usually is a reference to the company's management. In blunt terms, this section is the "executive rap sheet" for prospective investors. Contained in it is a summary of the professional background of key executives in the organization, as well as information about their age, education, and previous positions held. Upon reading the section, it can be ascertained whether executives in the prospective IPO are being compensated in cash or stock, whether they have participated in previous IPO transactions, and whether they possess the necessary education and training to provide investors with a high degree of confidence that their investment will be well managed.[17]

In reviewing the red herring, investors need to take into account whether the company's top managers have actual experience within the industry in which they are doing business or whether they are merely figureheads. For example, in some cases it is a red flag when the IPO's prospectus indicates that the chief executive officer of the company never had any executive experience within a specific industry. Consider the proliferation of Internet deals last year that saw individuals from diverse business backgrounds suddenly thrust into top management positions. It was not uncommon to see former marketing professionals or topflight salespeople head Internet start-ups. While these situations are more frequent in "penny stock" deals (those offerings underwritten by smaller investment firms), sometimes even "bulge bracket" or recognized regional firms engage in this activity.

Finally, there is a chance that the management of the IPO may be inflating their resumes. In an age when many professionals, from politicians to executives to students in various walks of life, have lied outright about their academic records or military service or lack thereof, there exists the risk that some managers may not be telling the truth about their credentials. Such actions damage the IPO process, threaten the ability of honest firms to raise cash, and imperil shareholders by weakening the bond between management and investors.

COMPANY FINANCES: ROSY OR A BED OF THORNS?

Many analysts point to earnings as the primary barometer of future stock performance. If the outlook for earnings is robust, then the stock price should move in tandem. Alternatively, if earnings are cyclical or subject to revision, then the stock price is less likely to be a strong gainer over time. However, more often than not, a typical IPO does not have any earnings, since many such companies are in emerging sectors or are spending capital at a rapid pace in order to gain market share, with the expectation that earnings will soon follow. Moreover, there often is no direct relationship between earnings and stock performance in the early stages of an IPO. Simply stated, investors are looking ahead several years and are willing to pay today what may seem to many to be inflated prices for a company whose earnings may catch up to its present price in the next two to three years. Hence, it is not unusual to read a red herring for a company's IPO and find that the company is gushing red ink.

Consider, for example, one of the biggest and most profitable domestic IPOs to be completed: the 1998 offering of Conoco, which was spun off from DuPont. An examination of the firm's preliminary prospectus would indicate that the company was enjoying respectable margins as well as a healthy market share in its industry. Yet, some six months after its IPO was finalized, investors who got in at the offer price only realized a modest double-digit gain. On the other hand, consider almost every Internet IPO that came to market in 1999. Nearly each one was beset by a vast amount of red ink and the prospects of widening deficits in the future, as each of the companies' business models called for spending enormous amounts of cash up front in order to gain customer loyalty in the years ahead. However, many investors looked beyond today's balance sheet and income statement and were betting on a strong performance down the road, perhaps in three to five years. Those investors who managed to get into some of these deals at the offer price saw gains of over 100 percent in the first few months after the offering.

Yet how can investors judge which is the more suitable investment, the money loser or the cash cow? Simply stated, there is no general rule investors can follow to hang their hat, except for the commonsense statement that if it looks suspicious, then it likely should be avoided.

THE UNDERWRITING TEAM: ALL-STARS OR BUSH LEAGUE?

To some, underwriting an IPO may seem a rather straightforward operation. One simply identifies a worthwhile candidate to go public, assembles the necessary documents to satisfy regulators, lines up a group of bankers to aid in selling and distributing the offering, and, finally, prices the deal and collects the fees. Unfortunately, such a scenario doesn't occur in the real world. Companies often walk a proverbial minefield in the path to completing their IPO. At its most primary level, the selection of an underwriter is perhaps one of the most critical steps a company may take. The proper choice may result in a long-lasting relationship in which the initial underwriter will handle subsequent public offerings for the company and negotiate M&As. On the other hand, a poor selection may translate into a tumultuous association between banker and company that could lead to the former walking away from supporting the IPO price in the aftermarket, thus imperiling the value of shareholders' stock, as well as the company's long-term financial prospects.

Yet, how do the company seeking an IPO and the underwriter get together in the first place? Often, the relationship is cultivated months and years prior to the actual IPO. For example, ties are forged when the venture-capital arm of a particular investment bank commits seed financing to a developing company with the expectation that once the business is mature, the bank will underwrite the offering. In addition, some venture-capital firms enjoy strong working relationships with a select number of underwriters. A case in point is Menlo Park, California–based Benchmark Capital's (www.benchmark.com) ties with the investment bank Goldman Sachs. Of the 80 IPOs managed by Goldman between 1998 and 1999, nearly half had received funding or investments from Benchmark Capital, including Juniper Networks, 1-800-Flowers.com, and Ashford.com, among others. Finally, some companies take themselves on the road to knock on doors, make presentations, and, hopefully, make a positive impression in order to find a willing underwriter.

Yet, the IPO road is still paved with other pitfalls in the choice of underwriters. One issue investors should be aware of is the experience of particular underwriters in handling certain types of IPOs in particular industries. Restaurant IPOs, for instance, are an excellent example of how what appears to be a relatively simple industry to understand, and thus finance, has nonetheless frustrated many on Wall Street. The top underwriter for IPOs in this sector over the past two decades has been Montgomery Securities, now a division of Banc of America Securities. Of the firm's 14 deals since 1981, several have multiplied several times over in value. Among the winners are Lone Star Steakhouse and Saloon, The Cheesecake Factory, and Papa John's International. In contrast, consider the case of Merrill Lynch. Throughout the 1990s, the firm ranked among the leaders in underwriting IPOs by amount of capital raised. Yet, its performance in certain sectors, in this case restaurant deals, illustrates the fact that even the biggest and best capitalized firms can back clunkers. For example, since 1979, Merrill's restaurant IPOs have been limited to just five deals. Its most dubious offering, in retrospect, was Boston Chicken, the one-time high-flying food chain that eventually went bankrupt in 1998.

Similarly, just as an also-ran baseball team can be transformed into a pennant contender by tapping the free-agent market, so, too, can a firm that had just a modest track record in a particular industry in one year jump into the top ranks upon the addition of a new crop of bankers and analysts. Consider, for example, CS First Boston. Up until recently, the firm had been, at best, an unassuming factor in the "league" rankings in technology IPO underwriting. Prior to 1997, the company did not rank in the top 10 among investment banks underwriting tech IPOs; in fact, based upon its number of issues, it managed to rank only 27th in 1996 and 16th in 1997. Yet, when the technology team at Bankers Trust/Alex. Brown & Co., led by Frank Quattrone, George Boutros, and Bill Brady, were to be folded into the operations of the major German commercial bank Deutsche Bank, the three bankers bolted and cast their lot with CS First Boston in July 1998.[18] The result was that the firm saw its volume of IPO underwriting in general, and technology deals in particular, soar as companies flocked to it. As a consequence, the firm's rank in IPO underwriting, based on number of deals, climbed from 7th place in 1998, to a 1st place showing in 1999, when CS First Boston closed the books on 49 tech IPOs, the best ever single-year showing by any underwriter.

By contrast, consider the role that Internet analyst Henry Blodget played at his former and current employer. Previously, Blodget was employed by CIBC Oppenheimer & Co., but presently he is under contract to Merrill Lynch. In the one-year period prior to his joining Merrill in early 1999, Oppenheimer and Merrill could both brag of holding about a 5 percent market share each in Internet IPO proceeds. Merrill was responsible for underwriting two Net IPOs in 1998 with total proceeds of $69.2 million, while CIBC Oppenhiemer's tally was $65 million from a single IPO. In the time after Blodget joined Merrill, the firm's Internet IPO business climbed to more than $534 million in proceeds from seven deals, whereas Oppenheimer could boast of only two issues, with proceeds of under $130 million. Thus, like a baseball franchise that pays a free agent millions of dollars to join the team, Merrill paid money to Blodget that, apparently, the company thought was well spent, despite the views of some skeptics.[19]

RISK FACTORS

If any one section of the red herring can be labeled as the by-product of a legal mind, for better or worse, then it would have to be the part laying out the risk factors associated with the offering. In what may also be called the "worst-case scenario" section, the risk factors portion of the red herring lists all the real, likely, and perhaps improbable events that could cause the company to go swirling out of control and into insolvency the day after the IPO is completed. These eventualities typically include a dependency on a limited line of customers, a reliance on key executives to manage the operation, and the possibility that a competitor will emerge with a similar or better product or service. Furthermore, it's not uncommon for the company to declare in this section, with such language as "we may fail...," "we may be unable...," or "we may lack resources...," that a high degree of risk is associated with the offering. While it is generally assumed that the risk factors section of the prospectus is designed to insulate the company from liability by disclosing known and potential risks, one interesting caveat has begun to emerge: Some documents are carrying language indicating that the company is at risk of securities class action litigation due to volatility in the IPO price. Hence, companies are acknowledging that there will be price swings in their stock (perhaps this is good news for day traders!) and that they do not wish to be punished for such movements.

REVIEW AND COMMENT

The process of registering a security for a public offering is not limited to simply assembling the facts and figures contained in the documents and arranging such information in a proper form. Rather, once the document has been drafted, it must be forwarded to the SEC's Division of Corporate Finance for review. Here, regulators will probe the document to determine whether there is any deficiency in the "material facts" presented that would affect investment decisions. Material facts may include, but are not limited to, financial statements and the section of the prospectus highlighting management's discussion and analysis of the firm's financial status and results of operations. Often, regulators may object to a particular way revenues or profits are booked by the company or to an unusual accounting practice that is employed. Once the agency has completed its examination of the firm's prospective IPO filing, it will forward a "comment letter" notifying the company of any shortcomings that may exist in the document.[20]

HERE, THERE, AND EVERYWHERE

There once was a time when receiving a red herring was tantamount to being on some privileged list of those entitled to special treatment. Prior to the Internet Age and other communication and delivery improvements, brokers would tease their clients and prospects by dangling a red herring in front of them as if it were some sacred text or holy scripture to be read only by a chosen few. When the red herring finally was mailed, the broker usually stapled several of his business cards to the document, making it difficult or impossible to open. And there were those who, rather than ship the red herring by the trusty U.S. Postal Service, delivered the document to a client by overnight courier. Of course, the broker never mentioned to his prospect that the reason for the special handling was not a case of premium service, but rather a means to avoid mail-fraud charges if a disgruntled client ever filed a complaint!

But the recent liberalization of investing now allows the red herring to be obtained instantly through a variety of Web sites. Among those that provide investors with such documents are www.edgar-online.com, www.ipo.com., and www.freeedgar.com. Furthermore, investors may log onto the academic libraries of various university business schools, such as MIT's Sloan School of Management (www.sloan.mit.edu), to access public filings.

One of the most active proponents of widespread dissemination of the preliminary prospectus, as well as practically all relevant financial information, is the SEC. On three occasions, the agency has issued releases regarding the electronic delivery of information. Its first declaration was the October 1995 SEC Release 33-7233, the body of which stated that information distributed electronically must be equivalent to its hard-copy counterpart. In addition, the SEC requires that recipients of the electronic version of a prospectus be offered the opportunity to permanently save that information.

AMENDMENTS, LOCKUPS, AND THE QUIET PERIOD: ISSUES BEFORE AND AFTER THE DEAL

IN A SIMPLE, IDEAL WORLD, IPOS WOULD OPERATE AS FOLLOWS: A COMPANY DECIDES THAT IT REQUIRES CAPITAL TO EXPAND ITS OPERATIONS. THE COMPANY FILES THE NECESSARY PAPERWORK TO COMPLY WITH REGULATIONS, HIRES AN INVESTMENT BANK TO OVERSEE THE ISSUANCE OF STOCK, AND, FINALLY, RECEIVES THE FUNDS FROM THE COMPLETED OFFERING. THE COMPANY THEN PROCEEDS TO EXECUTE ITS BUSINESS PLAN. SUCH IS NOT THE CASE, HOWEVER, IN A WORLD OF CHANGING CONDITIONS, SHIFTING MARKETS,

AND GYRATING PRICES. MORE OFTEN THAN NOT, AN ORIGINAL REGISTRATION STATEMENT MAY SEE CHANGES IN SUCH ITEMS AS SHARES OFFERED, THE ANTICIPATED PRICE RANGE FOR THE OFFERING, AND, IN SOME RARE CASES, THE UNDERWRITER. INVESTORS NEED TO BE AWARE OF THE IMPACT OF SUCH REVISIONS ON THE PROSPECTIVE PRICE OF THE IPO, AS WELL AS ON THE COMPANY'S FUTURE OPERATING PERFORMANCE.

Likewise, just as changes in pricing frequently take place in the days and weeks prior to the completion of an IPO, so, too, are there "lockups," which are designed, at least in theory, to limit price changes after the offering is final. Then, after the deal is done, during a time called the "quiet period," restrictions apply that limit what can be discussed by the relevant parties to the offering, as well as what shares can be bought or sold. These restrictions frequently are aimed at limiting or eliminating price volatility. Yet, all too often, such caps have the opposite effect, resulting in price gyrations analogous to a pressure cooker exploding when its lid is opened prematurely or left on too long over a hot range. This chapter's objective is to examine some of these developments, which may occur either before or after the IPO becomes effective.

Perhaps the most critical development affecting an IPO prior to its completion is a decision by the banker or other issuer to withdraw or postpone the offering.[21] Although not always fatal or harmful (witness theglobe.com's offering discussed earlier or the Goldman Sachs 1999 IPO, originally filed in the spring of 1998), a delay in the offering often spells difficulty for the firm. Expenses are likely to rise if documents must be refiled with regulators and, subsequently, new prospectuses delivered to likely investors. In addition, given that the purpose of the IPO is to raise capital for the company, any delay may inhibit operations and erode both confidence and the firm's financial resources. The erosion of confidence may be compounded if the postponement is the result of an individual problem, such as auditing troubles or the loss of a key customer, and not a mass withdrawal of IPO deals from the marketplace by underwriters. The latter occurred in late October 1987 and in the summer of 1998 when the overall investing climate soured. Still, whether the delay is the result of poor market conditions or specific misgivings about the individual deal, a postponement nonetheless may trouble investors enough to lower their confidence in the offering.

DAYS BEFORE THE DEAL

As noted earlier, the process of completing an IPO, from filing a registration statement with the SEC, to printing and distributing a prospectus, to the actual pricing of the deal, may run from a few weeks to several months before it is declared effective. Typically, it was considered reasonable for a company planning an IPO to endure a 60- to 75-day period that included filing the offering, responding to any queries from the SEC, amending the original document, and completing the transaction. Yet, as deals proliferated, terms became more complex, and administrative resources have remained stagnant or, in some cases, have been reduced. It is not surprising to see an increase in the average number of days an IPO remains in registration before the deal is finalized.

As we shall see later, the average number of shares offered by an IPO in its registration statement has steadily been on the increase.[22] IPOs completed in 1995 had an average of 3.5 million shares filed. The following year the figure inched up to 3.7 million, and in 1997 it reached over 4.4 million. By 1998 the average number of shares filed for an IPO was up to 5.9 million, by 1999 it cracked the 7 million mark, and in the opening days of 2000, buoyed by John Hancock Financial Services' 102-million-share offering (which, incidentally, ranked as the 12th leading IPO in terms of shares offered), the number exceeded the 10-million-share mark.

RAISING PRICES BEFORE THE CLOSE

As a prospective IPO is readied for public and regulatory review, the underwriter arrives at an expected price range for the deal. For example, when the Foundry Networks' offering was completed in September 1999, the firm's underwriter, Deutsche-Alex. Brown, initially expected to price the offer between $14 and $16 per share. In the days prior to the opening, the expected price range had jumped to between $22 and $24. By the time the IPO was actually completed, the offer price was $25, some 60 percent ahead of the midpoint range from where the deal was first thought to start trading. Such changes are not unusual, given the strong institutional and individual investor demand for many IPOs.

What is noteworthy is that, while throughout the 1990s approximately one out of every five IPOs that came to market was priced above the high end of the deal's original filing range, 1999 saw an unprecedented proportion of IPOs being priced at exceptionally higher prices. Nearly 40 percent of all IPOs completed in 1999 were priced above the high end of the offering's original high filing price.[23] One may point to the proliferation of Internet and e-commerce IPOs as the fuel fanning these pricing fires: Last year, more than one-third of all IPOs were Internet related. However, one may also suggest that the vast supply of Internet IPOs should not have resulted in extreme volatility, but rather should have served to mitigate price swings, as investors had a greater range of choices among portfolios and thus could have been more discriminating had there been fewer Internet IPOs available. In fact, what apparently occurred was that those issues which were dropping in value found few supporters, whereupon investors flocked to those issues which posted gains and, in the process, bid them to even higher ground.

Yet, as evidenced by available data, when an underwriter of an IPO announces a change in the prospective deal's expected price range, investors are presented with a strong and reliable clue as to what the future prices will likely be. For example, since 1991, those IPOs which experienced a cut in their original high filing price typically underperformed those deals whose high end of the price range was raised. Hence, in 1998, 76 IPOs had the high end of their original filing price reduced, and in the subsequent 12 months, those issues gained, on average, 27 percent. The 1991–1998 figure compares with 44 IPOs completed during 1998 alone, which saw an increase in the high end of the filing range. In the one-year period following the completion of those high-end deals, they appreciated an average of 142 percent. Likewise, during 1999, no fewer than 54 IPOs saw a reduction in the initial high filing price, whereupon those deals gained an average of 15 percent on their first day of trading and after 2 months of trading had appreciated about 28 percent from the final offer price. However, the 166 IPOs priced that year and that saw price hikes prior to the actual completion of their deal had a first-day increase of over 127 percent and jumped more than 180 percent after 60 days of trading.[24]

These results match those of an analysis by Kathleen Weiss Hanley[25] that appeared in the *Journal of Financial Economics*. In an article entitled "The Underpricing of Initial Public Offerings and the Partial Adjustment Phenomenon," she put forth the proposition that the connection between the final offer price of an IPO and its range as disclosed in the red herring is a reliable indicator of returns.

SILENCE IS GOLDEN

As the wide media coverage of some notable trials has turned the average citizen into an armchair expert on the rules of civil procedure, so, too, has one "road show" provided investors with a quick education in the SEC's rules with respect to the public disclosure of information.[26]

In what one day may be a business school case study as to how management should *not* perform prior to the completion of an IPO, let us examine the case of Webvan, Inc. This California-based e-commerce grocer, which previously had been the recipient of the largest private financing by a U.S. company, was poised to go public in early October 1999. Its underwriters and comanagers had solicited indications of interest from investors and had arranged several road shows (i.e., meetings with pension fund and money managers). These meetings, which are intended for management to adhere to the facts contained in the prospectus, are supposedly limited to financial and investment professionals only. Yet, a financial journalist gained entry into the road show's conference call and subsequently reported on Webvan's presentation. Among the issues raised were matters concerning the so-called double standard whereby institutions attending the road show gain access to facts and information not available in public documents, while an average investor's only source of information is contained only in those public documents. In this instance, professional investors gained access to information about Webvan's on-time delivery rates, as well as some of the special contractual relationships the company enjoys. In addition, in the days and weeks prior to the expected date of the IPO, Webvan management was highly visible in such financial publications as *Business Week* and *Forbes Magazine*. As a result, the SEC was compelled to act in the belief that Webvan had violated the "quiet period" guidelines, which mandate that the management of a company issuing securities limit its comments to what is contained in the prospectus and nothing else. Furthermore, as various financial television programs compete aggressively for audiences, it is not uncommon for a CEO of a newly minted IPO to appear on a program discussing his or her company's debut. Yet, the underwriter cannot issue any research reports on the IPO for 25 days after the offer. In this regard, whereas a decade ago it would have been unthinkable for management to speak publicly on the merits of an IPO until a printed report was issued by an underwriter, it has become an everyday occurrence to see a CEO on CNBC, CNN, or Bloomberg TV talking about the IPO.

At a cursory glance, the delay in the Webvan IPO resulted in some short-term costs. First, from a monetary statement, prospectuses and related documents had to be reprinted to include the information that Webvan's management had discussed at the road show and that was subsequently leaked by the press. Second, investors who had anticipated completing their orders in early October now had to seek alternative offerings. However, in the long term, the incident gave rise to questions regarding the merit of a regulation crafted in an age prior to financial cable television programming and investment chat rooms. Although a thorough examination of SEC guidelines and regulations is beyond the scope of this book, it may nonetheless be stated that because technology moves faster than regulation, it is the latter that must change in order to serve the public's interest.

Still, as mentioned earlier, the underwriter cannot issue any research reports on the IPO for 25 days after the offer.

Furthermore, research departments of investment banks are finding new means of offering recommendations on IPOs even before they are traded. Specifically, certain companies that have yet to issue an IPO, but that have publicly traded fixed-income instruments (primarily high-yield or "junk" bonds) and whose financial results are reported to the SEC, may be classified as a "reporting company" by statute. Thus, based upon a strict interpretation of securities law, investment banks not involved in the public offering may issue a research report on the company despite the fact that no public stock was traded. Such was the case when the New York investment bank Bear Stearns & Co. issued a research report on the on-line auction company FreeMarkets, Inc., prior to the completion of the firm's IPO in early December 1999. Incredibly, an analyst writing the report forecast a target price of $300 per share in the upcoming 12 months even before a single share of the company ever began trading![27] That development comes on the heels of the SEC's 1999 announcement that it is seeking to write specific regulations for investment road shows, with keen attention given over to the degree to which information is made available to the general public as well as the investment community.

Notwithstanding the monetary costs associated with the Webvan, Inc. episode, the true expense was the loss of confidence some investors endured, as well as the damaged relationship that ensued between the issuer and the underwriter. Besides clearly illustrating in the minds of investors that there exists a double standard when it comes to the disbursement of information regarding IPOs, some investors questioned the merits of the IPO process itself. In the aftermath of the Webvan IPO incident, SEC chairman Arthur Levitt cautioned companies planning IPOs that the agency would not consent to the continued practice of "material nonpublic information" being forwarded to institutions during the road-show period, to the exclusion of individual investors. Nonetheless, lines still continue to be blurred as the agency is being forced to address such basic issues relating to the road show as whether information distributed at these events must first be filed with the SEC and whether an on-line event should be classified as an "oral communication or writing." The latter issue clearly illustrates the fact that many securities regulations were crafted specifically for written or oral presentations and that regulators are still pondering how to address investor concerns in an electronic age.[28]

In a noteworthy postscript to this affair, the Webvan offering was finally completed in November 1999, after about a month's delay, at a price of $15 per share. Whatever misgivings or concerns investors had concerning the road-show detour, it was apparent that they were short lived. Responding to strong institutional demand, underwriters raised the initial filing range from between $11 and $13 to between $13 and $15. At the close of Webvan's first day of trading, its shares rallied over 65 percent, to close at about $25 each, placing the company in the 67th percentile in terms of first-day trading gains by IPOs in 1999. Yet, the shares subsequently headed lower as investors began to have misgivings over the long-term prospects of some e-commerce IPOs. By early March 2000, Webvan shares were trading at under their offer price and some 50 percent off their all-time high.

An additional effect of Webvan's faux pas has been an embrace by some investors of Internet road shows as a means of distributing information about an upcoming IPO. Various electronic broadcasters, such as Bloomberg and Yahoo!, offer recorded video and audio presentations of IPO road shows, while a leading provider of business-to-business communications, Seattle-based Activate.net Corp., received approval from the Securities & Exchange Commission in September 1999 to transmit financial information live over the Internet through a password-protected user-controlled presentation rather than on a tape-delayed basis. This service, entitled "Activate Roadshow Service," allows viewers to electronically submit questions to road-show participants that can be answered during the broadcast. The use of the password and other security measures are designed to prevent unauthorized investors from sneaking a peek at the proceedings. Perhaps in part due to this development, Activate.net was acquired by CMGI, Inc., one of the world's leading "incubators" of Internet companies. Another response was the move by the on-line investment firm Wit Capital to allow open access to all press conferences, in addition to posting transcripts of the calls on the company's Web site.

But perhaps the most comprehensive and complete answer to the road-show issue is to simply broaden the audience by allowing individual investors into the presentation. In early 2000, SEC Commissioner Laura S. Unger[29] stated that the commission may mandate that prospective IPOs provide the general public unrestricted access to promotional material used in road shows.

RESTRICTED SALES AND LOCKUPS

One might expect that, given the large number of IPOs that have dramatically risen in price, insiders, company employees, and beneficial owners of the new offering would be quick to unload their shares to ensure their gains. Yet, just as it is difficult for the average investor to gain entry into the IPO club, so, too, is it complicated for the insider to sell shares on the open market. Specifically, since in many cases the number of shares being offered in an IPO represents only a small portion of the outstanding number of shares of the company, it is commonly believed that if insiders and other pre-IPO investors (e.g., institutions, venture capitalists, etc.) were permitted to sell soon after the deal was closed, the result would be mildly disruptive at best and tumultuous at worst, as well as damaging to the company's ability to raise capital in the long run.

Hence, once the offering is complete, many companies restrict the sale of stock by shareholders who secured their holdings prior to the actual IPO. These shareholders may be able to sell such restricted shares only if the shares are registered or if they meet the criteria for exemption from registration under three sections of the Securities Act of 1933. First, under Rule 144, beneficial owners of restricted shares for at least one year may sell a certain number of shares 90 days after the completion of the offering, given that certain conditions pertaining to the percentage of shares they may sell and the amount of notice they must give are met. Second, under Rule 144(k) of the act, a person who, for 90 days prior to the completion of the offering, is not viewed as an affiliate of the issuing company and who has owned his or her shares for at least two years may sell those shares upon the completion of the IPO. Put another way, Rule 144 shall not apply

> to restricted securities sold for the account of a person who is not an affiliate of the issuer at the time of sale and has not been an affiliate during the preceding three months provided a period of at least two years has elapsed since the later of the date of the securities.

It is noteworthy that, as defined, a person may be (1) a relative or spouse, (2) a trust or estate that controls a beneficial interest of 10 percent or more in the equity, or (3) a corporation or other organization that controls an interest of 10 percent or more in the equity. Finally, under Rule 701 of the Securities Act, titled as an "exemption for offer and sale of securities pursuant to certain compensation benefit plans and contracts relating to compensation," shares of common stock attained through the exercise of rights under the issuing company's stock plans, including options, may be resold by individuals, other than affiliates, 90 days after the completion of the offering, subject to restrictions found in Rule 144(a).

Similar to requiring restricted sales, many IPOs enact lockup agreements, which are arrangements between the company's directors, officers, stockholders, and option holders not to sell any share in the offering for a specified period without the express consent of the underwriter. The purpose of such a covenant, at least in theory, is to limit volatility in trading, as well as to maintain a loyal shareholder base. Essentially, an underwriter who has put up cash to buy shares under a firm-commitment offering is looking to avoid any dumping of shares once the deal is done. As noted in Table 3-1, throughout the 1990s there was a near-universal embrace of lockup agreements, with over 90 percent of IPOs since 1996 incorporating such agreements into their plans.

Yet, even with the trend to place a lockup agreement in the company's prospectus, there has been a corresponding decline, on average, in the number of days the agreement can remain in effect. The duration of the lockup agreement is measured from the date of the prospectus. Throughout the 1990s, until 1999, a typical lockup agreement was in effect, on average, for nearly 250 days, or about eight months, as indicated in Table 3-1. Thus, insiders and officers affiliated with an IPO that was completed, for example, in June 1997 were not able to trade their shares without restrictions until February 1998. By 1994, the length of the typical lockup agreement was 275 days, or about nine months; thereupon, the average duration of the lockup began to decline until 1999, when, for the first year

Table 3-1 IPOs with Lockup Provisions

Year	Number of IPOs	Percentage of All IPOs	Average Days before Expiration
1988	164	92.1	278
1989	176	93.8	176
1990	123	71.5	258
1991	328	89.4	254
1992	483	93.4	255
1993	627	88.7	254
1994	536	87.9	275
1995	518	89.3	248
1996	803	92.1	239
1997	579	91.8	234
1998	363	97.1	226
1999	543	94.1	184
2000*	246	91.1	184

* Through June 30.
Source: Thomson Financial Securities Data

since 1989, it fell to less than 200 days (about 185 days, or nearly six months). This reduction in the number of days before a lockup agreement expired corresponded with an unprecedented appreciation in IPOs in their opening days.

Yet, large investors remain concerned that a pending lockup expiration may trigger selling. As a result, some have offered to extend the duration of a lockup with respect to their own holdings. For example, Vulcan Ventures and General Atlantic Partners, two early backers of the e-commerce Web site Priceline.com, reportedly arranged for a partial sale of their holdings in exchange for an extension of the lockup period for the rest of their holdings.

Besides the rapid appreciation of many IPOs contributing to the decline in the duration of the lockup, so, too, is executive compensation a factor. Since many employees of start-ups—especially Internet operations—are wooed with stock options to join a new enterprise, it is not uncommon to see an official at a firm whose IPO skyrocketed become a millionaire on paper, but a pauper at the bank. Shortening the lockup period allows that individual to readily cash out some shares.[30]

In contrast, some argue that the lockup agreement is designed not entirely to lock in insiders from selling early, but to limit the available supply of stock on the open market and thus artificially drive up the price of the stock and, consequently, lock out smaller retail investors. For example, the results of a study by Michael L. McBain and David S. Krause[31] published in a 1989 article in the *Journal of Business Venturing* indicate that an IPO's stock price is directly related to the proportion of insider ownership. The premise is that lower insider ownership indicates higher risk and thus adversely affects the price of a share. Accordingly, for as long as insiders maintain their level of ownership, outsiders will bid the shares higher.

It would be a mistake, though, if one were to argue that the IPOs with the shortest lockup agreements outperform those with longer ones. Based upon available information, 1999 saw several IPOs, including Bluestone Software, Salon.com, KPNQwest, and Fashionmall.com, come to market with expiration dates of just 90 days or less on their lockup agreements. In nearly every case, those IPOs with shorter lockup agreements, on average, performed no better, if not worse, than the typical IPO.[32] For example, Salon.com, which priced its IPO at $10 a share, had a 90-day lockup period in force. However, at the expiration day, the shares had already dropped over 40 percent in value. Analysis revealed that those IPOs with lockup agreements of 90 days gained approximately 13.1 percent by the time the lockup expired. This figure compares with a 26.2 percent gain, on average, for those IPOs whose lockup agreement came to an end 180 days after the offer date. Furthermore, IPOs with 90-day lockups that were completed in 1999 gained 128 percent, on average, by the close of that year, compared with a 210 percent average gain for IPOs with lockup durations of 180 days or more. Results such as these, however, may be swayed by the higher number of IPOs with 180-day lockup periods compared with those with a shorter duration. Nonetheless, several facts are irrefutable. First, the average length of a lockup agreement has been on the decline. Second, the number of IPOs with 90-day or shorter lockup periods is on the rise, doubling from just 11 in 1995 to 22 by 1998 and increasing to a near-record high of 31 in 1999, second only to 1997's 38 IPOs. Apparently, institutions and insiders are eager to exit one deal to move to another. Finally, venture-capital-backed IPOs typically have shorter lockup periods than those issues not backed by such funding. For example, of the 77 venture-capital-supported IPOs issued in 1998, the corresponding lockup duration was 184 days, compared with 239 days for IPOs that lacked such funding. The following year, the average lockup period of venture-capital-supported IPOs was 177 days, while all other IPOs had an average lockup period of 192 days.[33]

One reason the lockup expiration periods have dropped is that venture-capital firms and institutional owners of IPOs are less willing to keep their full investment intact for any extended period because of the need to commit capital to new investments. As one money manager noted, in today's IPO market venture funds must quickly return some of their gains to their partners and then must turn out more deals to remain competitive, after which they quickly move on to the next deal. In part, the rapid appreciation of IPOs in the past few years has made it imperative for institutions to "lock in" gains whereby they can document a strong return on capital to their own investors and partners in order to garner more capital to fund more IPOs. Hence, the contraction in the lockup period takes on a life of its own, with institutions needing to exit ever more quickly from their investments to get more cash to fund more deals. Another factor that may cause the shorter expiration time of lockups to be viewed favorably is that, in some cases, fund managers are prohibited from owning a stock with limited liquidity. Once the supply of stock increases upon expiration of the lockup, these managers may surge in to buy shares, thus increasing the demand, and perhaps the price, of some issues.

But what happens after the lockup period expires? An examination of recent IPOs reveals interesting results. For example, among IPOs priced in 1998 with lockup agreements of 180 days, the average gain at the time of expiration was approximately 19 percent. However, in the next 180-day period, those IPOs gained about 42 percent. As for those deals with lockups of 90 days, the average gain at the time of the agreement's expiration was under 10 percent, while in the next 90 days after the lockup expired, their average gain was a paltry 2.7 percent.

IPO Observations: As a general rule, if an IPO is trading under its offer price in the first month of dealings, it is unlikely that it will soon return to its offer price. Of nearly 1200 IPOs issued in the 1990s that traded at prices lower than the offering price in the first month after they were issued, only 367, or about 31 percent, posted any positive returns by the end of their first year of activity.

IT'S NOT WHO YOU KNOW... MOST OF THE TIME

ARMED WITH THE KNOWLEDGE OF THE MECHANICS OF AN IPO, THE ABILITY TO READ A PRELIMINARY PROSPECTUS, AND THE INSIGHT TO DETERMINE THE IMPACT OF VARIOUS REVISIONS, AMENDMENTS, AND AGREEMENTS RELATING TO THE DEAL, AN INVESTOR MAY NOW BELIEVE THAT HE OR SHE IS WELL EQUIPPED TO PURCHASE AN IPO. DON'T OPEN YOUR CHECKBOOK, YET, HOWEVER. THE NEAR-UNIVERSAL RESPONSE INDIVIDUAL INVESTORS OFTEN RECEIVE WHEN TRYING TO BUY A PENDING DEAL FROM A TRADITIONAL STOCKBROKER WOULD BE AT BEST A CHUCKLE, OR MORE LIKELY, AN OUTRIGHT REJECTION. JUST AS MEMBERS OF A POSH COUNTRY CLUB OR AN EXCLUSIVE SOCIETY OFTEN PLACE VARIOUS RESTRICTIONS ON ASPIRING MEMBERS, SO,

TOO, DO INVESTMENT BANKS PLACE ROADBLOCKS BEFORE INVESTORS SEEKING TO GAIN ACCESS TO IPOS.

Yet, at one time, IPOs were a somewhat difficult item for retail stockbrokers to sell. In earlier years, when the typical profile of a stock investor was that of an older white male who put his money in such established blue chips as Goodyear Tire, Westinghouse Electric, and U.S. Steel, it was rare to find stocks of newly established companies in one's portfolio. Much of the decision-making process in creating an investment strategy or assembling a portfolio was left to the discretion of one's broker or "company man," who often held the same values and backgrounds as his client. But as the workplace has become diverse, so, too, has the investment world. Today's investors are increasingly younger, more affluent, better educated, and, most importantly, anticipating higher returns than investors of earlier generations. Furthermore, technology has put institutional-quality equity research at one's fingertips, while lower commissions have driven investment expenses to the bare bottom.

However, in part, one of the costs associated with the popular deep discount-stock trades at $5 each, or electronic trading, is that the importance of an alliance with a stockbroker has been significantly downplayed. Thus, it has been argued, mostly by established proponents of full-service brokers, such as John Stephens of Merrill Lynch, that Internet stock executions are a threat to the financial security of investors.[34] By contrast, those firms promoting low-cost and individually controlled investment decisions maintain that only those high-commission producers at Wall Street firms are threatened. As an example, some of the common excesses include full-service brokerage firms often charging handling fees greater than those some e-commerce sites charge for a single trade.[35] Furthermore, it has been documented that some brokers have pushed clients into such high-commission, yet low-return investments as real-estate partnerships, master-limited trusts, and yes, even IPOs. Yet, there are a couple of relevant facts to consider. First, Forrester Research has forecast that, by 2003, more than 10 percent of IPO volume will be sold to investors through on-line firms. And second, the number of individuals with on-line brokerage accounts is expected to double to more than 20 million by 2003, according to Jupiter Communications, while assets handled by on-line brokerages are likely to increase to nearly $3 trillion, from under $1 trillion in 1999. Yet, despite those expectations, the majority of individual security transactions will still be handled by individual brokers.[36]

The reality is that if you're seeking to purchase an IPO from a broker with whom you do not have an existing relationship, the chances are perhaps only somewhat better than being able to walk up to a ticket window the day of a championship sporting event and trying to gain entrance into the stadium or trying to purchase the most popular toy on December 24th. Moreover, even establishing an ongoing relationship with a broker doesn't guarantee that you will gain access to an IPO: The fact is that, until recently, access to IPOs was extremely limited, not only for individual investors, but also for the individual brokers of the leading underwriters of the IPO itself, as well as among various mutual funds and institutions. For example, in an exposé reported in *The Wall Street Journal,*[37] the existence of "pot lists" was revealed, indicating which institutional investors get the lion's share of hot IPOs. But more importantly, it also was uncovered that the Boston-based mutual fund giant Fidelity Investment regularly sought and received IPO allocations twice those of its closest competitor. Apparently, the investment firm exercised its might in controlling commissions and restricting orders to friendly IPO underwriters. In sum, those firms which provide greater trading activity to the sales desks of the underwriters in question are likely to get a better allocation of IPOs than mutual funds and asset management firms that have a relatively low turnover in their portfolio. In essence, if you trade, you get to play.

The reasons for such limited access vary. A study by Richard B. Carter and Frederick H. Dark[38] hypothesized that the so-called bulge-bracket investment banks (e.g., Morgan Stanley, Goldman Sachs, and Merrill Lynch) exploit their power of determining who gets what in allocating IPOs and seek to restrict IPO sales to primarily those investors with a long-range perspective, in order to limit "flipping" as well as to maintain market control. Such limited access for retail investors was parodied in an ad campaign by FRB.com, the on-line division of Friedman Billings Ramsey, a Virginia-based broker. In the commercial, the sound of a small knock on the door gives way to louder pounding as the announcer comments on investors being shut out of IPOs. The message is clear: For many years, access to IPOs has been by invitation only.

Others maintain that the IPO market, while lucrative in terms of both fees for the underwriter and returns for the investor, is but a small slice of the investment banking and overall equity market.[39] Thus, when the IPO is put into the context of the broad array of financial products, from mutual funds, to individual stocks, to direct stock-purchase plans offered by the likes of such blue chip companies as Merck, Home Depot, and Exxon, it becomes clear that individuals have an abundance of choices. Yet, in any given year, the number of IPOs issued is in the hundreds, a paltry figure compared with the several thousand issues that trade daily on the New York Stock Exchange, the NASDAQ National Market, or the American Stock Exchange. Plainly, the overwhelming demand for equities in general is magnified by the paltry supply of available IPO shares.

First, let's briefly examine how IPOs have traditionally been distributed internally within investment banks. Typically, an IPO would be divvied up by a pecking order established by the headquarters of a firm. Hence, if a 5,000,000-share offering by Merrill Lynch was in the wings, it was not unusual for a certain percentage of the shares to be allocated to a New England regional office and another portion to a Southeast office, while still other portions were assigned to West Coast shops. After that, sales managers in the respective offices would divide their allocations among top commission-producing representatives, based upon internal indications of interest submitted by the broker. Thus, if the Charlotte, North Carolina, office had 50,000 shares on hand, a million-dollar producer might receive 5000 shares to dangle before his or her most prized clients, while a rookie broker might be hard pressed to get 100 shares. And that doesn't even take into account comanagers of the deal or other managers who are part of the syndicate or selling group and who are also lining up to receive a portion of the offering.

For the average investor seeking a piece of a new offering, the chances of success are somewhat akin to that of picking the correct six numbers in a state lottery drawing. Likewise, as seen in Table 4-1, even some investment firms have difficulty in receiving a slice of a particular IPO. Based upon the fact that the so-called big-producing brokers would receive the largest allocation of an IPO to distribute, it is clear that the likely candidates for getting IPOs would the high-income clients of such brokers. Thus, it is not surprising to learn that when Netscape, one of the hottest IPOs of 1996, went public, it was reported that NBC news anchor Tom Brokaw was one of the lucky few who managed to get in at the opening price.[40] On the other hand, it is unlikely that the weather reporter from the NBC affiliate in Akron, Ohio, was successful in gaining access to shares. By and large, if

Table 4-1   Allocation of Shares for Selected IPOs

Issue	Wit Capital	Charles Schwab	E*TRADE	E*OFFERING	Datek	Ameri-trade	DLJ-Direct	Total Shares in Offering
barnesandnoble.com	940,000	0	0	0	0	0	0	25,000,000
eToys	178,000	0	0	0	0	0	0	8,320,000
Goldman Sachs	57,500	57,500	0	57,500	57,500	57,500	57,500	55,200,000
Junipter	48,000	48,000	0	0	0	0	0	4,800,000
Webvan	198,000	0	0	0	0	0	0	25,000,000
F5 Networks	0	80,000	0	0	0	0	0	3,000,000
Internet Capital Group	0	0	0	150,000	0	0	0	14,900,000

Source: Company prospectuses.

you do not have assets of at least $100,000 in your brokerage account, it would be difficult to convince a broker to fulfill your request for an IPO. Deals that are viewed as "hot" and likely to rise dramatically are more prone to end up in a high-asset account, rather than one with a few thousand dollars. The reason is that the IPO allocation process is very much a discriminatory operation whereby those who have the resources to purchase other financial products from the brokers, rather than small retail investors, will be the recipients of a new stock offering. For the broker, discriminating in this manner simply makes good business sense: Reward my top accounts and don't bother with the small ones.

A MARKET RESPONSE

While we have not quite come to underwriters having a rallying cry of "IPOs for the people!" providing greater access to IPOs is one of the primary objectives of some recently formed investment firms. Among these firms are WR Hambrecht + Co., started by a San Francisco investment banker, Bill Hambrecht, formerly of the technology boutique Hambrecht & Quist (which, incidentally, was acquired by the money-center bank Chase Manhattan in October 1999 for $1.4 billion), Wit Capital (in which the investment firm Goldman Sachs has a 22 percent stake), and E*OFFERING (which is partially owned by the electronic broker E*TRADE). However, it would be presumptuous to label such underwriters as "new breed," "new age," or some other clever description indicating that they are trailblazers of some sort. These enterprises recognize that individuals have long been frustrated with the way IPOs have traditionally been marketed and thus are seeking to carve out a niche in the financial services marketplace. Are they motivated by altruism? Of course not.

Rather, firms that are offering the possibility of latching onto an IPO are simply responding to customers' wishes and providing a service for a perceived need. In addition, for the most part, these firms are acting neither as book managers on an IPO nor as comanagers, but rather as members of the domestic syndicate that they are dependent on, developing and maintaining relationships with the major underwriters of IPOs, notably Goldman Sachs, Morgan Stanley Dean Witter, and Merrill Lynch. Featured next are summaries of some of the leading "e-managers," firms that rely on e-commerce as a means of distributing IPOs and building their businesses.

WIT CAPITAL

For some firms, the road to riches takes peculiar turns. A case in point is Wit Capital. The firm began after ads appeared in newspapers such as *USA Today* featuring an offer to purchase shares in a New York–based firm called Spring Street Brewery at $1.85 each. In 1995, the company completed a Regulation A offering that raised nearly $1.6 million through the sale of more than 844,000 shares in what was heralded as the first "digital IPO." Shortly thereafter, the microbrewer evolved into Wit Capital, an on-line investment bank. Wit's mission was to slash the costs firms must endure when going public, according to the company's founder, Andrew Klein, a onetime associate at the New York law firm of Cravath, Swaine & Moore. The catalyst of this move was a trading mechanism whereby Spring Street Brewery's shares were to change hands through an electronic bulletin board called Wit-Trade.

However, over time, the company began to take on the image of a traditional Wall Street firm. Its first major step was going public itself. In June 1999, Wit Capital issued 7.6 million shares at $9 each in an IPO that raised $68.4 million for the firm before fees and expenses. However, rather than doing the job itself, Wit tapped the services of Bear Stearns to underwrite the offering. Since the debut of the offering, Wit's stock price has more than doubled. Also, Wit began a hiring spree to staff its operation with key personnel, including Ronald Readmond, former vice chairman of Charles Schwab and managing director at Alex. Brown & Son, who joined Wit as its co-CEO, and former Merrill Lynch Internet analyst Jonathan Cohen. Other signs that the so-called rebels were looking much like the establishment were managerial appointments such as George Lieberman, formerly the director of technology and strategy at Merrill Lynch and one-time head of capital markets at Salomon Smith Barney, as chief information officer, and Mark Loehr as director of investment banking. In March 2000, the company hired Mack Rossoff, who had served as JP Morgan's chief of media and entertainment banking, as head of its mergers and acquisitions operations. Hence, professionals from the very establishment organizations that Wit was supposedly not going to replicate were in fact added to the Wit "dream team." And the push to tap into Wall Street's old guard wasn't cheap: Wit Capital announced that in the nine months ending September 30, 1999, compensation and benefit expenses soared from $2.7 million in the previous year to over $25 million, and total expenses soared from under $7 million to over $40 million in the same period. During the same time, the firm's revenues rose from $1.3 million to more than $28 million.[41]

In early 1999, it was reported that the company had more than 15,000 accounts and had assembled a network of online brokers, including Datek, Quick & Reilly, National Discount Brokers, and Mysdiscountbroker.com, a subsidiary of Southwest Securities Group, that could reach an investor population of over 2 million. Within six months, Wit's accounts grew to more than 52,000. Investors seeking to open a Wit capital account are required to deposit a minimum of $2000. For those seeking IPOs, Wit advises that investors have at least $2000 in assets at the time the offering is declared effective. However, one episode resulted in a change in Wit operations. When an investor first indicated an interest in an IPO, after reviewing the preliminary prospectus, he or she would enter a "conditional offer" to purchase the shares when they were issued. Such offers would be accepted by Wit only if the IPO was declared "effective" by the SEC. It was at this point that Wit stumbled in the eyes of some, since the firm would notify investors who bid on the deal that the offer was effective, whereupon a reply was required to reaffirm the original order. If no response was tendered, either because the investor was unavailable or because the bank had the incorrect E-mail address, then the offer was often not filled. This procedure was made more burdensome when investors sometimes had to determine when an IPO was being priced and await notification from Wit. However, the procedure was revamped when the SEC relaxed its rules concerning the on-line distribution of IPOs. The new rules allowed Wit, and effectively all firms, to collect final client confirmation orders for IPOs up to two days prior to the time the offering was declared effective by the agency.

Also disturbing to some investors are the small allocations Wit itself receives on IPOs. It has been estimated that in a typical IPO with several million shares being offered, Wit would be fortunate to receive a few hundred thousand. Thus, as Wit Capital's Andrew Klein conceded, "we may receive 40,000 or more requests on a hot deal but can only satisfy a fraction." For example, in the third quarter of 1999, the company reported that the number of shares it had retained for sale to its customers (including designated shares) actually fell to 6.8 million, from 6.9 million in the previous quarter. Still, it must be recognized that any "democratization" of the IPO process represents progress from the closed-door policies that were in place just a few years ago. Furthermore, Wit has participated in some brand-name IPOs, as illustrated in Table 4-2, and has been a comanager of several offerings in 1999, as well as part of a syndicate on over 70 IPOs, according to information tallied by Thomson Financial Securities Data.

Besides its activity as a broker and distributor of IPOs, Wit has engaged in some savvy acquisitions. Late in 1999, the company acquired the Connecticut-based SoundView Technology Group, an institutional investment banking and research boutique with a concentration in high-tech issues, for a reported $325 million. SoundView was founded in 1979 as part of the consulting firm Gartner Group and subsequently became an independent company in 1985. The move was seen as a strategic step by Wit in its efforts to both penetrate the institutional market and gain larger IPO allocations for subsequent distribution to its retail clients. However, if published reports hold true, then Wit's attempt to provide retail clients with greater access to IPOs is meeting a brick wall.[42] In the aftermath of the SoundView deal, Wit has seen fewer, not more, allocations of IPOs. Mark Loehr, head of investment banking for the newly formed Wit SoundView, concedes that while the firm had previously averaged 200,000-share allocations for IPOs, three deals in early 2000—for MatrixOne, Switchboard.com, and Register.com— each averaged about 100,000 allocated shares.

WR Hambrecht + Co.

The cofounder of San Francisco-based investment boutique Hambrecht & Quist, W. R. (Bill) Hambrecht has a long history of bringing innovative and technologically driven companies public. In March 1968, along with George Quist, he

Table 4-2 Wit Co-managers IPOs in 1999

Issue Date	Issuer	Business Description	Proceeds Amount in This Market ($ mil)	IPO	Book Manager(s)
1/21/99	Covad Communications Group Inc	Provides communications services	140.4	Yes	BEAR
1/28/99	American Axle and Mnfrg	Manufacture automobile axles	95.2	Yes	MERRILL
2/4/99	Delphi Automotive Systems Corp	Manufacture automotive components	1445.0	Yes	MSDW
2/10/99	Korn/Ferry International	Provides executive search services	164.5	Yes	CS-FB
2/12/99	United Pan-Europe Comm NV	Provides telecommunications services	576.9	Yes	GS
2/22/99	Corporate Executive Board Co	Provides business research	124.4	Yes	SALOMON-SMITH
3/29/99	MKS Instruments	Manufacture process control instruments	91.0	Yes	NATION-MONT-SEC
3/29/99	Priceline.com Inc	Online travel agency	160.0	Yes	MSDW
4/8/99	Hugoton Royalty Trust	Oil and gas exploration, production	142.5	Yes	GS
4/13/99	MIH Ltd	Provides pay-television services	81.7	Yes	MERRILL

Date	Company	Description	Amount		Underwriter
4/15/99	StanCorp Financial Group Inc	Insurance company	283.1	Yes	GS
5/3/99	Goldman Sachs Group Inc	Investment firm	2925.6	Yes	GS
5/11/99	WESCO International Inc	Construct industrial buildings	140.0	Yes	LEH
5/14/99	Nextcard Inc	Provide credit services	120.0	Yes	DLJ
5/19/99	eToys Inc	Web-based retailer of toys	166.4	Yes	GS
6/3/99	Zany Brainy Inc	Own, operate toy stores	61.0	Yes	DLJ
6/9/99	Azurix Corp	Provides water services	556.3	Yes	MERRILL
6/16/99	SBA Communications Corp	Provides wireless telecommunication services	79.4	Yes	LEH
6/18/99	Goto.com	Provides Internet search services	90.0	Yes	DLJ
6/23/99	Globespan Inc	Manufacture semiconductors	48.8	Yes	BOSTON-ROBERTS
6/24/99	Internet.com Corp	Provide Internet services	47.6	Yes	US-PIPER
6/28/99	E-Loan Inc	Provides Internet mortgage services	49.0	Yes	GS
6/29/99	Network Plus Corp	Provides telecommunications services	128.0	Yes	GS
7/1/99	Commerce One Inc	Develop e-commerce solutions	69.3	Yes	CS-FB

Table 4-2 Wit Co-managers IPOs in 1999 (Continued)

Issue Date	Issuer	Business Description	Proceeds Amount in This Market ($ mil)	IPO	Book Manager(s)
7/7/99	Interliant Inc	Provide Internet services	61.3	Yes	MERRILL
7/20/99	Insight Communications Co Inc	Operate cable TV systems	563.5	Yes	DLJ
7/21/99	Voyager.Net Inc	Internet Service Provider (ISP)	135.0	Yes	DLJ
7/22/99	Insweb Corp	Provides insurance services via Web	85.0	Yes	GS
7/26/99	Freeserve PLC (Dixons Group)	Internet Service Provider (ISP)	144.9	Yes	CS-FB
7/27/99	Drugstore.com Inc	Provides online retail svcs	90.0	Yes	MSDW
7/28/99	Focal Communications Corp	Provides local telephone services	129.4	Yes	SALOMON-SMITH
7/29/99	Digex Inc	Provides Internet hosting services	170.0	Yes	BEAR
8/4/99	Homestore.com Inc	Real estate website on Internet	140.0	Yes	MSDW
8/10/99	Braun Consulting Inc	Deliver e-Solutions	28.0	Yes	DLJ
8/12/99	IXnet Inc(IPC Information)	Provides global networking services	97.5	Yes	DLJ SALOMON-SMITH

8/12/99	Quest Software Inc	Develop computer software	61.6	Yes	BOSTON-ROBERTS
8/18/99	NovaMed Eyecare Inc	Provides health care consulting services	32.0	Yes	DLJ
8/19/99	HeadHunter.NET Inc	Provides web-based employment services	30.0	Yes	FIRST-UNION-CAP
8/19/99	LaBranche & Co	Security brokers & dealers	147.0	Yes	SALOMON-SMITH
9/22/99	ICICI	Government agency	273.9	Yes	MERRILL MSDW
9/23/99	eGain Communications	Develop Internet software	60.0	Yes	BOSTON-ROBERTS
9/23/99	Netzero Inc	Internet Service Provider(ISP)	160.0	Yes	GS
9/23/99	Trintech Group Plc	Provides computer related services	53.6	Yes	DEUTSCHE-ALEX-B
9/24/99	Interspeed Inc	Provides data communication services	42.0	Yes	US-PIPER
9/27/99	Medscape Inc	Provides medical resource Website	48.0	Yes	DLJ
9/28/99	Spinnaker Exploration Co	Provides oil, gas exploration services	116.0	Yes	CS-FB
9/29/99	InterNAP Network Services	Develops Internet connection	190.0	Yes	MSDW
10/1/99	Daleen Technologies Inc	Provides computer services	49.2	Yes	BOSTON-ROBERTS

Table 4-2 Wit Co-managers IPOs in 1999 (*Continued*)

Issue Date	Issuer	Business Description	Proceeds Amount in This Market ($ mil)	IPO	Book Manager(s)
10/1/99	Williams Communications Group	Provides fiber optic communication services	544.6	Yes	SALOMON-SMITH LEH
10/6/99	DSL .net Inc	Provides data communications	54.0	Yes	DEUTSCHE-ALEX-B
10/6/99	Neuberger Berman Inc	Provides investment advisory services	200.0	Yes	GS
10/7/99	Illuminet Holdings Inc	Provides telecommunication services	74.1	Yes	MSDW
10/7/99	TriZetto Group Inc	Develop software	37.8	Yes	BEAR
10/8/99	E-Stamp Corp	Develop Internet software	119.0	Yes	DLJ
10/8/99	Jupiter Communications Inc	Provides research services	65.6	Yes	DLJ
10/18/99	Martha Stewart Living	Design "how to" related products	103.7	Yes	MSDW
10/18/99	Radio Unica Communications Cor	Owns, operate Spanish radio stations	109.4	Yes	SALOMON-SMITH
10/20/99	Aether Systems Inc	Provides telecommunications services	96.0	Yes	MERRILL

Date	Company	Description			
10/26/99	JNI Corp	Provide fibre channel software	93.1	Yes	DLJ
10/27/99	Predictive Systems Inc	Provide network consulting services	72.0	Yes	BOSTON-ROBERTS
10/28/99	Akamai Technologies Inc	Provides website services	234.0	Yes	MSDW
10/28/99	Allied Riser Communications Co	Provide communications services	226.8	Yes	GS
11/3/99	Be Free Inc	Provides e-commerce services	67.2	Yes	DLJ
11/3/99	City Telecom (HK) Ltd	Provides telecommunication services	41.6	Yes	CS-FB
11/4/99	WebVan Group Inc	Online grocery store	375.0	Yes	GS
11/8/99	Charter Communications Inc	Provides cable TV broadcasting services	2745.5	Yes	GS
11/9/99	Data Critical Corp	Develops data transfer technology	35.0	Yes	DLJ
11/10/99	Edison Schools Inc	Provides services to public schools	97.9	Yes	MERRILL
11/16/99	Quintus Corp	Develops customer support software	81.0	Yes	DLJ
11/17/99	Rainmaker Systems Inc	Provides relationship management services	40.0	Yes	DLJ THOMAS-WEISEL

Table 4-2 Wit Co-managers IPOs in 1999 (*Continued*)

Issue Date	Issuer	Business Description	Proceeds Amount in This Market ($ mil)	IPO	Book Manager(s)
11/18/99	Symyx Technologies Inc	Provide physical research	77.5	Yes	CS-FB
11/19/99	SciQuest.com Inc	Provides online scientific products	120.0	Yes	DLJ
11/22/99	Digital Impact Inc	Provides online marketing	67.5	Yes	CS-FB
11/23/99	Official Payments Corp	Provides electronic payment options	75.0	Yes	DLJ
12/7/99	Classic Communi-cations Inc	Provides cable television services	206.3	Yes	GS
12/8/99	Andover.net Inc	Manage a network of websites	72.0	Yes	W-R-HAMBRECHT
12/9/99	Freemarkets Inc	Provides online retail services	172.8	Yes	GS MSDW
2/9/99	MedicaLogic Inc	Develops medical related software	100.3	Yes	DLJ
12/13/99	Tritel Inc	Provides communications	168.8	Yes	GS
12/15/99	Xpedior Inc	Provides computer consulting services	162.2	Yes	DLJ

Source: Thomson Financial Securities Data

formed Hambrecht & Quist (H&Q), an investment banking firm concentrating on emerging growth companies. During his tenure at H&Q, Hambrecht brought such companies as Abode Systems, Network Solutions, and Lycos public. H&Q, too, went public in August 1996 in a $56 million transaction that the company itself underwrote, a deal that was one of only a dozen IPOs by security dealers or investment banks which went public since 1980 and acted as their own underwriter. Rather than representing a conflict of interest in that these firms underwrote their own offering, such self-directed deals may be interpreted by some as a sign of financial strength, indicating that they have the means and ability to get their own deal completed. However, in January 1998, less than two years after bringing his company public, Hambrecht broke away from the firm he helped develop and went out on his own to create WR Hambrecht + Co.

But unlike his competitors, who were either offering lower costs or the chance of boarding the IPO ship, Hambrecht proposed a radical approach to the IPO allocation process. The objective of the new plan was to allow companies to raise capital at a much lower cost than the traditional 7 percent fee charged by many underwriters, as well as to give investors greater opportunities to get into an IPO. Labeled OpenIPO, the auction-based method, rooted in a design by the economist William Vickrey, was intended to offer four key benefits. First, the investors who purchased the IPO would more likely be long-term holders of the stock rather than day traders or flippers (those who purchase an IPO only to quickly sell it or "flip it back" to the underwriter in order to lock in a fast gain). Thus, the potential for price swings would be limited. Second, various expenses associated with an IPO, from managers' fees to accounting, legal, and printing costs, should be lower. Third, rather than the investment bank deciding the final offer price of the deal, it would be decided by how investors determined the merits of the issuing company. Finally, the OpenIPO method would do away with the so-called IPO discount, enabling offerings to be more "rationally" priced.

The OpenIPO approach works as follows. First, all bids are entered secretly: Investors privately forward the price they would be willing to pay for the stock. Second each bid, be it institutional or individual, is on equal ground. Thus, even if some bidders seek 100 shares while others are after 100,000, each stands on the same footing. Third, a mathematical model is employed, setting the optimal price for the IPO whereby the highest bidders win when that price is reached. Finally, the offering is completed when the amount set out to be raised is attained. The objective of an OpenIPO is twofold: (1) The enormous price jumps often associated with IPOs would, at least in theory, be reduced, and (2) small investors would be put on an equal footing with institutions with respect to bidding for shares.

In May 1999, Instinet, the largest agency-only broker and a subsidiary of the global information giant Reuters, acquired an 11.4 percent stake in WR Hambrecht + Co. for $20 million. In addition, Fidelity Investments, the Boston-based mutual funds powerhouse, made five equity investments in the firm, totaling some $50 million. The purpose of the investments was to enable customers of Fidelity's discount brokerage business to have access to WR Hambrecht deals. Finally, an investment arm of Rubert Murdoch's News Corp. took a position in WR Hambrecht. The firm also expanded into the East Coast in early 2000 when it tapped Matthew Regan, formerly of BHC Financial, to run Hambrecht's retail brokerage operation located in Berwyn, Pennsylvania.

The company's activities as a book manager, comanager, and domestic syndicate member have shown mixed results to date. The firm's first IPO, a $10.5 million deal for

Ravenswood Winery, was priced at $10.50, based upon the OpenIPO system. In the next 30 days, the issue was trading flat from its offer price, a performance that compares unfavorably with the better than 80 percent advance by the four IPOs which were completed on the same day that Ravenswood priced its own IPO. WR Hambrecht's next deal, for on-line community and Web site Salon.com, met with an even chillier response. The IPO was completed in June 1999 at a price of $10.50. In the following month, Salon.com's stock price managed to climb by 11 percent. However, soon thereafter the shares began to fall, ending the year more than 40 percent below their offer price and leaving the company ranked as one of the bottom 10 Internet IPO performers in 1999.

The situation went from bad to worse as WR Hambrecht's OpenIPO strategy lost some of its luster when it was reported that the company had been aggressive buyers of Ravenswood Winery since its debut in April 1999. Although aftermarket support by underwriters is common and even counted upon by issuers, the level at which WR Hambrecht was investing its own capital in its own deal was seen as rare and uncommon. SEC filings intimated that the underwriter and its founder had increased their position in the winery to over 13 percent in the six months following the completion of the IPO. Furthermore, it was revealed that on some days nearly all of the trading volume of Ravenswood, which averaged about 6400 shares daily, was from buy orders from WR Hambrecht's own account. Greatfood.com, an e-commerce retailer, was scheduled to complete its IPO by WR Hambrecht in the summer of 1999. However, that deal was postponed due to "market conditions." Interestingly, in a subsequent filing for a convertible preferred offering, Greatfood.com revealed that WR Hambrecht had an estimated 10 percent position in the company.

One deal, which, on appearance, would seem to have been the firm's crowning moment, could very well lead to an unraveling of the OpenIPO process. Late in 1999, the company acted as lead manager of Andover.net, Inc.'s IPO. The deal was priced at $18 per share and closed at over $63 on its first day, trading for a 252 percent gain. The trouble was twofold. First, the OpenIPO process, as mentioned earlier, was supposedly designed to mitigate or even eliminate such lofty initial-day price pops. In this regard, some market observers claimed that the firm's two previous deals worked according to plan, but that Andover.net was involved in the Linux operating system, which had seen phenomenal growth. Second, and perhaps more critical, was the fact that it was reported that, based on the Dutch auction process, Andover.net's effective price should have been $24, not $18. Thus, the company elected to give up $6 per share, or some $24 million in proceeds. The reason for this monetary sacrifice, according to a WR Hambrecht spokesperson, was that without it, Andover.net's offering would have been delayed due to the company's having to refile documents with the SEC, as well as having to notify investors to reconfirm their orders.

Adding insult to injury, in early February 2000, Andover.net was acquired by VA Linux Systems, which holds the record for the best performing first-day gain by an IPO, for an estimated $54 per share, some 17 percent off Andover's first-day closing price. Hence, many early investors likely lost money on the deal, since Andover.net completed its IPO on December 8, 1999, at which time the company had a history of less than 60 days as an independent public firm before being acquired. Although the stock did drop as low as $25 in late January 2000, indicating that those who were successful at getting in at the bottom scored impressive gains prior to the merger announcement, the fact that Andover.net was acquired so soon after the completion of its own deal raised many eyebrows on Wall Street.

Yet another stumble by WR Hambrecht occurred in December 1999, when the firm was dropped from the VA Linux Systems IPO domestic underwriting syndicate by lead underwriter Credit Suisse First Boston. A stake in VA Linux that WR Hambrecht had acquired when it participated in a private placement for the company was not disclosed in the deal's prospectus. The nondisclosure created a dispute between the company and VA Linux's lead manager, resulting in Hambrecht's removal. In addition, a Denver-based money manager filed suit against WR Hambrecht in the aftermath of the firm's Andover offering, alleging that its bid was rejected while others, similarly priced, were accepted. On a brighter note, the firm scored a coup when three dozen equity research investment bankers and other personnel bolted from rival Prudential Securities' Prudential Volpe Technology Group to join Hambrecht.

The true test of WR Hambrecht's capacity to break into the upper ranks of IPO investment banking will come down the road as the company manages more IPOs and as investors gain experience in working with the OpenIPO concept. Currently, with just a handful of deals under its belt, the firm has yet to demonstrate that potential issuers are beating a path to its door. As evidence, one may examine the early 2000 IPO registration filings. Of the more than 250 issues that have filed to go public, only one, Nogatech Inc., opted to have WR Hambrecht manage its deal. In contrast, such bulge-bracket firms as CS First Boston and Goldman Sachs have won the business of several dozen or more IPO candidates each. The effectiveness of the OpenIPO approach beyond any technology-related deals would be significant, since, in the financial world of the late 1990s, nearly any tech IPO blossomed. The question for Hambrecht is whether any nontech offerings managed by the firm would sprout new investors or, instead, wither on the vine.

E*OFFERING

In a world where the terms "e-commerce," "e-brokers," and "e-trading" have become commonplace, it should come as no surprise that the first to claim the title of being a "netcentric" banking firm was E*OFFERING (www.eoffering.com). Like Wit Capital and WR Hambrecht, E*OFFERING seeks to provide retail investors with greater access to the IPO market, at the same time cutting underwriting costs to issuers and offering strong institutional-style research. Led initially by Walter Cruttenden III, a cofounder of the California-based investment boutique Cruttenden Roth,[43] E*OFFERING negotiated a relationship in January 1999 with on-line broker E*TRADE, which now owns some 28 percent of the firm, for a reported $10 million. E*OFFERING claims that up to half of the public offerings it receives will be distributed to its own retail on-line investors, while the remainder will be allocated to E*TRADE. In fact, on E*OFFERING's Web site, the firm is identified as the investment banking arm of E*TRADE. While E*OFFERING's only book-managed IPO in 1999 was a $73 million deal by First Sierra Financial, E*OFFERING has served as a comanager on several high-flying issues, including Red Hat, which gained over 700 percent in its first month of trading, and Bamboo.com, which soared some 200 percent in its opening month. Furthermore, nearly half of the IPOs that E*OFFERING either led or comanaged in 1999 were completed with an underwriting fee of under 6 percent, below the industry norm of 7 percent. In the case of First Sierra, which carried a gross spread of 5 percent, the company realized a savings of more than $1 million in underwriting fees.

As a member of the domestic syndicate, E*OFFERING has participated in some of 1999's hottest IPOs. Among the deals in which it received allocations are Merrill Lynch's managed deal for Internet Capital Group (E*OFFERING received 40,000 shares), Internet software developer TIBCO Software (a Goldman Sachs–led offering), and business software provider Viador, Inc., whose IPO was underwritten by Bear Stearns. In total, six of the IPOs in which E*OFFERING received an allocation doubled or more in value on their first day of trading, while two-thirds rose by double or more from their offer date. Among the firm's past acquisitions is the purchase of California-based securities brokerage firm Meridian Capital Group for $2.5 million. Still, reports of rising expenses imperiled the company as a new round of financing was arranged, including another $10 million from E*TRADE and an infusion of capital from venture-capital firm General Atlantic Partners of Greenwich, Connecticut, for a total of $52 million. In May 2000, E*OFFERING was acquired by Wit Capital for $328 million in a transaction that called for E*TRADE to acquire the retail brokerage operations of Wit, along with a 2.2 percent stake in Wit for an estimated $10 million.

E*TRADE

E*TRADE has done an admirable job as a leader in liberating investors from the chains of full-service brokers. The company has gathered millions of dollars in assets, has established various trading relationships, and has aggressively acquired numerous firms from banks to brokers. Moreover, as regards its own IPO, it has been more than stellar. The E*TRADE IPO (NASDAQ-EGRP) raised $59.5 million and was completed in August 1996 at a price of $10.50 per share. Sixty days from the initial offering the shares were trading above $15, and they reached an all-time high of over $70 in the summer of 1999. Yet, by early 2000, the shares had slipped to about $20, representing more than a 70 percent decline from their high. Yet, despite that fall, E*TRADE has its proponents, in part because of the firm's low-cost commission, wherein the rate is as low as $4.95 for customers who make 75 or more transactions per quarter.

Of the more than 500 IPOs completed in 1999, E*TRADE was a book manager on none, a comanager on 18, and a member of the domestic syndicate on 34. Of the latter, its allocation ranged from a high of more than 3.3 million on Priceline.com's (NASDAQ-PCLN) March 1999 IPO to a paltry 50,000 shares for Be, Inc.'s July 1999 deal. The average first-day trading gain of those IPOs E*TRADE participated in during 1999 was over 98 percent, while those it comanaged gained about 85 percent.

Charles Schwab

As the nation's largest discount broker, and one that has edged out the full-service giant Merrill Lynch in terms of market capitalization, Charles Schwab began to offer IPOs to its on-line clients in 1997. By 1999, the firm was a part of the domestic syndicate on more than 60 IPOs, whose average first-day gain exceeded 85 percent. In addition, Schwab has been in the underwriting group of some of the all-time top first-day-gaining IPOs, including Akamai Technologies, Wireless Facilities, and Efficient Networks. On the downside, almost a dozen of the IPOs in which Schwab has been allocated shares to distribute to its on-line clients have turned south, including Hoover's, Inc., Autoweb, Inc., and Valley Media.

If your portfolio is modest or if you're not an active trader, don't look to Schwab as a convenient source of IPOs. In early 2000, the company imposed stringent guidelines whereby IPOs would be allocated to individuals with $1 million or more in their portfolios, compared with a previous requirement of $500,000. Alternatively, IPOs may be allocated to those who have made at least 48 commissioned trades and have a balance of $50,000 or more in their portfolios.

An examination of the IPOs in which Schwab has managed to receive allocations reveals a dependence on two specific underwriters: Credit Suisse First Boston and the San Francisco–based Hambrecht & Quist. Furthermore, Schwab's choice of IPOs is almost entirely geared towards high-technology issues. With the exception of two of 1999's "supersize" deals, Goldman Sachs' $3 billion offering and United Parcel Services' $4.4 billion IPO, and a handful of other deals, Schwab has focused on e-commerce and Internet-related issues in its IPO choices for its retail clients. That comes as no surprise, given the strength of that particular market segment in 1999. But for those investors seeking IPO opportunities beyond technology, the choices were limited.

In 1999, Charles Schwab was a comanager on 8 IPOs and a participant in a domestic syndicate on no fewer than 68. For that total of 76 IPOs, the average first-day trading gain was over 92 percent, while the overall appreciation by the end of 1999 was over 100 percent. Schwab customers may indicate their interest in a particular IPO by logging onto www.schwab-ipos.com and informing the firm.

Sometimes, even the most well-oiled ship runs aground. In the case of Schwab, the firm settled complaints from customers relating to the execution of on-line trades associated with the day theglobe.com went public. Specifically, some Schwab customers who placed premarket orders to purchase the high-flying IPO attempted to cancel their orders as the stock soared from its offer price of $9 to over $90 at one point in its trading day. With the extremely fast market that persisted that fateful day, some investors wound up with filled orders at a price far and above what they ever expected or what they could cover in their accounts.

In the aftermath of the complaints, Schwab,[44] as well as many other on-line and traditional brokers, began to impose limits with respect to margin requirements on specific Internet IPOs and even classified some offerings as "unmarginable." Thus, some individuals who sought to day trade some of 1999's top IPOs were deliberately left on the sidelines. Yet, within a year of such measures, Schwab announced its intention to purchase the day-trading firm CyBerCorp, Inc., for a reported $488 million. Furthermore, Schwab announced a cut in its flat Internet trading rate of $29.95 to $14.95, matching such competitors as Fidelity Investments.

DLJ Direct

As the on-line trading unit of Wall Street firm Donaldson, Lufkin & Jenrette, DLJ Direct, whose genesis began with the first on-line brokerage firm, PCFinancial Network, has close ties to its parent. DLJ's role as a comanager of IPOs has extended to some of those managed by the so-called DLJ, the Elder. Among these IPOs are JNI Corp.'s $93.1 million offering, launched in October 1999, and Official Payments Corp.'s IPO, completed the following month. Both IPOs gained nearly 250 percent from their offer price by the end of 1999. Other IPOs to which the firm provided access for its clients were Data Critical Corp. (up 49 percent in 1999), Nextcard, Inc. (up 44 percent), and Medscape (up 25 percent). With more than 300,000 active accounts, DLJ Direct received a ranking of 12 among 21 on-line brokers in a survey conducted in the spring of 1999 by *SmartMoney* magazine. DLJ also received high rankings in the "Staying Out of Trouble" category. Furthermore, in thestreet.com's "2000 Online Broker Survey," DLJ Direct ranked first in IPO availability for its clients.

Since its debut, DLJ Direct has been a joint book manager on two IPOs (its own offering and Fastnet Corp.'s IPO, which it managed with ING-Barings), a comanager on a dozen, and a member of a domestic syndicate on another two dozen. The firm has received, on average, an allocation of more than 50,000 shares for IPOs in which it has participated. The average first-day trading gain was about 57 percent, while the overall gain through the end of 1999 was over 130 percent.

fbr.com/ Friedman Billings Ramsey

The on-line arm of Virginia-based investment bank Friedman Billings Ramsey was rolled out in the summer of 1999 to much fanfare. At the time, the company claimed to be one of the most bountiful suppliers of IPOs on-line, and in news reports it was being called "the nation's first public on-line investment bank." That may be true; however, an examination of the parent company's lead-managed IPO may give investors pause. Of the 36 IPOs of which Friedman Billings Ramsey has been the primary underwriter, most have been in such nontechnology sectors as real estate investment trusts, mortgage banks, and other financial companies. On average, these deals gained about 10 percent on their first day of trading and under 50 percent from their offer date. While those figures may have been acceptable to most investors in an earlier era, in the white-hot world of IPOs circa 1999 such results are considered substandard. In fact, Friedman Billings Ramsey's own IPO, for which the company acted as lead manager in December 1997, lost more than two-thirds of its value from its offer price of $20 after two years of trading activity. Moreover, the firm's performance shows a stark split personality. On the one hand, on the basis of proceeds raised,

Friedman Billings Ramsey ranked as the 18th leading firm throughout the 1990s. However, when it comes to performance, it's another picture altogether: Of 43 book managers who handled at least 22 deals in the past decade, the firm ranks 26th in terms of aftermarket performance of IPOs, with an average gain of under 4 percent through late February 2000.

Friedman Billings Ramsey's on-line entity, fbr.com, offers a service called IPODesktop that allows clients to place and execute IPOs and secondary equity offerings through the Internet and that has the stated intention of providing up to half the shares the firm receives in an offering available to investors. To participate in an IPO that fbr.com is managing as part of a domestic syndicate, an investor must first open an account and submit a conditional bid to purchase shares in the offering. Within 48 hours before the IPO is declared effective, an investor will be requested to reconfirm his or her conditional bid, and a computer program randomly selects the investors whose orders will be accepted. Once selected, the investor will again be notified and queried as to whether his or her offer should be accepted. The order is finally executed when the investor notifies fbr.com by E-mail.

Friedman Billings's role as a member of a domestic syndicate handling IPOs during 1999 saw both lofty gains as well notable losses. The firm received 120,000 shares in the Red Hat, Inc., IPO, which gained more than 400 percent in its first day of trading. Likewise, in February 1999 the firm secured 70,000 shares in Web-site operator VerticalNet's $56 million IPO, which went on to enrich investors with more than a 2,600 percent jump over the initial price by the one-year anniversary of its offering. On the other hand, such IPOs as consulting services provider Nextera Enterprises and Consolidated Energy both suffered double-digit losses in their first day of trading. However, if each successful client of the firm whose order was accepted for those two deals were limited to just 100 shares each, then fewer than 2000 individuals would have gained access to the deal, a situation likely to frustrate many and further reinforce the belief held by some investors that the IPO process is an insider's game. In response, the company created a new system called "Offering Marketplace" to distribute IPO shares to its retail customers. The system was designed to permit investors to directly approve a previously placed conditional offer to purchase an IPO, as well as to place an order based on a particular price range rather than at a specific limited price.

COMING TOGETHER

Frustration at not receiving any significant allocation of IPOs from leading underwriters compelled Charles Schwab to join forces with industry competitors TD Waterhouse and Ameritrade to form an on-line investment bank in order to get a larger slice of the IPO market. Backed by venture-capital powerhouses Benchmark Capital, Trident Capital, and Kleiner Perkins Caufield & Byers, the objective of the new entity, currently called Epoch, was to boost its allocation of IPOs from the low levels the individual firms had been receiving. For example, it was reported that among IPOs in which Schwab participated, the firm's clients received, on average, about 2.5 percent of the issued amount. Thus, for a typical 4-million-share offering, Schwab customers may look to receiving only about 100,000 shares. Obviously, even if a Schwab customer were able to purchase a mere 100 shares, just 1000 individuals would be able to purchase the IPO at its offer price—and that from a firm which ranks as the leading on-line broker, with more than

2 million customer accounts. Based upon those facts, it is no wonder that some IPOs skyrocket. Simple supply and demand would suggest that as on-line brokerage accounts burgeon while allocations remain stingy, and as more investors demand spectacular returns, IPOs will be bid to ever higher levels.

However, one effect of Schwab's move was the company's withdrawal from many preexisting relationships with investment banks issuing IPOs. After that, many Schwab customers went from being able to bid on numerous IPOs in 1999 to almost zero in early 2000.

Further evidence of the paltry distributions some firms receive can be seen upon examining some of the year's hot IPOs. Consider, for example, Marketwatch.com's offering of 2.75 million shares in January 1999. The stock gained more than 470 percent in its first day of trading as investors clamored for shares in the on-line financial information company that was part of broadcaster CBS's entrée into the Internet world. Yet, firms such as Wit Capital and Hambrecht & Quist received just 60,000 each, or about 2.2 percent of the available shares. Thus, based on the fact that Wit had an estimated 52,000 accounts at the time of the offering, it easy to see that many orders are surely destined to go unfilled. Similarly, when Foundry Networks completed its 5-million-share offering in September 1999, on-line broker E*OFFERING could secure only 60,000 shares, or about 1.2 percent of the issue, for its clients' accounts. (The figure is even lower, considering that E*OFFERING is obligated to turn over a portion of any IPO allocations it receives to E*TRADE.) The way the IPO game is now designed, the odds of, for example, a typical Schwab customer getting his or her order filled on a hot IPO would be about 1 in 2000. With the emergence of the new trilateral alliance, perhaps those odds will be reduced.

WHO GETS WHAT

In war, spoils go to the victor. In politics, it's the candidate with the greatest number of votes who will assume office. In sports, the fastest wins the race. Yet, in the IPO world, there are no clear-cut ground rules as to who will win or lose in the allotment of IPOs. Clearly, relationships count, but when a hot IPO arrives on the scene, often the ties that bind would just as soon be severed than to give up a few thousand extra shares. Probably the foremost factor that puts some underwriters ahead of others is that they will take the unpopular deals as well as the most coveted IPOs. A top-tiered institution often seeks dependable and reliable customers to "spread a deal" if necessary, whereupon the customers are "rewarded" for buying some unpopular IPOs by getting a greater allocation in a "hot" deal.

IPO Observation: Many on-line brokers promise access to IPOs, but as a general rule, the success rate for access is correlated with one's assets and trading activity. Despite what is featured in marketing campaigns, televised ads, or postings on chat rooms, investors with more assets will have better chances of getting into an IPO than will those with more modest accounts.

STATISTICAL SPOTLIGHT

I F YOU LOOK AT THE SIDELINES OF A FOOTBALL GAME OR IN A BASEBALL DUGOUT, YOU'RE LIKELY TO SEE COACHES AND MANAGERS PORING OVER STATISTICS OF HOW A SPECIFIC HITTER PERFORMS AGAINST A CERTAIN PITCHER OR HOW ONE TEAM RESPONDS DEFENSIVELY WHEN AN OPPONENT CALLS A RUN OR PASS PLAY. FOR EXAMPLE, WHEN HOME RUN KING MARK MCGWIRE OF THE ST. LOUIS CARDINALS STEPS TO THE PLATE AGAINST NEW YORK METS PITCHER KENNY ROGERS, BOTH MANAGERS ARE LIKELY TO HAVE A DETAILED PRINTOUT ON HOW EACH PLAYER HAS PERFORMED WHEN FACING THE OTHER. SIMILARLY, WHEN FOOTBALL'S DALLAS COWBOYS ARE PLAYING ON THE ROAD ON A GRASS SURFACE AGAINST AN AMERICAN CONFERENCE TEAM, YOU CAN BE SURE THAT THE HEAD COACH WILL CONSULT DOCUMENTED PERFORMANCE STATISTICS INDICATING HOW WELL OR POORLY THE TEAM FROM TEXAS PERFORMS UNDER SUCH CONDITIONS.

So it is with stocks, especially IPOs, as various trends or repetitions often indicate that a pattern exists which investors can readily exploit for profit. For example, the uptick in the number of IPOs doubling on their first day of trading, as shown in Table 5-1, fosters the belief among some investors that many IPOs are a "sure thing." It is not surprising that analysts and portfolio managers will examine the size of the impending deal, choices of manager, and changes in anticipated prices in an attempt to glean signals as to whether the IPO will fly or die. While many market commentators often claim that past performance is not a guarantee of future success, the fact is that certain deals of a particular type often enjoy strong aftermarket support, while others languish. In sum, there are deals to avoid, deals to consider, and deals that are a slam dunk. This chapter focuses on identifying IPOs of a particular characteristic and examining their overall performance. Later in this book, a review of how particular underwriters rate in the IPO performance contest, as well as how certain industries perform, will be presented.

SIZE MATTERS...NOT!

The IPO market has long been noted for big deals. Such headline-grabbing deals have often been the catalyst for heightened investor interest in IPOs. Throughout the 1990s, there were no less than two dozen IPOs of $1 billion or more in the United States.[45] Among recent offerings of this magnitude were United Parcel Services' $4.4 billion issue completed in November 1999, New York-based Goldman Sachs' $2.9 billion debut offering in May 1999, and Du Pont's $3.96 billion spin-off of its Conoco unit to shareholders in October 1998. As such IPOs have become more

Table 5-1   IPOs Doubling or More First Day after Offer Date

		YEARLY VOLUME TOTALS	
Year	**Issues**	**Year**	**Issues**
1986	7	1994	3
1987	3	1995	13
1989	1	1996	10
1990	1	1997	5
1991	2	1998	12
1992	3	1999	97
1993	4	2000*	76

Source: Thomson Financial Securities Data.
*Through September 1, 2000.

frequent, so, too, have they commanded a larger share of both the underwriting volume totals and the fees associated with new equity offerings. For example, of the $69 billion worth of IPOs raised in the United States in 1999, about 32 percent came from deals of $1 billion or more. This figure contrasts with, for example, 1993, when deals of $1 billion or more accounted for less than 8 percent of the domestic IPO market proceeds.

Yet, that's only a small part of the picture. For instance, up until May 1999, British Petroleum's October 1987 IPO was ranked as the top IPO that sold a portion of its offering in the United States. However, the $2.86 billion amount represented only that slice of the offering sold in the U.S. domestic market: Almost another $9.6 billion was picked up by investors in Europe, Asia, and elsewhere. If one takes into account the fact that some deals sell shares to overseas investors, then, based on worldwide proceeds, the number of multibillion-dollar IPOs in the past decade soared to 53 from only 7 in the

1980s. Such megadeals are usually found, not in the ranks of smaller or emerging-growth companies, but rather in mature industries and long-established concerns.[46]

But what of performance? Upon examination, despite all the hoopla, many of these IPOs are laggards if not outright losers. Consider that the average gain of a multibillion-dollar IPO priced during the 1990s 30 days after its debut was about 15 percent. Now consider all other deals. Subtracting these mega-offerings, non-multibillion-dollar IPOs gained more than 22 percent, on average, in their first month of trading. The results are even more impressive when one examines smaller deals. For example, the price per share of IPOs that raised between $100 million and $249 million during the 1990s increased about 30 percent in the first month of trading and 33 percent in the first 60 days. The results are comparable for deals under $50 million: Those IPOs which raised between $25 million and $49 million gained over 28 percent in the first month of trading and 31 percent, on average, by the close of the second month of trading. The lesson is that size may bring bragging rights for some issuers and underwriters, but for investors' portfolios, it may be a weight too heavy to bear. However, as we shall see later, a driving force in an IPO is not necessarily the size of the company undertaking the offering, but rather how many shares are being put forth on the block for investors.

Summary: Big IPOs may gain the spotlight, but size is not an indicator of future performance. Rather, it is earnings, or, more accurately, the expectation of future earnings growth, that is the driving force behind higher stock prices.

MADE IN THE U.S.A.

As the wave of immigration at the turn of the previous century brought individuals with new talents, skills, and hopes to the shores of America, so, too, at the dawn of the 21st century, new foreign companies have entered U.S. capital markets to raise funds to fuel their dreams. The level of foreign IPOs issued in the United States reached an unprecedented volume in 1999 as a record $12 billion was raised by foreign companies offering portions of themselves to American investors. From privatizations such as Deutsche Telekom's November 1996 $11 billion deal to the numerous Canadian, Korean, and Israeli IPOs priced here, foreign IPOs have been a considerable factor in the IPO market. Moreover, nearly one of every five dollars raised in the United States from IPOs in recent years has come from foreign businesses propelled by the draw of institutions seeking above-average returns and the marketing power of such entities as the New York Stock Exchange, which embarked on a campaign to encourage more foreign companies to list themselves with the exchange.

However when it comes to shareholder value, many foreign IPOs that are listed in the United States come up as second-class citizens. Collectively, more than 500 foreign companies sold a portion of their IPOs in the United States during the 1990s. (Incidentally, the world's largest IPO in terms of proceeds, NTT Mobile Telecommunications' $18 billion offering, did *not* sell any shares in U.S. capital markets.) In the first month of trading the price of a share in these deals rose, on average, about 11.6 percent, compared with more than 23 percent by U.S.-headquartered concerns. Even after a year of trading history, foreign IPOs still lag behind U.S. deals, with domestic offerings having gained an average of 25 percent, compared with about 20 percent for non-U.S. deals. Among some notable crackups of foreign IPOs are Grupo Tribasa, Petroleum Securities Australia, and Telex-Chile, each of which has lost more than 90 percent of its value since going public.

Yet, all this is not to say that foreign investing, especially in IPOs, should be ignored. Rather, many noted asset managers, such as Jimmy Rogers, Mark Mobius, and John Templeton, are strong proponents of seeking out some obscure company, be it a South African brewer, a Vietnamese food company, or a Polish power plant. In fact, an examination of IPO issuance outside the United States reveals some interesting facts. For example, between 1995 and 1999, more than $400 billion was raised by issuers in countries outside of North America, nearly double what was raised in the United States and Canada from IPOs over that same period. One of the nations outside of North America that saw the greatest volume of IPOs during this period was China, with more than 580 issues that raised over $39 billion. (This figure includes issues located in Hong Kong, which was absorbed by China in 1997.) Among these issues were a $323 million offering by Faw Car Company, whose shares trade on the Shenzhen Stock Exchange, and a $224 million IPO by Jiangsu Yongding Company, a manufacturer and wholesaler of telecommunications equipment, whose shares trade on the Shanghai Exchange.[47]

Investors interested in developing companies may also consider taking a look at shares that list on the London Stock Exchange's Alternative Investment Market (AIM). Created in 1995, the AIM seeks to allow small, growing start-ups to raise capital and have an organized and open forum for the exchange of their shares. In 1999, nearly $1.5 billion was raised by 67 new companies that traded on the AIM. Companies that list on the AIM are granted waivers from the size and trading requirements that typically are necessary for being listed on the London Stock Exchange (LSE). More than 340 companies list on AIM, including such American companies as Globalnet Financial.com, Inc., Offshore Tool & Energy Corp., and Electronic Retailing Systems, and have a total market capitalization of approximately $10 billion, with most firms having a market cap between $8 million and $25 million.

Other foreign stock exchanges, recognizing that investors have developed a burning desire to own the latest high-tech offering, as well as growing companies seeking a place to raise capital, have created new "submarkets." Besides London's AIM, a handful of small-capital exchanges are either in the works or already in business. Among these financial institutions are Germany's Neuer Markt, which was created in 1997, France's Le Nouveau Marché, and Italy's Nuovo Mercato.

Summary: While portfolio managers "talk the talk" of adding international holdings in a portfolio as a means of diversifying or finding undervalued offerings, the fact is that such issues underperform relative to domestic companies. Among the reasons for their poor showing are lack of information, confusion about accounting practices, and lack of liquidity. As Warren Buffett once stated, when it comes to investing internationally, he'd rather put his money where his mouth is...namely, with the Coca-Cola Company, which derives a large share of its revenues and operating profits from overseas operations.

YOUTH VERSUS AGE

In the contest between the generations, there are varying degrees of success and achievement. Companies with a long track record of operation may be able to claim that their management has weathered recessions, wars, and shifting consumer preferences to get these firms where they are today. For this reason, they claim they are worthy of shareholders' respect and money. On the other hand, some companies that may still have wet ink on their papers of incorporation claim that the past is irrelevant with respect to their day-to-day operations. For these new corporate kids on the block, speedy technological change and rapid product development are what count.[48]

In fact, how old a company is does matter when it comes to the performance of IPOs, in that newly formed enterprises are more likely to be flexible in responding to market conditions and to post substantially higher rates of earnings growth than firms that are burdened by bureaucracies, layers of management, and a structured reply to business matters. But a key factor with respect to the age of a company going public is why the company is issuing an IPO in the first place. That is, when one thinks of IPOs, the common reference is either a new idea or concept being manifested in a company or some entrepreneurial spirit embarking on a mission to provide the proverbial better mousetrap. The aging industrial cyclical concern or the restaurant chain with tired and faded stores is not what comes into mind among some investors who are thinking of IPOs. A casual observation of some past IPOs would suggest that those deals in comparable industries—such as Friendly's Ice Cream (NASDAQ-FRND) or Ben and Jerry's Ice Cream (NASDAQ-BJICA)—are actually akin to competing generations and rival markets wherein a company's longevity may be held as a disadvantage. And those results show up in the stock prices. In the case of Friendly's, founded in 1935, since its IPO in November 1997, the company's stock has actually dropped over 70 percent from its offer price of $18. Furthermore, financial woes forced the firm in March 2000 to announce the closing of nearly one-quarter of its 600-plus stores. On the other hand, Ben & Jerry's, which has been serving scoops since 1978, has provided its early investors with better than a nine-fold gain since the IPO was priced at $13 per share ($4.33 a share adjusted for stock splits) as the company was acquired in June 2000 by Dutch consumer products giant Unilver for nearly $340 million.

A casual observation of some recent IPOs reveals that those which have been in business for a greater period of time have lagged those of more recent vintage. For example, in 1998, the Shoe Pavilion (NASDAQ-SHOE), Cultural Access Worldwide (NASDAQ-CAWW), and Select Comfort (NASDAQ-AIRB) went public after being in business for 10 years or more. Yet, by early 2000, each of these issues had declined by 70 percent or more from their offer price. Alternatively, many companies that went public in 1998 did so after about only one year of operation. Among these firms were ISS Group (NASDAQ-ISSX), which was founded in December 1997 and went public less than four months later, Allegiance Telecom (NASDAQ-ALGX), which was started in April 1997 and went public in June 1998, and 24/7 Media (NASDAQ-TFSM), which was founded in January 1998 and went public the following August. Each gained more than several hundred percentage points from their offering price.

Summary: It should come as little surprise that newer companies often see their stock price do better than more established concerns when it comes to IPO activity. One reason is that investors may perceive the newer entrant as providing a different and unique service or product whereby earnings growth may accelerate. In contrast, a more mature company offering an IPO may demonstrate a track record of predictability in earnings, which may provide evidence that earnings growth is likely to be restrained.

LISTINGS...LOCATION MATTERS

Just as the choice of an underwriter is important in the success of an IPO, where the deal will trade is a barometer of future performance. Specifically, the selection of an IPO's listing will aid in bringing it to market, minimizing administrative costs, and perhaps most importantly, keeping it visible to investors. Throughout the 1980s and 1990s, the

NASDAQ National Market reigned as the primary beneficiary of most IPOs, including many high-flying technology
issues. Of the more than 5000 IPOs completed in the 1990s,
over 4000 are still trading on either the NASDAQ National
Market or its small-capital counterpart. On the other
hand, while some 1,100 IPOs have listed on the New York
Stock Exchange (NYSE) in the past decade, more than one-
third have been either closed-end funds or real estate
investment trusts (reits). Furthermore, the Big Board has
been on a three-year slide as U.S.-based IPOs, excluding
REITS and closed-end funds, totaled just 39 in 1999, off
from 56 in 1998, 75 in 1997, and a record 82 in 1996. In
addition, with the steady stream of IPOs sometimes doubling or tripling in value on their first day of trading, it is
noteworthy to mention that not a single NYSE-listed IPO
has made the grade as among the best opening-day performers. In fact, until Martha Stewart Omnimedia's deal
in the Fall of 1999 and the February 1999 IPO by Perot
Systems, the best showing for a Big Board–listed IPO on
its first day of trading was a September 1991 deal by
General Physics (NYSE-GPH), which was offered at $13
and gained 103 percent on its opening day. It is noteworthy
that General Physics ended up being acquired by National
Patent Development Corp. in September 1996 in a transaction that wound up valuing GPH under its initial offer
price. In its entire history, the NYSE could boast of only 10
IPOs by U.S. companies that gained 50 percent or more on
their first day of trading.[49]

In fact, according to an exchange spokesperson,[50] up until
1984 the NYSE did not permit IPO listings, and only three
"new companies" prior to that time were allowed to enter:
U.S Steel, Ford Motor Co., and Comcast. In contrast, the
NASDAQ had been home to many fast-growing companies
such as Intel, Microsoft, Dell Computer, and Cisco Systems,

to name just a handful. Consequently, NASDAQ-listed IPOs have been bigger winners for investors than those on the NYSE. Of the top 50 all-time IPO gainers, nearly all have been listed on NASDAQ; just 2 NYSE-listed IPOs have made the grade: motorcycle manufacturer Harley Davidson's July 1986 IPO, which has gained more than 10,000 percent after stock splits, and technology company Jabil Circuit, whose April 1993 IPO has appreciated more than 3800 percent since its debut at $7.

Some still maintain that NASDAQ IPOs are underperformers, despite evidence to the contrary. In an April 1993 study published in the *Journal of Financial Economics*, Tim Loughran[51] presented evidence that in the period between 1973 and 1988, NASDAQ IPOs lagged in performance to similarly sized NASDAQ securities with a trading history of six years or more. Furthermore, the analysis indicated that, after adjustment for the size of the deal, NYSE-listed securities in the same period outperformed both NASDAQ equities and IPOs overall. Nevertheless, it should be pointed out that, by taking as a starting point prices from the early 1970s, when the country was in a recession and the Dow Jones Industrial Average was under 800, the results may have been skewed. In fact, several points should be raised as to why those results need not be an indictment of NASDAQ IPOs in general. First, the period under examination was one in which the IPO market did not receive the degree of investor interest that has occurred in the late 1990s, so it is likely that many IPO investors simply bought and held their holdings then, thus limiting the volatility of the stock and the momentum of their prices. Second, research on IPOs in that period was more likely to be limited to just the underwriting firm, leaving out third-party brokers who would be interested in making a market in the IPO. As a result, investor interest in the offering was likely to be limited to just the underwriter firm's investor base.

Summary: Most IPOs begin trading on the NASDAQ National Market or some other over-the-counter market. Although the NYSE has seen an uptick in IPO listings in recent years, many are American depository receipts, which have traditionally underperformed domestic issues, while others have provided less explosive gains than those which trade over the NASDAQ. Hence, investors seeking IPOs that are likely to appreciate quickly are more apt to find such issues being traded on the NASDAQ than on the NYSE.

PRICING AND TOP GAINERS

Often, inexperienced investors confuse a company's stock price with its inherent value or lack thereof. Sometimes an investor may claim that a stock trading at over $100 per share is too expensive. On the other hand, a stock trading at $3 per share is viewed as a bargain. But such an analysis, failing to take into account the fact that the higher-priced shares may actually be trading at a relatively low price-to-earnings ratio while the firm whose shares are at $3 may have neither earnings nor any immediate prospects of profitability, is wrongheaded. Still, there is some validity ito the contention that stocks of a certain price range may behave one way while those of another may perform in an opposite fashion.[52]

During the 1990s, more than 1400 IPOs, excluding unit offerings, were priced at under $10 per share. In the month that followed their offering, on average, deals priced at that level gained about 16.2 percent, and by their first anniversary of being a public company they had gained 17.5 percent. Moving down the price scale, those IPOs priced at

$5 or less, excluding unit offerings again, climbed more than 21 percent in the first four weeks of trading, but could manage only a 16 percent gain after one year.

At the other end of the spectrum, IPOs priced at $30 per share or higher in the past decade have lagged in performance. With fewer than four dozen such deals so priced in the 1990s, the average gain after four weeks of trading was 14.1 percent, while after a full year of activity the IPOs with the highest offer price registered an 11 percent gain. Therefore, it can be inferred that higher-priced IPOs have less room for upside appreciation than those that are more modestly priced. The reason may be that those IPOs which are higher priced may be either larger or more established companies with less room for immediate growth.

In this regard, the pricing of an IPO, at least with respect to the number of shares and the offer price, affects the liquidity of the offering, which in turn affects future prices. For example, an issue offered at $5 or less per share is not marginable and thus would not be considered by institutions or day traders. Similarly, IPOs composed of less than 1 million shares would be viewed as too susceptible to volatility and price manipulation as well as unacceptable by some institutional investors, many of which are prohibited from owning more than a 5 percent stake in any individual company. In a Stanford Graduate School of Business research paper entitled "What Type of IPOs Do Underwriters Support and Why," N. R. Prabhala and Manju Puri argue that those IPOs which are larger have lower gross spreads and higher offering prices and are more likely to be supported in the aftermarket than those at the other end of the IPO spectrum.

Likewise, those investors who attempt to grab the brass ring on an IPO that shows explosive price gains on the first day or one that ranks among the year's top gainers more often than not will be disappointed. For example, of the 10 best performing IPOs that were priced in 1996, half lost ground the following year. Similarly, of those IPOs that stood as the leaders in 1997, only 5 of the top 10 managed to add to their gains in the following year. By way of example, information obtained from Thomson Financial Securities Data clearly illustrates that, in some cases, the prudent strategy may be to sell short one of the leading top IPO gainers of the previous year. As for those IPOs which soared on their opening trading day, some have recently been disappointing. By way of illustration, in 1998 11 IPOs at least doubled their value on the day they were offered. By the close of 1999, three of those issues were trading off their initial gains, while another, Realax Software AG, had actually declined dramatically, to below its offer price. Moreover, in 1999, when almost one of every five IPOs doubled in value or did even better on their first trading day, six such high flyers ended the year below their offer price.

Summary: Stay clear of low-priced IPOs. And don't expect high-priced deals to quickly surge ahead.

IT'S HARD TO STAY AHEAD WHEN YOU START DOWN

Handicappers of sports events are keen collectors and interpreters of information. For example, if the Green Bay Packers are leading in a game going into the fourth quarter, based on past performance, they usually win the contest 75 percent of the time. However, if the Packers are traveling and their opponent is an American Conference team and the field surface is grass, then whenever they enter the final quarter ahead, history shows that their winning percentage increases to over 90 percent. So it is with IPOs with respect to winning and losing. That is, if a stock is trading under its offer price soon after the deal is completed, then, more often than not, the chance of getting back on track is slim at best. Since 1990, about one-fifth of all IPOs have lost ground in their first 30 days of trading, averaging about a 12 percent decline. By the close of their first year of trading, this group could only generate a modest recovery, as their average loss still was about 6 percent.

Now consider the other side of the coin. Over the same period, nearly twice as many IPOs gained 10 percent or more on their opening day, averaging about a 48 percent move to the upside. From then on, collectively, this group moved ahead and wound up with an average advance of about 52 percent by the end of their first year of trading. From this evidence, investors infer that once an IPO gets off to a slow start, it's difficult for it to recover.

As indicated in the Table 5-2, these results hold up consistently. Since 1990, those IPOs which lost ground in their first four weeks of trading in every year except 1992 and 1995 came up short for investors by the end of the first full year of trading. For example, in 1990, 50 IPOs declined in value from their offering price, with the average loss exceeding 13 percent. By the close of the first full year of trading, the group was still averaging a decline, although of only 4.4 percent. By contrast, those IPOs which gained 10 percent or better in their first four weeks of trading demonstrated strong double-digit gains in their first full year of trading. These strong early gainers continued to be popular with investors at the end of the first full year of trading and, in every year except 1990 and 1996, managed to post further gains.

Summary: Even in the most powerful year for IPOs, those deals which failed to jump ahead on their first trading day demonstrated lackluster results further on. Borrowing an oft-used quote from the technical analyst's handbook, "If a stock breaks trend, it's likely to continue to trend lower"...until it no longer does so.

VENTURE-BACKED IPOs

Just as the unprecedented gains by IPOs have made investors stand up and take notice, the explosive inflow of cash into venture-capital funds has turned heads from Wall Street to Silicon Valley. From 1990 through 1999, an estimated several billion dollars was raised by venture capitalists, who then turned around to provide seed financing and, later, funding to

Table 5-2 IPO Aftermarket Performance

AVERAGE CHANGE FOR ISSUES DECLINING IN FIRST MONTH OF TRADING AND ONE-YEAR PERFORMANCE

Year	Number of IPOs	Percent Change Four Weeks after Offer Date	Percent Change One Year after Offer Date
1990	50	−13.1	−4.4
1991	64	−10.2	−8.1
1992	137	−11.7	1.3
1993	141	−10.7	−12.4
1994	144	−10	−5.3
1995	94	−9.1	3.7
1996	185	−12.5	−9.6
1997	159	−12.1	−4.9
1998	104	−15.5	−10.4
1999*	72	−15.7	−17.4

*Deals priced through August 31, 1999.

Table 5-2   IPO Aftermarket Performance (*Continued*)

AVERAGE CHANGE FOR ISSUES ADVANCING
10 PERCENT OR MORE IN THE FIRST MONTH OF
TRADING AND ONE-YEAR PERFORMANCE

Year	Number of IPOs	Percent Change Four Weeks after Offer Date	Percent Change One Year after Offer Date
1990	57	31.8	30.8
1991	181	35.3	40.3
1992	195	33.4	56.6
1993	287	33.2	36.4
1994	192	29.7	80.5
1995	302	46.6	76.4
1996	390	43.5	35.7
1997	274	33.8	41.8
1998	169	54.2	73.4
1999*	42	154.8	308.9

*Deals priced through March 31, 1999.

Source: Thomson Financial Securities Data.

emerging companies in such industries as biotechnology, communications, and information technology. But the prize that the venture-capital firms seek is not merely to witness the birth and development of a new company or the emergence of a leading-edge technology. Rather, the windfall is when a financed company goes public and its stock price jumps to higher ground.

Since 1990, no fewer than 1700 IPOs, or about one-third of all IPOs completed in that decade, received some degree of venture-capital backing at some stage prior to the public offering. To almost no one's surprise who followed market activity in 1999, nearly one-half of the 544 IPOs priced that year received some degree of venture-capital backing, according to the National Venture Capital Association (NVCA). This aid may have come in the form of "seed financing," "later-stage" support, or infusions of private equity.[53] In any case, the level of such backing has steadily grown as the number of venture-capital-backed IPOs has risen from less than 60 in 1990, to over 200 by 1995, to a record 271 in the final year of the decade. In 1999, venture capitalists invested over $48 billion, more than double 1998's total of $19 billion, according to the NVCA and Venture Economics.

With respect to performance, to claim that venture-capital-backed IPOs, in total, outdistance non-venture-capital-backed deals would be an understatement: During the 1990s, a typical venture-capital-financed IPO gained about 35 percent in its first four weeks of trading and over 240 percent by the close of the decade. In contrast, non-venture-capital-backed IPOs gained almost 16 percent after four weeks, nearly 19 percent through the first year of trading, and 53 percent at the end of the 1990s. Thus, over the intermediate to long term, venture-capital-backed IPOs historically have outperformed non-venture-capital-backed deals by several fold.

Furthermore, on the basis of results disclosed by the NVCA, a typical venture-capital-backed IPO completed in 1999 raised $87 million in its offering, and upon completion of the deal, the value of the company, on average, was more than $500 million. In comparison, an average venture-capital-backed IPO consummated in 1998 brought $49 million upon offer and was valued at $229 million upon completion. Overall, returns on venture-capital-backed IPOs have been stunning. NVCA statistics reveal that the one-year average return for such an offering in 1999 was nearly 93 percent, compared with a 25 percent gain by the Dow Jones Industrial Average. Similar results have been achieved over the intermediate term, with venture-capital-backed IPOs posting an average annual return of over 41 percent for the three-year period ending 1999, versus a 20.8 percent rise for the Dow Industrials. Not surprisingly, venture-capital-backed IPOs have taken on a decidedly Internet flavor: In 1999, nearly 70 percent of the proceeds raised by such IPOs went to Internet-related companies in contrast, only about 10 percent of 1996's total proceeds from IPO underwriting went to that kind of deal.

Yet, within the venture-capital industry, there is a hierarchy. Such notable firms as Benchmark Capital, Accel Partners, and Sequoia Capital have backed IPOs that have outpaced their counterparts several fold. For example, of the more than 130 IPOs that Sequoia Capital has backed, the average gain after one year of trading was over 100 percent, while overall, the deals jumped by more than 2000 percent, on average, from their offering price. One study suggests a number of reasons for the better performance of venture-capital-backed IPOs. William Magginson and Kathleen Weiss, in a *Journal of Finance*[54] article, maintain that venture-capital funding assists the issuing company by lowering the overall cost of going public and maximizing net proceeds to the issuer. In addition, in a report published in the same journal entitled "The Role of Venture Capital in the Creation of Public Companies," evidence is presented indicating that venture capitalists take significant equity interests in IPOs, serve on the boards of the new companies, and maintain their investment in the IPO over time. Such guidance may provide venture-capital-backed firms with more highly skilled managers and easy access to capital, in virtue of which those firms are better equipped to navigate through rough waters than companies without such backing.

Over the past few years, several underwriters have been among the leaders in underwriting venture-capital-backed IPOs. Among these firms are Deutsche Alex. Brown, formerly BT Alex. Brown, Banc Boston Robertson Stephens, and

Hambrecht & Quist. With respect to aftermarket performance, the impressive gains are clear-cut. For example, those venture-capital-backed IPOs which were underwritten by Deutsche Alex. Brown gained an average of 24 percent on their first day of trading, compared with an 18 percent gain for the firm's non-venture-capital-backed offerings. Likewise, a venture-capital-backed Banc Boston Robertson Stephens IPO gained 39 percent on the day of its debut, compared with 29 percent for IPOs the firm underwrote that were not backed initially by venture-capital firms.

Venture-capital firms that participated in the IPO market both during the period 1997–1999 and in 1999 itself saw strong returns. Kleiner Perkins ranked as the top venture-capital firm in terms of the number of companies it financed that issued IPOs during the three-year period ending in 1999. The total amount raised by these firms was in excess of $2.46 billion, while the total valuation of the companies, including insider shares, was nearly $24 billion. By the end of 1999, the 39 IPOs those companies issued had a market capitalization of over $94 billion and had generated an average annual return of more than 280 percent. San Francisco-based Hambrecht & Quist Private Equity Group, the venture-capital arm of H&Q, placed second, with 35 companies that it backed eventually going public and raising $1.92 billion. At the time the deals were completed, their value reached $12.5 billion, and by the end of 1999, they attained a market capitalization of almost $52 billion, a figure that translates into an average gain of 241 percent. The third-place firm that provided venture capital for IPOs between 1997 and 1999 was not a venture-capital firm per se, but chipmaker Intel Corp., which, through its venture-capital financing arm, backed 24 companies which went public during that period and raised $1.7 billion. By the end of 1999, these deals saw their market cap climb to almost $32 billion, posting an average gain of 295 percent. It is notable that 21 of those 24 IPOs were completed in 1999 and raised $1.51 billion, which put the firm in first place among venture-capital firms that saw their deals go public that year.

Recently, institutional money managers and investment bankers joined the ranks of the disgruntled to voice their displeasure over the preferential treatment some venture-capital firms receive when it comes to getting IPOs—especially those firms which had previously financed the IPO candidate. Indeed, the scramble for IPOs has even hit the ranks of the well-heeled fund managers, in that allocations which were once common have become rare. In sum, venture-capital firms are using their muscle to elbow out other investors in IPOs. In doing so, those firms often enjoy a windfall and, more importantly, can inflate their fund's investment returns, improving their performance as they shop for more clients. For example, it was reported that Baker Communications Fund,[55] a New York–based venture-capital firm, was able to purchase 400,000 shares of Akamai Technologies at the offer price, despite the fact that the fund had by that time owned 7.4 million shares of Akamai.[56] (As an aside, the Akamai IPO had not only disappointed retail investors, but also probably caused some tension at upcoming alumni and faculty meetings at the Massachusetts Institute of Technology. The reason was that Akamai was the offshoot of a collaboration between MIT Professor of Applied Mathematics Tom Leighton and ex–graduate student Daniel Lewin that enriched both by some $1.5 billion when the offered closed in October 1999. Moreover, it was reported that several MIT students associated with the two and who worked on the company's development ended up holding equity positions in the company valued in excess of $10 million. This, to some, gave Akamai another reason to maintain close ties with their alma mater.)

That incident led to questions about whether it was permissible under federal securities law for an issuer of an IPO to pledge prior to an offering being declared effective that an investor, in this case a venture-capital firm, can receive shares in an IPO. Such "directed share programs" have come under the inquisitive eye of regulators, since it may very well be an infraction of Section V of the Securities Act of 1933. Although it is a common occurrence for a venture-capital firm to have the opportunity to purchase private equity in any future financing, the dilemma is whether such a program may be translated into public shares. Whether the demand would still persist when IPO performance falters remains to be seen.

Summary: Look to see if the offering has received prior financial support from venture-capital firms. If so, it's likely that the IPO's performance in the aftermarket will be better than a similar offering that did not receive such backing.

LEVERAGED BUYOUTS

During the 1980s, there was a surge in the number of leveraged buyouts (LBOs) as corporate raiders, aided by high-yield debt financings, aggressively acquired companies and subsequently sold off parts of them to pay down the debt. Such transactions as New York–based buyout firm Kohlberg Kravis Roberts's acquisition of grocer Safeway Stores in 1986 for $5.3 billion and food and tobacco producer RJR Nabisco for nearly $30 billion in 1988 made financial headlines. In the years ahead, several of these LBOs resurfaced as IPOs, including such companies as children's book publisher Scholastic Corp., specialty tea producer Celestial Seasonings [which, incidentally, was acquired in early 2000 by Hain Food Group (NASDAQ-HAIN)], and radio broadcaster Infinity Broadcasting. In total, more than 250 such offerings were completed in the past decade, raising nearly $21 billion, with Goldman Sachs and Merrill Lynch each responsible for more than $3 billion in underwriting activity.

Yet, while the original backers of deals like these frequently saw a windfall, the investing public more often than not was left with little gain. Issues such as Sunbeam-Oster, AMF Bowling, and Polo Ralph Lauren each declined in value by nearly one-third or more from their offer price. Similarly, one-time LBOs apparel maker Warnaco Group and lottery services firm GTECH Holdings have lagged behind the leading market averages since issuing IPOs. One likely factor that may be responsible for the lackluster performance of these companies is that, as former LBOs, they may have balance sheets which are heavily weighed by enough debt that inordinate interest payments limit the likelihood of any cash falling to the bottom line. Another possibility, arising out of an examination of many of the issues that have reemerged as IPOs, is that too few of them are high-technology issues. Rather, the assortment of LBOs that have returned to the IPO route reveals various "brand name" companies that once commanded customer loyalty, but are marked by a decline in allegiance. Hence, as investors paid increased attention to firms that could generate the potential, or at least the expectation, of high profits, they almost in tandem gave scant interest to those firms which offered value in the form of a highly recognizable brand. (Witness the accelerated valuation paid to nearly any e-commerce or Internet company, while, in contrast, such stocks as Berkshire Hathaway or McDonald's floundered as they traded at 52-week lows in early 2000.)

Summary: As IPOs, LBOs have tended not to be big winners, because of their excessive debt loads and their tendency to be mostly in "brand name," nontech sectors in which earnings growth may be muddled.

TRACKING STOCKS

Tracking stocks have come into vogue in the past few years as some companies have resorted to so-called financial engineering to "unlock shareholder value." Basically, a tracking stock is typically a distribution of shares, or an issuance of new shares in a public offering, in a particular business segment of a company whereby the performance of this unit is "tracked" through the new offering. The intent behind such moves is the belief that the market is undervaluing the company, which may have a particular fast-growing unit, and in order to unleash this hidden value, a new stock must be issued. Recently, companies such as publisher Ziff-Davis, brokerage firm Donaldson, Lufkin & Jenrette, and retailer Circuit City have completed a tracking stock offering. Among those that are contemplating or have already completed such an offering are Walt Disney & Co., for its Go.com Internet business, office supply retailer Staples, for its Staples.com operation, J.C. Penney, for its Eckerd drugstores chain, and *The New York Times*, for its electronic and Internet-related media properties.

However, detractors of tracking stocks claim that such offerings expose investors to several possible several pitfalls. First, shareholders of tracking stocks are not considered to be owners of the targeted company. Instead, the parent company retains control by virtue of a common board of directors. In addition, should the parent company of the tracking stock fall into financial hardship and declare bankruptcy, it is likely that the owners of the tracking stock would be left out in the cold. This is because, under statute, in a reorganization of a corporation, the secured creditors have first rights in having their claims satisfied, versus those of unsecured creditors (i.e., common equity holders). In the case of owners of a tracking stock, their claims would probably even fall junior to those of a common equity holder, because a tracking stock owner owns essentially no equity in the company, but rather is a holder of an instrument whose appreciation is tied not directly to earnings per se, but to the performance of the parent company's own stock. Second, and perhaps most critical, the proceeds raised from the issuance of tracking stocks need not be used for the operations of the targeted company. For example, AT&T's move to issue a tracking stock for its wireless business generated over $10 billion for the company. However, it was reported that the firm's total wireless capital expenditures during 2000 would exceed only $4 billion. What would the remainder of the money be used for? The answer is acquisitions, primarily to build market share, but also to reduce debt, in light of AT&T's recent flurry of takeovers.

Of the nearly two dozen tracking stock issues, only a handful have scored strong gains. Most have lagged behind the general market averages. For example, publisher Ziff-Davis, Inc., issued shares in its Internet business ZDNet as a tracking stock. Since going public in March 1999 at an offer price of $19, the offering, by early February 2000, has lost about 17 percent in value from its first-day closing price of $36. Over the same period, the Dow Jones Industrial Average gained about 8 percent to close above 10,600, while the NASDAQ Composite nearly doubled in value over the same period. Furthermore, as was the case in the late 1980s and early 1990s when Wall Street was embracing so-called equity-linked preferred stock deals such as PERCs, DECs, and MIPPs, the prospects for substantial gains in such offerings were halted by the fact that many of the issuing firms were from industries experiencing modest to sluggish earnings growth at the time, thereby reducing the prospects that these stocks would appreciate. By early 2000, Ziff Davis had decided to reincorporate its tracking stock back into its parent company, while other companies, such as Pittson, had reevaluated the merits of their tracking stock issue.

Perhaps the sharpest barb against tracking stocks came in a critique by Burton G. Malkiel, author of "A Random Walk Down Wall Street," published in *The Wall Street Journal*. [57] Specifically, Malkiel cited several dangers associated with tracking stocks. First, the complex structure of such issues often delivers less than what appears to the eyes of many investors. Second, the aftermarket pricing of the tracking stock will be greatly influenced by the performance of the parent company. Finally, management may have divided loyalties between the parent company and the tracking stock wherein one may be favored over the other. In the words of Malkiel, "Financial engineering is often the sign of a late-stage bull market. ...[S]uch innovations ...settle back to discounts as the drawbacks become more apparent."

Summary: Investors are still trying to educate themselves on how to value tracking stocks and what place they should play in a portfolio. For now, despite Wall Street bankers' push for such deals, the outlook is uncertain as to whether they may be practical investment choices.

SELL HIGH...TAKE A LOOK AT BUYING LOW

As happens many times after a spectacular party, the revelers often stagger about, looking for direction. The same may be said of some IPOs in the aftermath of incredible first-day trading gains. Over the past few years, a successful strategy would have been to *sell short* the top-performing first-day IPO gainer. An argument in favor of this approach would be that such firms as theglobe.com, as noted earlier, and, more recently, VA Linux, have delivered negative shareholder value in the days following their offering. Likewise, companies such as Secure Computing, Paravant Computing, and Univec, each of which finished its year as the best first-day gainer, subsequently yielded negative returns to shareholders. Even a stock such as Shiva, Inc., which more than doubled on its first day of trading, failed to follow through for investors despite being acquired by Intel. Indeed, the company had the dubious distinction of actually being "taken under," since its acquisition price of $6 per share ($12 per share before a stock split) was less than its offer price of $15.

In contrast, a trolling of some of the worst first-day performers reveals some gems among the tarnished. While such companies as Vetco or Java Centrale may no longer be actively traded, and others, such as Innotrac, have plunged even further from their initial downturn, a few firms have rebounded from an early drop.

Statistical Summary: IPOs often present clues as to their future performance based upon their size, their location or the longevity of their operations. While each factor is not, in and of itself, a definitive determinant of how the offering will fare, together they serve investors well by pointing them in the probable direction the deal is headed.

IPO Observation: Investors must always be able to answer two basic questions when looking at IPOs as an investment. First, what is the objective of the contemplated move? Is it for long-term gains for retirement, or is it simply a speculative and impulsive action designed for quick profit? In addition, investors need to be able to answer the "pain" question: How low can an investment go before one feels the pain of the loss? For some individuals, a two-point drop in a stock's price may cause a panic attack and sleepless nights; others, by contrast, are hardly bothered by a 30-percent, 40 percent, or even 50 percent decline. As shown in Table 5-3, the average first-day gains of IPOs, while impres-

Table 5-3 Average First-Day Aftermarket Performance for IPOs*

| | PERCENTAGE OF CHANGE ONE DAY AFTER OFFER | | | | | | | | | | |
Month	1990	1991	1992	1993	1994	1995	1996	1997	1998	1999	2000
January	6.95	19.79	20.7	10.66	9.46	9.88	17.55	13.7	16.45	100.47	110.6
February	7.26	22.11	14.55	16.85	12.12	20.45	18.6	8.46	15.8	54.63	106.64
March	11.06	19.86	12.01	12.59	7.41	18.26	18	9.63	18.55	74.15	80.24
April	9.97	15.52	4.58	12.78	5.29	18.9	21.58	14.54	22.47	66.13	38.5
May	20.33	11.8	6.15	8.16	6.71	23.43	26.99	15.74	9.52	50.41	31.7
June	19.22	6.74	2.73	13.99	5.08	17.6	12.36	14.87	9.4	35.07	46.1
July	6.93	8.21	7.18	12.6	4.77	20.16	9.32	15.88	17.57	54.45	57.62
August	6.17	11.67	5.35	11.49	6.17	26.9	12.6	14.13	15.38	45.01	26.4**
September	7.58	21.43	9.05	19.18	16.94	20	18.25	21.72	75.84	64.84	
October	0	13.6	13.44	14.41	8.91	12.76	11.95	19.29	9.46	70.2	
November	0	13.92	14.79	9.44	10.94	29.74	11.25	6.49	53.31	102.3	
December	13.42	13.31	16.53	7.57	9.05	16.89	12.38	7.53	40.78	118.9	
Year Avg.	11.41	12.84	10.41	12.08	8.26	20.52	15.96	13.4	18.89	66.52	

* Excluding closed-end funds.
** Through August 15, 2000.
Source: Thomson Financial Securities Data.

sive of late, nonetheless, have been seen periods of frailty. In sum, investors must be honest with themselves and be able to answer how much of a paper loss they can tolerate before bailing out.

TOP PERFORMING AND LAGGING INDUSTRIES

Nearly every observer of the financial world, from the most visible commentator on the cable television financial news programs to the fixed-income pensioner who longs for the day when he clipped coupons on his bonds, is aware of the tremendous gains registered by high-tech and Internet-related IPOs in the closing years of the 1990s. Yet, the underwriting world is more than the latest dot-com deal or the newest on-line seller of widgets. In fact, from 1990 until 1999, high-technology IPOs lagged behind nontech deals in terms of number of offerings. As seen in Figures 6-1 and 6-2 the technology IPO issuance at the start of the 1990s was anything but dynamic. Furthermore, until recently, investors in IPOs were just as likely to rush into a trendy retailer's offering or a popular food chain's stock deal as they were to back some new technology

IPO. FOR EXAMPLE, IN THE EARLY 1990S, INSURANCE COMPANY IPOS[58] WERE POPULAR, AS EVIDENCED BY THE FACT THAT BETWEEN 1990 AND 1995 THE INSURANCE SECTOR RANKED IN THE TOP FOUR AMONG OVERALL IPO GROUPS, BASED UPON PROCEEDS RAISED. WHAT'S MORE, IN THE PAST DECADE THE LEADING IPO PERFORMER FOR ANY INDIVIDUAL YEAR WAS DECIDEDLY NON-TECH RELATED, AS A PASSENGER AIRLINE, A CLEANING SERVICE, AND A MAN-UFACTURER OF INDUSTRIAL CHEMICALS EACH SAW THEIR IPO SCORES EARN TOP HONORS AS THE BEST PERFORMING ISSUE IN THEIR DEBUT YEAR.

An examination of the historic performance of IPOs throughout the 1990s may give one further insight into the shifting sands of investing and a realization that what was a popular decision one year may be disastrous the next. Alternatively, much as a rookie ballplayer may display signs of brilliance that will last throughout a career, so, too, have some IPOs demonstrated a resilience in their debut year that puts them into the investment hall of fame. For example, in 1990 the best performing IPO was Implant Technology, whose business was listed as manufacturing surgical implants. The $3.3 million deal was managed by now-defunct broker–dealer F. N. Wolf and priced at $1 per share. At the end of 1990, the stock was changing hands at $3.125, a better than 200 percent gain. A couple of notches down on 1990's list of IPO top gainers was a company called Cisco Systems, whose stocks were purchased in a $50.4 million deal by blue-chip firm Morgan Stanley and priced at $18 each. At the close of the year, the shares were trading at nearly $45 each, an almost 150 percent gain. Needless to say, in subsequent years Cisco went on to become one of the all-time best performing IPOs, not only enriching its early backers, but still generating wealth to new investors. As regards Implant Technology, its shares no longer trade, and no information is available on its demise.

The following year saw a commercial cleaning service company nose out a biotech company as the best performing

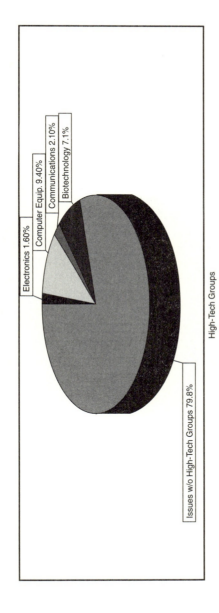

Electronics 1.60%

Computer Equip. 9.40%

Communications 2.10%

Biotechnology 7.1%

High-Tech Groups

Issues w/o High-Tech Groups 79.8%

Figure 6-1 High-Technology Totals: January 1 to December 31, 1990

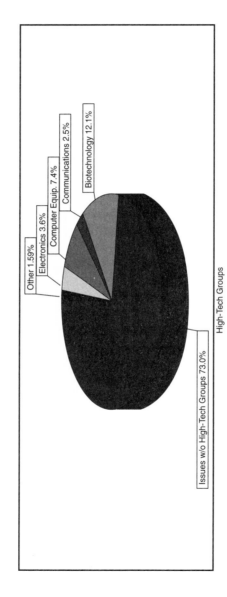

Other 1.59%

Electronics 3.6%

Computer Equip. 7.4%

Communications 2.5%

Biotechnology 12.1%

High-Tech Groups

Issues w/o High-Tech Groups 73.0%

Figure 6-2 Technology IPOs 1991

IPO completed in 1991. The company, Valley Systems, Inc., was a $5 million offering led by Laidlaw Equities whose year-end price rose 385 percent from its offering cost of $5 per share. As for 1991's second-place finisher, MedImmune, the Morgan Stanley–managed IPO gained 373 percent that year. In the years ahead, Valley Systems wound up being acquired by HydroChem Industrial Services in September 1998 for about $38 million, while MedImmune skyrocketed to above $170 a share by early 2000, good for a gain of over 3500 percent from its offer price. In 1992, investors, perhaps still harboring memories of People's Express, the one-time high-flying IPO of a decade earlier, flocked into shares of Reno Air, a regional passenger airline. The $5.3 million IPO, led by a now-dissolved underwriter called Paradise Securities, was offered at $3 per share and ended the year at over $17, a better than 400 percent gain. Yet, the skies were hardly friendly for Reno Air, as increased competition, fare wars, and unprofitability forced the company on the selling block. It was acquired by American Airlines in November 1998, with common shareholders receiving $7.75 for each share owned. However, while 1992's best perform-ing IPO subsequently was grounded, the IPO that took sec-ond place among market leaders that year, Lone Star Steakhouse & Saloon, still is delivering a satisfying return and often has portfolio managers and individual investors returning to load up on shares. Lone Star's $18.9 million IPO was priced at $13.50 per share and, with a stock split in 1992, closed the year at over $37, a gain of 457 percent. Further stock splits reduced the offer price, so that by 1999 the adjusted offer price was $3.375,which translated into an overall gain of about 160 percent for Lone Star's initial investors since the debut of the company.

As a new president entered the White House in 1993, so, too, was new leadership forming among IPO price perform-ers. Unlike the previous three years, during which no tech

IPO reigned as the performance champion, 1993 saw tech firms come in as four of the top five gainers. Heading the list was Microchip Technology, a manufacturer and wholesaler of semiconductors, which gained a stunning 500 percent in its inaugural year. That IPO was followed by Casino Data Systems, a developer of accounting systems for casinos. Although the company's stock rose 425 percent from its $5 offer price in 1993, in later years the firm's performance drew mixed results, as the company returned to where it started by spring 2000. The year 1994 saw continued strength in technology issues, as such firms as Network Peripherals, FORE Systems, and Cascade Communications went public, with each gaining more than 300 percent by the close of their first year of trading. While 1994 was marked by only a modest increase in the number of tech IPOs over the previous year's figures, in terms of performance investors placed their foot on the pedal, and these shares surged dramatically ahead. The average gain by year's end for the 188 tech IPOs offered in 1994 was 38 percent, compared with 32 percent for those 183 tech issues which came public in 1993.

The year 1994 also was notable for two other events. In the first, in a history-making development, an Internet service provider (ISP) for the first time registered as among the year's better performing IPOs. Netcom On-Line Communication went public at $13 and closed the year above $28, for a 118 percent gain. The company ended 1994 as the 24th-leading IPO among more than 600 issues. In the second event, CMG Information Services debuted at $8 and finished the year up over 190 percent, to rank as the seventh-best gainer. The firm would later go on to become CMGI, a leading "incubator" of Internet and e-commerce companies, and would see the price of a share in it rise several thousand percentage points from its initial offer price. By middecade, tech issues, the Internet wave, and the dot-com fervor came into focus, as four of the top five gainers among the IPO class of 1995 included such companies as communications equipment manufacturer Premisys Communications and Internet software developers Spyglass, Netscape Communications, and UUNet Technologies.[59] Although 1995's best performing IPO was a small manufacturer of industrial chemicals, Technical Chemicals and Products, Inc., whose stock price, after being split, ended the year up 900 percent from its offer price, the strong gains posted by many issues in the tech sector overshadowed that company's performance.

In 1996, underwriters unleashed technology financings, with more than $20 billion in tech IPOs flooding the market, more than double the volume of a year before and triple 1994's level. The numbers also marked a new record for tech IPO volume that stood until 1999. All but a handful of the top 20 IPO performers were tech related. However, while issuance was strong and short-term performance exceptional, investors were beginning to experience the early signs of intermediate tech weakness. At the end of 1996, the average tech IPO priced that year gained 22 percent. However, by the end of the following year, only 119 of the 269 tech issues that came to market in 1996 managed to post a further gain. The tech slump in 1997 was magnified by the first significant drop in the number of tech IPOs that decade, as issuance declined by more than one-third, from 369 in 1996 to 238 in 1997, while dollar volume was nearly cut in half, to just over $11 billion. In addition, the lofty gains of previous years gave way to more "muted" gains. Specifically, one of the top IPO gainers in 1997, chipmaker Rambus, gained 281 percent that year, a figure that would have registered as only the eighth-best performing IPO of 1995. Nonetheless, among those top gainers in 1997, one small offering would in the months and years ahead be on either the most beloved list of investments or the most reviled stock concept ever foisted on investors.

For 1997 was the year e-commerce powerhouse Amazon.com became public at $18 in a $54 million offering managed by Deutsche Morgan Grenfell. In that year, Amazon.com climbed by better than 230 percent, to close above $60. After several stock splits, the shares now trade at more than several thousand percentage points above their original offer price.

Although 1998 saw continued softness in technology IPO issuance as the number of tech deals slumped to just 138, the lowest volume since 1990's 53 deals, investors remained confident in selected issues, bidding higher the shares of such companies as Inktomi, VeriSign, Inc., and Broadcom, among others. However, underwriting that year was hampered by political and social unrest in Asia and currency dislocations in Russia, and gains in the IPO market were likewise dampened by investor concerns. By the close of the year, just 25 IPOs that came to market in 1998 managed to gain 100 percent or more, compared with 43 from the previous year that doubled or did even better by the end of 1997. In the following year, much of what was considered the norm was cast aside, as 1999 marked the first time in the 1990s that the manufacturing sector did not top the list as the leading IPO group, based upon the amount raised by underwriters. Leading the way in 1999 were personal and business service firms.

RETAIL IPOs

Often, it has been stated that the most powerful individual in the economy is not the chairman of the Federal Reserve Board, but rather the American consumer. Armed with cash and credit, consumers have adopted habits of spending that have fueled the profits of numerous retailers while closing the doors on others. With respect to investing opportunities in retail IPOs, perhaps the best were in those companies which radically reshaped the way Americans shopped and the reasons they did so. For example, Home Depot, whose $44.2 million IPO was completed in October 1986 at a price of about 50 cents per share, adjusted for stock splits, empowered shoppers as do-it-yourselfers as they grabbed hammers and tape measures to renovate America. Likewise, Amazon.com, while seen in some quarters as an Internet or e-commerce company, may be still viewed as a retailing concern whose mission is to build a brand name and a location for consumers to buy books, videotapes, and assorted electronic gear in a convenient and cost-effective place.[60]

Except for 1990, when just 8 IPOs were completed, the retailing sector has always been well represented among first-time equity financings. With a decade-high 44 retailing IPOs priced in 1993, there has been a consistent level of companies seeking to sell shares to the investing public and underwriters willing to assist them in their mission. Among the notable brand names that went public in the past several years are women's retailer Ann Taylor, children's educational toy store Noodle Kidoodle, and sporting goods retailer Coleman. Recently, the move into e-commerce companies has led to a blurring of the lines, as retailing and technology hybrids have become more commonplace, as evidenced by such offerings as eToys, Stamps.com, and pcOrder.com. Yet, among the more than 280 retailing IPOs that went public in the 1990s, only 3—General Nutrition Companies, Bebe Stores, and Amazon.com—registered among the top performers in any given year. General Nutrition Companies went public in January 1993 at $16 per share and ended the year at $28.50, good for a 256 percent gain. Bebe Stores was a 1998 issue that came public at $11 and closed the year at almost $35, for a 215 percent gain and a spot on the top 20 list of best performing IPOs of the year. Only about one-third of all retailing IPOs are trading above their offer price, while a like number are trading below.

IPOs in the retailing sector have been marked by remarkable successes, as well as failed concepts. Abercrombie & Fitch, a 1996 spin-off from women's retailer The Limited, gained over 200 percent in its brief history as a public company, with many teenagers being drawn to the store's clothing line. (Recently, though, signs indicate a slowing of this once-rapid growth.) Similarly, bookstore chain Borders Group, a spin-off of Kmart in 1995, has nearly doubled in value since going public. In addition, several retailers that had launched IPOs have been acquired in the past few years. Among these firms are Orchard Supply Hardware Stores, Petstuff, and Baby Superstore.

On the other hand, investors in some ill-fated IPOs have endured several retailing bankruptcies, including those of Filene's Basement, footwear retailer Just for Feet, and Garden Botanika. Finally, several one-time high-flying retailing IPOs have subsequently suffered hard times. For example, several retailers have seen their IPOs double in value in their first year of trading, only to tumble in the months ahead. As a case in point, consider Garden Ridge. The 1995 offering for this chain of home furnishings stores was completed in May 1995 at $15 each ($7.50 when adjusted for a two-for-one stock split). Within a year, the stock was up 270 percent. However, competition from Home Depot contributed to the company's woes as, by late 1999, the stock was trading below its offer price and the company's board of directors was on the verge of accepting an offer from management to go private. In early 2000 that deal closed, whereupon Garden Ridge shareholders received $11.50 for each share they owned, or a 23 percent *discount* off the original offer price! Similarly, Restoration Hardware, a retailer of high-end home accessories and "nostalgic" items, drew rave reviews, but little in the way of customer traffic as its IPO slumped nearly 70 percent after debuting in June 1998 at $19.

IPO CLUES: DISCOVERING THE NEXT HOT COMPANY

If one were searching for clues to identify successful retailing IPOs, the following would be sensible guidelines: First, avoid those issues where there's an 800-pound gorilla already on the scene. All too often, some promoter will be hawking the next Home Depot or the next Starbucks in markets where those companies already have a dominant position. For example, New World Coffee, a New York–based franchiser of coffee shops, has failed to see its stock price move beyond the single digits. Second, just because there's a ".com" associated with a retail IPO, investors should not expect immediate windfalls, especially where companies are having a difficult time developing an identity. Of those e-commerce IPOs trading under their offer price, deals such as 1-800-Flowers.com, FTD.com, Musicmaker.com, and Musicland Stores may be having difficulty getting investors to identify their service and product with the underlying stock. Being one of several on-line book, gift, food, or widget merchants bodes poorly for the performance of a company's stock. Instead, it is the company that can motivate a client to purchase through its Web site rather than the competition's that will prosper. The motivation may come in the form of customer rebates, client satisfaction, ease of use, reliability, or building allegiance through celebrity endorsements.

Finally, trends come and trends go, but it's companies that can create and maintain a market, whether they are "brick-and-mortar" issues, "e-tailers," or some combination of the two, that will prosper and enrich shareholders. For example, stocks such as Wet Seal and Rag Shops enjoyed strong run-ups, only to retreat as store traffic softened and earnings weakened. In such cases, customers initially were drawn into the store, but as time went on, other retailers became more attractive. By contrast, merchants such as Bed Bath & Beyond or Linens-n-Things have managed to carve out a niche that transcends spur-of-the-moment fads, as each caters to new homeowners, as well as those couples becoming empty-nesters, and both middle- and upper-income groups.

One likely development in the near term is an increase in the number of brick-and-mortar companies issuing shares in their e-commerce units to the investing public. Already, book retailer Barnes & Noble has created barnesandnoble.com, while fragrance company Perfumania has created perfumania.com as a publicly traded company. Among those companies planning similar offerings are office supply retailer Staples, for its on-line business, and Kmart, for its own e-commerce site labeled Bluelight.com.

Summary: Whether it's in e-commerce or brick-and-mortar companies, the success of a retail IPO will largely rise or fall as goes ithe sales growth rate of its store.

HEALTH-CARE IPOs

With prescription drug costs skyrocketing and medical expenditures a hot topic from Washington to the family kitchen table, it would seem likely that health-care IPOs—essentially, those companies providing medical services and operating health-care facilities—would be booming. However, the reality is that health-care IPOs have been hampered by cost containment policies enacted by the public and private sectors and by federal probes into the practices of several hospital management companies. As a result, margins have been squeezed, payment schedules have been drawn out, and investors have decided to stay on the sidelines. In addition, efforts to introduce e-commerce to prescription drug sales encountered some stumbling blocks in light of reports that retired physicians were being hired solely to "write" prescriptions for on-line clients whom they never actually examined. Furthermore, given that some prescriptions have a limited number of refills, the prospect of repeat orders was dampened, forcing analysts to trim revenue forecasts and push out the expected date of profitability for several on-line drug retailers.

In total, of the nearly 200 health-care companies, excluding biotechnology firms, that have gone public in the 1990s, all but about 10 percent either are no longer trading or are changing hands at below their offer price. And while nearly two dozen health-care IPOs subsequently were acquired (including some of the decade's largest deals, such as HealthTrust, Inc., and Hospital Corp. of America), about one-quarter of the decade's deals (including many assisted-living and nursing home companies) have lost money for investors.[61]

Yet, the real telltale sign of the difficult time health-care IPOs have had of late is the fact that, during a time when IPO fervor has swept many business sectors, only a handful of new issues, excluding on-line health information sites such as drkoop.com and Healthcentral.com and prescription and medical supply retailers such as Mothernature.com and Drugstore.com, have emerged from this group in the past year. In the opinion of many market observers, the group, while not on life support, is in a damaged condition and in need of repair. However, while other groups passed it by with respect to the performance of their stocks, only those investors who are willing to commit risk capital are venturing into this field.

Summary: Much as there are diverse groups within the medical industry, from health-care providers to drug manufacturers to biotech research-and-development firms, so, too, are there disparate performers among IPOs within the sector. For investors, the lesson learned from these deals is that, more often than not, they rarely prove to be a "magic bullet" for one's portfolio. Rather, they often must nurse their earnings before any explosive price appreciation is seen.

NATURAL RESOURCES IPOs

As oil prices and the cost of an ounce of gold climbed in late 1999 to their highest levels since the start of the decade, the prospects for a revival of natural resources IPOs would appear good. As for what took place during the 1990s, one could claim that, at best, it was a mixed performance. Only about one-quarter of the 120-odd natural resource–related IPOs priced in the past 10 years are trading above their offer price, while a like number are changing hands at less than what they started out at. In fact, of the five largest natural resources IPOs, three have lost money for investors, while the best performer, ENI,[62] is an Italian-American depository receipt whose gain may be more attributed to a play as an international equity holding rather than a natural resource selection. (An American depository receipt, commonly referred to as an ADR, is simply an issue that represents shares in an already-public company trading in a foreign stock exchange.)

Also of note is that, with the surge in IPO issuance and the unparalleled price gains of many issues in the later years of the 1990s, natural resource IPOs lagged considerably. While more than 30 issues were completed between 1997 and 1999, fewer than a half dozen such deals managed to trade at a gain. Furthermore, of those natural resource IPOs which came to market in the past decade and subsequently were trading at a loss, nearly two-thirds went public in the past three years. And the lackluster performance has not been limited to oil-and-gas issues: Those particularly hard hit were mining shares, as prices for precious metals remained at a level where operations for many producers were marginally profitable at best. Of the eight IPOs in the gold and silver mining business during the 1990s, only one—Cia Minas de Buenaventura—was trading above its offer price.

Summary: Even when the price of a barrel of oil surged above $30 in early 2000, there was little in the way of IPO registrations in the oil-and-gas sector.

LEISURE-TIME IPOs

Americans spend billions of dollars per year on tickets for movies, sporting events, and assorted kinds of entertainment. A like amount is wagered at casinos and racetracks. So with such a built-in revenue base, it would seem that IPOs in the leisure-time sector would be an attractive investment opportunity. Not so: Of the more than 100 companies that went public in the 1990s whose primary business included motion picture distribution, casino operations, or professional sports teams, only about one-fifth are still trading above their offer price. Perhaps the best explanation why investing in leisure-time companies has been anything but pleasurable for many investors is that those companies are forced to consistently deliver new and exciting products in order to keep an audience's attention. For example, consider a major food or beverage company. If its product is a household staple or a fixture in the culture, then the company may simply have to be able to generate consistent sales and profits. However, in the case of a filmmaker or record producer, yesteryear's film or CD, as well as yesterday's artist, may no longer bring in the cash in the years ahead. Rather, this kind of firm must produce an even more exciting or desirable product in order to both retain its past audience and attract new attendees. Likewise, consumers' tastes change: In 1987, nearly half of the record albums sold were in the rock 'n' roll genre; today, just about a quarter fall into that category, while rap and, surprisingly, gospel are among the fastest growing styles of music.

In total, the average gain from the offer date of an IPO during the past decade in the leisure sector is about 50 percent. Among the leading issues are video rental store Hollywood Entertainment, whose shares have risen about 600 percent since their debut in 1993, and Anchor Gaming, whose IPO has jumped over 400 percent in less than six years. At the other end of the spectrum, such issues as racetrack operator Colonial Downs, casino owner Ameristar Casinos, and fitness club operator Sports Clubs Co. have each seen the price of their IPO drop by one-half or more since their debut. The New York–based investment firm Donaldson, Lufkin & Jenrette has chalked up the greatest number of losing issues of any single underwriter in the leisure-time group. Four of the firm's six lead-managed deals in the group have seen their stock price turn south, with three—American Skiing Co., Groupe AB S.A., and Film Noble—each dropping by 70 percent or more.

Summary: Traditional leisure-time and entertainment IPOs, excluding software companies, have been nerve-racking investments for many. Perhaps that is why, to some investors, the best entertainment is trading stocks, not owning entertainment companies.

7

BETTING ON THE JOCKEY

INVESTORS MAY CONSIDER THE ABILITIES OF SPECIFIC UNDERWRITERS AS A CLUE TO THE FUTURE PERFORMANCE OF ANY IPOs THEY UNDERWRITE. FOR EXAMPLE, IF A CERTAIN FIRM HAS AN ESTABLISHED TRACK RECORD IN BRINGING CERTAIN TYPES OF COMPANIES PUBLIC, WHETHER IN A PARTICULAR INDUSTRY OR MARKET SECTOR, THEN INVESTORS MAY BE ABLE TO JUDGE WITH A DEGREE OF AUTHORITY HOW FUTURE DEALS MAY PERFORM.

The aim of this chapter, however, is to go beyond merely claiming, for instance, that the firm of Robertson, Stephens, now a division of FleetBankBoston, concentrates on technology issues, while the investment bank PaineWebber has brought public only 16 high-tech IPOs out of more than 160 issues during the past few years, so that the latter's deals may pose a greater risk for investors. Rather, the chapter will examine which banks lead in particular IPO underwriting and why companies gravitate to those firms. Sometimes, a firm will hire a particular banker because of his or her past work on another type of financing or because of the personal relationship that banker enjoys with a key member of the underwriting team and the issuer of the IPO. Alternatively, companies occasionally seek out investment banks with experience in a particular regional setting.

One recent trend, if it continues, may give way to fewer and fewer choices for both investors and issuers in selecting which investment bank to do business with.[63] As the dollar amount of IPOs has reached record highs, there has been a corresponding decrease in the number of underwriters acting as lead managers on IPOs. In both 1994 and 1996, 154 individual managers acted as a book manager for at least one IPO in a given year, but since then, the number of underwriters participating in the IPO market as a lead manager has steadily declined. In 1997, 139 book managers made up the overall IPO market; by 1998, the number had dropped to 110, and it fell to just 80 in 1999. The latter figure was the second lowest of the decade, with only 1990's showing of 59 separate IPO book managers completing deals that year representing a lower participation in the market.[64]

Besides the drop in the number of underwriters underwriting IPOs, activity has become concentrated among a handful of investment bankers. The dollar volume of IPO underwriting among the top five firms reached the most condensed level ever in 1999, as more than 66 percent of the amount raised from IPOs came from Goldman Sachs, Morgan Stanley Dean Witter, Merrill Lynch, CS First Boston, and Donaldson, Lufkin & Jenrette. In 1998 the top five firms accounted for less than 62 percent of IPO volume, while in 1997 the figure was slightly above 50 percent. Two reasons may be responsible for such developments. First, given that most of the IPOs under examination in this book are firm-commitment deals (which, as previously mentioned, require that the firm put up its own capital to complete a deal), many firms may be too undercapitalized to complete IPOs at today's lofty levels. Second, since many IPOs are of the high-technology variety and may therefore have some venture-capital backing, investment companies without strong relationships to venture-capital firms may have little success in having a deal go their way. For example, of Goldman Sachs' 27 IPOs managed in 1999 that received some degree of venture-capital backing, 7 were backed in part by Kleiner Perkins. Likewise, of Morgan Stanley Dean Witter's 30 of 49 IPOs completed that year which had venture-capital financing, most were orchestrated in part by Sequoia Capital.

THE LEADERS

Just as battle-worn combatants struggle for supremacy inch by inch over a battlefield or beachhead, so do investment banks engage in maneuvers to gain an advantage in the so-called underwriting league tables. Whether it's backing an IPO of dubious distinction or adding more shares to inflate the offering, banks are keenly aware of where their rivals stand. Thus, it's perhaps no surprise to see an increased number of multibillion-dollar IPO deals as underwriters seek to put some distance between themselves and their competitors by dealing at any cost and for any size. During the 1990s, more than $340 billion was raised in the United States from IPOs, or nearly $10 million daily, including weekends. However, more than half of that amount, or about $174 billion, was generated by just four firms: Goldman Sachs, Morgan Stanley Dean Witter, Merrill Lynch, and Salomon Smith Barney. As evidence of the recent increased concentration in the underwriting business, consider the fact that in the 1980s the four leading IPO managers accounted for about 35 percent of the industry total, while by September 2000 the top four IPO underwriters accounted for 67 percent of the market's share for proceeds.

Perhaps the most dramatic contrast in underwriting between the 1990s and the 1980s is with respect to the size of the deal. In the 1980s the typical amount raised from an IPO was about $21 million, compared with $76 million in the 1990s. Nonetheless, even the latter figure has been surpassed by 1999's activity, as the average size of a deal in that year was over $125 million. This increase in volume illustrates the expanding need for capital, when the question is examined from the point of view of individual firms. For example, Merrill Lynch, which underwrote less than $6 billion in IPOs during the 1980s, saw its underwriting volume exceed $41 billion the next decade, while the amount underwritten by Morgan Stanley jumped from less than $3.4 billion to more than $48 billion during the same period.

Several reasons are offered as to why this development has occurred. First, given that the average size of a deal has increased, some firms may not have the capital resources to underwrite deals. As noted earlier, a firm-commitment offering requires the underwriter to put up its own capital, in essence "buying the shares" from the issuer, before selling the deal to institutional and individual investors. Second, some issuers may be flocking to institutional "brand name" investment firms, such as Goldman Sachs or Morgan Stanley, at the expense of some lesser known or regional firms. Finally, and perhaps most important, potential IPO issuers can retrieve reports from firms, such as Thomson Financial's Autex,[65] that document the so-called aftermarket support of a book manager in handling the offerings that he or she brought public. Indeed, if it can be documented that one manager consistently acted as a buyer and seller and maintained an orderly market for a particular stock, than the investment bank may have an advantage over a rival whose track record in the aftermarket is less consistent.

LEADERS LEAD...OTHERS DON'T

During the 1990s, more than 300 individual underwriters participated in the IPO market as a book manager of at least one deal. Some names, such as Monroe, Parker, and Sentra Securities, are unfamiliar, others, like Kidder, Peabody, have faded into the backdrop of financial history and eventually merged with other underwriters, and still others, such as Drexel Burnham Lambert, are best forgotten; the fact remains that the better performing deals are unwritten more often by "brand name" firms, and not by others. For example, of all the underwriters of IPOs in the 1990s, a group of seven has outpaced its competitors. On the whole, deals led by Goldman Sachs, Merrill Lynch, Morgan Stanley, CS First Boston, Donaldson, Lufkin & Jenrette, Lehman Brothers, and Alex. Brown exhibited better gains than those of all other managers. For example, IPOs brought public by this group, which was responsible for about one-third of all IPOs underwritten in the past decade, gained an average of 25.5 percent in their first day of trading, compared with 15 percent for IPOs brought by all other firms. Furthermore, since their offer date, IPOs underwritten by the group have gained more than 240 percent, on average, versus 68 percent for deals underwritten by all other firms.

Consider the top 100 best performing IPOs of the 1990s. Of these, 17 were managed by Goldman Sachs, while Morgan Stanley was responsible for bringing 19 of those deals public. In only 11 instances will one see an underwriter with just one issue to its credit within this list. Thus, it is apparent that the better performing issues tend to gravitate to selected "brand name" underwriters and rarely to lesser known firms.[66]

GOLDMAN SACHS

As the leading underwriter of IPOs in the 1990s, Goldman Sachs[67] already had a distinguished track record in managing top-performing deals. Chief among these was its March 1986 underwriting of a $58.7 million offering by a Washington state developer of computer software named Microsoft. As the decade came to a close, Goldman Sachs could look back and take pride on its stellar performance as shown in Figure 7-1. Among its notable achievements were handling Yahoo!'s $33.8 million IPO, which skyrocketed over 17,000 percent from its April 1996 debut, and bringing out eBay, whose stock price has risen over 2500 percent. In addition, the firm was lead manager on several multibillion-dollar offerings, including Sears, Roebuck & Co.'s $1.8 billion spinoff of its insurance subsidiary, Allstate Corp.; Ford Motor Co.'s $1.65 billion spin-off of its financial services arm, Associates First Capital, in May 1996; and the $2.74 billion IPO by cable TV operator Charter Communications. Of course, one must not forget that Goldman was lead manager of its own IPO, which raised over $3 billion for the firm and transformed it from one of the world's most profitable private partnerships to one of the world's most successful publicly traded companies.

During the 1990s, Goldman Sachs' IPOs gained, on average, more than 185 percent from their offer date through the close of the decade. On a year-by-year account, the IPOs

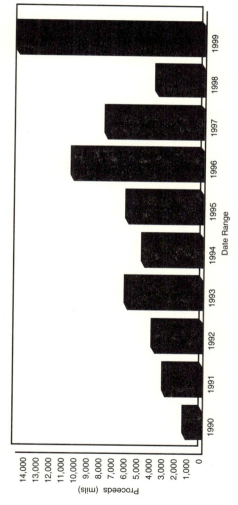

Figure 7-1   Goldman Sachs IPO Underwriting Volume

Goldman underwrote saw their best showing, as did those of many firms, in the final two years of the decade. For example, in 1998, the industry-leading 26 IPOs the firm underwrote that year rose, on average, 121 percent from their offer date to the year's end. Likewise, in 1999, a typical new equity issue brought public for the first time by Goldman gained over 175 percent from offer date to year end. That performance marked a major turnabout from the firm's showing at the start of the decade, when an IPO managed by Goldman Sachs *lost*, on average, nearly 5 percent in value at the end of the year for those issues brought public in 1990.

Aiding in the firm's performance has been a recognized presence in high-tech underwriting: Almost half of the IPOs Goldman has underwritten since 1990 were related to high technology. In contrast, during the 1980s, less than one-third of the IPOs the firm managed were of companies in the high-technology sector. And those high-tech issues brought results to Goldman and its clients: A typical one underwritten by Goldman in the 1990s gained 74 percent on its first day of trading and 141 percent after one year of activity. On the other hand, non-high-tech IPOs saw just a 12 percent gain, on average, on their opening day and 24 percent after 12 months of trading.

MERRILL LYNCH

As the nation's largest brokerage firm, in terms of its having the largest retail sales force, Merrill Lynch[68] ranks as one of the leading underwriters of IPOs in the past three decades, based upon number of issues. In total, excluding closed-end investment funds, Merrill has been the book manager for more than 510 IPOs since 1970, outdistancing its nearest rival, Lehman Brothers, by more than two dozen offerings. When the 1980s came to an end, Merrill Lynch could take pride in the fact that one of the IPOs it lead managed, Oracle Systems, which went public in March 1986, ranked as the top-performing IPO of that decade, with a gain of more than 1100 percent. And while it took nearly four years for Oracle to crack the 1000 percent mark, Internet Capital Group, which debuted in August 1999 at $12 per share, took less than four *months* to surge past that level, making it Merrill's best performing IPO of the 1990s.

That development stood as evidence that in the fast-moving IPO world, technology would lift even the most tied-down boat. What's more unusual is that, for the most part, Merrill had only a moderate attraction to high-tech underwriting in the past decade. Less than one-quarter of the company's IPOs were tech related. In contrast, many of Merrill's IPO deals were real-estate investment trusts, financial services companies, or foreign company offerings such as Argentine oil giant YPF, S.A., or Telefónica del Perú. Such deals, while ranking among Merrill's largest underwritings, have contributed to a lackluster aftermarket performance, as a typical IPO underwritten by the firm had risen only by about 51 percent towards the close of 1999 (excluding those issues with price information no longer available, because of either bankruptcy or acquisition). For example, while Merrill's 1991 underwriting of Kimco Realty's IPO has risen over 150 percent, excluding reinvested dividends, others, such as the firm's 1998 underwritings of ElderTrust Realty Group and Mills Corporation have been laggards for investors. Worse, among Merrill's recent IPOs are several notable bankruptcies, including children's play center Discovery Zone, fast-food operators Boston Chicken and Einstein Bros. Bagels, and retailer Bradlees Stores. On the other hand, several Merrill IPOs were subsequently acquired in the decade's M&A frenzy, including battery manufacturer Duracell International, soft-drink producer Snapple Beverage, and media company *Providence Journal*.

Yet, if one lesson could be drawn from Merrill's recent underwriting activities, it is that high tech matters. Of the firm's 25 best performing IPOs of the 1990s, nearly half were completed in 1999, and of those, all save one were tech related. Furthermore, Merrill has been steadily progressing into technology underwriting: In 1995, the firm underwrote just six high-tech IPOs; by 1999, the figure had jumped to 26 offerings.

MORGAN STANLEY DEAN WITTER

As one of the world's leading investment banking firms, Morgan Stanley Dean Witter[69] has a roster of IPO clients that includes many of America's top corporations, through the company's work on several notable deals involving companies spinning off divisions to shareholders. Such deals as AT&T's 1998 spin-off of its Lucent Technologies unit, Hewlett-Packard's issuance of shares in its Agilent Technologies, and Du Pont's shedding of its Conoco petroleum unit, each a billion-dollar-plus IPO, were managed by Morgan Stanley Dean Witter. Since 1990, in total, the firm has underwritten more than 310 IPOs and raised in excess of $50.5 billion in the United States from such transactions, as shown in Figure 7-2.

Technology underwriting has also been one of Morgan Stanley's strong suits. More than one-third of the proceeds it has raised for clients in the IPO market in the past decade has come from the tech sector, led by nearly $8 billion from the communications group. Perhaps the hallmark IPO underwritten by Morgan Stanley was its February 1990 deal for Cisco Systems. In the following decade, these

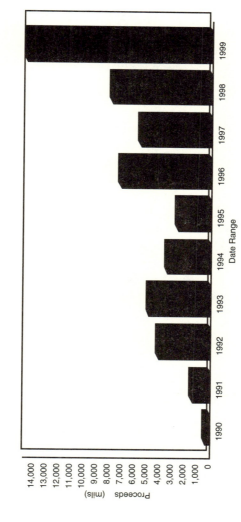

Figure 7-2 Morgan Stanley Dean Witter IPO Underwriting Proceeds

shares soared more than 80,000 percent, adjusted for several stock splits, from their original offer price of $18. Other notable IPOs managed by Morgan Stanley include the December 1996 offering by COLT Telecom Group, PLC, which has climbed more than 24,000 percent, and VeriSign, which, in its brief time as a publicly traded company since January 1998, has risen over 3600 percent.

Yet, the firm has seen its share of laggards. More than one-fourth of the IPOs underwritten by Morgan Stanley in the past decade are now trading below their offer price. True enough, several of these IPOs, such as Asia Pulp & Paper, China Eastern Airlines, and Empresas ICA Sociedad Control, are from foreign issuers, and weakening economies in those parent nations may have contributed to the downfall of the stocks, but such homegrown companies as Midway Airlines, Donna Karan International, and Yankee Candle also have turned in lackluster performances for both shareholders and the underwriter.

The firm's on-line arm, MSDW Online, is now being given greater access to the deals underwritten by its parent. Clients with account assets of $100,000 or more are given the right to indicate an interest in one of the firm's IPOs.

SALOMON SMITH BARNEY

The evolution of what is currently the investment house of Salomon Smith Barney[70] involves several twists and turns. The firm, which is a by-product of the 1998 $76 billion merger between insurance giant Travelers Group and commercial banking firm Citibank, was two separate concerns several years ago: Smith Barney Harris & Upham and Salomon Brothers. In the spring of 1987, Lama Holdings, an Arab investor group that held a 2 percent stake in Smith Barney, was seeking a buyer for its stake. Within months, consumer finance and insurance concern Primerica, formerly known as American Can, and now led by financial industry powerhouse Sanford Weil, purchased Smith Barney for a reported $750 million. Within a few years, Shearson Lehman Hutton, then a unit of American Express, became engaged in talks about the possible acquisition of Smith Barney. However, before a deal could be struck, negotiations were terminated. Then, in perhaps one of best known cases of a turn in financial tables, Primerica, with Smith Barney acting as its financial advisor, acquired Shearson Lehman Brothers from American Express for $1.15 billion. Subsequently, Primerica became Travelers Group, renamed Citigroup upon the completion of its merger with Citibank.

With respect to the firm's best performing IPOs of the past decade, it is surprising that one would have to go beyond the top 30 issues to find one that was completed in 1999, the industry's most supercharged year. Rather than pure Internet IPOs, Salomon Smith Barney's top deals derived from the telecommunications equipment and service sectors. For example, the firm's leading issue in the 1990s was telecommunications service provider Metromedia Fiber Network, whose offering gained more than 1700 percent from its debut in October 1997. While that gain would be a major accomplishment, the fact is that, of the 134 IPOs completed in the 1990s that gained 1000 percent of more in value from their offer price by the close of 1999, Salomon Smith Barney could boast of only five such offerings. In contrast, Goldman Sachs tallied 20, while rival Morgan Stanley brought an industry-leading 22 such IPOs public in the 1990s. Furthermore, while 1999 was a banner year for many underwriters, Salomon Smith Barney ended the year at its lowest level, ninth place, in underwriting league tables. Still, the firm ranked fourth among all book managers of IPOs in the 1990s, with nearly $25 billion in domestic proceeds from 300 issues.

JP MORGAN

Although JP Morgan[71] did not begin acting as a lead manager for IPOs until its 1992 deal for Riverwood International, the firm has recently come into its own in that regard. In 1999, JP Morgan acted as lead manager for Genentech's $1.94 billion IPO, which ranks as the largest IPO in the biotechnology sector and the 15th largest IPO ever in the United States. Of the nearly $9 billion in IPO proceeds JP Morgan was responsible for raising in the United States during the 1990s, about $4.1 billion came from high-tech issues, while the remainder was from such non-high-tech areas as finance, real estate, and natural resources. In fact, the firm's best performing IPO is decidedly non-high-tech: Capital One Financial Corp., a provider of credit and financial services, has seen its IPO climb by better than 800 percent since its debut in November 1994.

JP Morgan's penchant for large deals is evidenced by the fact that the size of its average deal is about $185 million, while competitors Merrill Lynch and Lehman Brothers have typical IPO offerings of about $155 million and $84 million, respectively. Indeed, among the top 10 IPO underwriters in terms of the size of their average deal, JP Morgan is second only to Goldman Sachs, which typically raised approximately $188 million in an IPO. By contrast, among the top 20 IPO underwriters during the 1990s, JP Morgan ranks next to last in terms of number of IPOs completed. Only Virginia-based Friedman, Billings & Ramsey, the 17th-ranked firm in terms of amount raised, had fewer offerings completed in the past decade, with 36. Still, the company's total business, including its M&A advisory work and debt underwriting, made it an attractive candidate for acquisition, whereupon in September 2000 Chase Manhattan Bank agreed to acquire JP Morgan in a $33 billion transaction.

DONALDSON, LUFKIN & JENRETTE

IPOs managed by the New York–based investment firm of Donaldson, Lufkin & Jenrette[72] in the 1990s, on average, have enjoyed strong gains, both on their first trading day and up to the present. Typically, a DLJ-backed IPO climbed nearly 22 percent in its first day of trading and more than 121 percent to today. The firm's mix of technology and non-technology issues falls within a pattern similar to that of many of its peers: About one-third of the overall proceeds it has raised from IPOs in the 1990s has come from the high-tech sector, while nearly 40 percent of the individual companies it has underwritten were from that sector. By far DLJ's best performing IPO was its March 1995 $38.4 million deal on behalf of semiconductor manufacturer SDL, Inc., at $16 per share; the issue has gained more than 8000 percent from its offer date in March 1995 to the end of 1999. The firm's largest IPO was a $563.5 million offering for cable TV systems operator Insight Communications Co., Inc., at $24.50 per share; the stock gained a relatively modest 20 percent from its July 1999 debut to the end of that year.

Among the several DLJ IPOs that have been acquired are OW Office Warehouse, RHI Entertainment, Inc., and Berg Electronics. On the downside, nearly three dozen of the nearly 200 IPOs DLJ has completed in the past decade are currently trading at less than 50 percent of their offer price. Among the firm's notable laggards are clothing retailer Joseph A. Bank Clothiers, Inc., hotel and casino operator Trump Hotels & Casino Resorts, and appliance store Tops Appliance City. Throughout the 1990s, the firm has underwritten more than $16.5 billion in IPOs from 195 deals. The year 1999 was the firm's best with respect to monies raised, with nearly $3.9 billion in proceeds, a figure that was up nearly 225 percent from its 1998 level. That year, DLJ matched its previous decade-high level in the IPO under-writing ranks of fifth place, last set in 1995. In August 2000, the investment banking firm Credit Suisse First Boston announced their intention to acquire DLJ for approximately $13 billlion.

LEHMAN BROTHERS

One of the darling stocks of the late 1990s, Qualcomm, Inc., is Lehman Brothers[73] top IPO performer. The manufacturer of communications equipment, which saw explosive earnings growth in virtue of Internet-related activities, was brought public by a $51.2 million lead-managed deal by Lehman Bothers in December 1991 at $16 per share. In the years that followed, Qualcomm's stock rose nearly 10,000 percent, to stand as one of the best performing stocks, not only of the 1990s, but also of all time. Those gains have aided in boosting Lehman's IPO aftermarket performance, which shows an average first-day trading gain of nearly 17 percent and an overall gain of more than 146 percent from its offer date for a typical IPO underwritten by the firm.

Throughout the 1990s Lehman Brothers brought public over 200 companies, excluding closed-end funds, and in the course of doing so raised more than $17 billion. That performance helped the firm capture the sixth position among all underwriters with respect to IPO activity in the past decade. Lehman Brothers ranked as high as third place in 1992, when it underwrote almost $3.2 billion in IPOs, and as low as 13th in 1998, when its IPO-related proceeds totaled under $800 million. Part of the firm's success lies in the fact that it has a slightly higher proportion of its under-writing in the technology sector than its contemporaries have. Still, while nearly 40 percent of the more than $18 billion the company has raised for IPO clients in the 1990s has come from the tech sector, with the communications industry representing the largest slice, there has been almost an even split with respect to the number of companies Lehman has represented in the tech and nontech sectors. The firm's largest IPO was a $966 million offering by PacTel Corp. in December 1993, as part of a spin-off from the company's parent, Pacific Telesis, The IPO was jointly managed with Salomon Brothers.

CS FIRST BOSTON

Throughout the 1990s, Credit Suisse First Boston[74] ranked in the top five in IPO underwriting volume. But the final year of the decade saw the institutional firm take top honors as the leading IPO underwriter, on the basis of number of issues managed, with 59, up from just 15 IPOs managed in 1998. That performance outpaced the showing of such competitors as Merrill Lynch, Morgan Stanley, and Goldman Sachs. Perhaps the prime reason for the firm's ascension was the hiring of powerhouse technology financier Frank Quattrane and his team of investment bankers. Formerly affiliated with Morgan Stanley, the group left Deutsche Bank in the summer of 1998 to join Credit Suisse and since then has delivered spectacular results. Between 1998 and 1999, IPO underwriting for the firm soared from $1.9 billion to nearly $6 billion. Furthermore, no less than 29 percent of the firm's total underwriting proceeds during the 1990s occurred in 1999 alone, while about one-quarter of all the IPOs the firm brought to market in the 1990s took place in the decade's final year. More than half of the firm's 12 top-performing IPOs in the past decade were priced during 1999 under Quattrane's management.

While Internet issues propelled Credit Suisse First Boston to higher ground in the industry's underwriting tables, some non-Internet deals were among the firm's top IPO underwritings of the decade. Among these are Sonic Corp., an owner and operator of drive-in restaurants whose IPO debuted in February 1991 at $16 and in the following nine-plus years gained nearly 400 percent, and Linens-n-Things, a retailer of home furnishings. Subsequently, such IPOs as sports apparel manufacturer Salem Sportswear and children's retailer Baby Superstore, Inc., were acquired. On the downside, CS First Boston has seen discount broker TD Waterhouse's IPO tumble more than 20 percent from its offer price, while medical device manufacturer Horizon Medical Products lost over three-quarters of its market value from its IPO offer price of $14.50.

BEAR STEARNS

If Wall Street is considered the theme park for capitalism, then perhaps Bear Stearns'[75] new 45-story office tower being constructed in midtown Manhattan may be viewed as capitalism's latest attraction. New York–based Bear Stearns & Co. ranks as the 10th-leading manager of IPOs since 1970, with nearly $9 billion in proceeds from 168 issues, and the 12th-leading IPO manager of the 1990s. More than one-third of the IPO issues it has underwritten, as well as more than one-quarter of the dollar amount this decade, has come from the technology area. Consonant with the fact that many underwriters enjoyed their best gains in 1999, Bear Stearns found itself enjoying a banner year that year with respect to IPO highfliers. That kind of performance is nothing new for the company, since it was the book manager for theglobe.com's IPO in November 1998, which soared over 600 percent from its offer price on its first day of trading. Of its 15 top-performing IPOs for the decade of the 1990s, 7 were completed in 1999, including Digital Island, the price of whose shares climbed over 1000 percent from a $10 offer price by the decade's close, and Viador, which gained over 340 percent by the end of 1999 after coming public at $9 in October of that year. In total, Bear Stearns priced 42 IPOs between 1998 and 1999, including, as noted earlier, on-line broker Wit Capital Group. Of these 42, one-third more than doubled in value by the end of 1999, 11 declined from their offer price, and a handful of others, including Xoom.com, which eventually merged with a subsidiary of General Electric to become NBCi, were acquired.

TECHNOLOGICAL TALENT

It is within those boutique investment houses that specialized in underwriting high-technology or emerging-growth companies that the most explosive growth was seen. Looking at the four leading firms in this area—Alex. Brown & Sons, Hambrecht & Quist, Robertson Stephens, and Montgomery Securities—one could easily foretell where the money was going and where the investment opportunities lay. In the 1980s, Maryland-based Alex. Brown was lead manager on 116 IPOs, raising $2.4 billion on behalf of its clients. In the following decade, Alex. Brown's underwriting activity in IPOs more than doubled, to 210 issues raising over $8.2 billion. Hambrecht & Quist's IPO underwriting activity rose from just $500 million from 34 issues to over $5.2 billion from 156 transactions, while Robertson Stephens, which completed just 3 IPOs during the 1980s, raising about $53 million, ended the 1990s with nearly $5 billion in IPO underwriting activity to its credit. Finally, Montgomery Securities' IPO business leaped from $354 million in the 1980s to over

$5.3 billion in the 1990s. In sum, these four firms' share of IPO underwriting, reflecting the growing funding requirements of high-tech companies, rose from 4.3 percent in the 1980s to 7 percent in the 1990s, while the amount they underwrote soared from about $4.2 billion to over $22 billion in the same period. However, what really puts these underwriters in a special class is their performance relative to that of their peers. Collectively, the four firms posted an average gain of about 26 percent on the initial day of trading for all their technology deals priced in the past decade and a gain of over 585 percent, on average, through the close of 1999. As regards all other firms that underwrote technology companies, their average first-day gain was 40 percent, and their stocks grew 331 percent at the end of the last decade. Thus, over the long run, these specific underwriters substantially outpaced their peers. Recently, such "establishment" firms as Morgan Stanley and Goldman Sachs have jumped to the leadership role, as shown in Table 7-1.

Even nonbrokers were getting into the act, as the California Public Employees' Retirement System, a $165 billion asset-rich pension fund commonly referred to as CalPERS, purchased a 10 percent stake in the investment banking firm of Thomas Weisel Partners for an estimated $100 million. The bought-up company, which was created by Thomas Weisel, a cofounder of San Francisco–based Montgomery Securities, now a unit of Banc of America. During 1999, Thomas Weisel Partners reportedly participated in 81 public equity offerings.

IPO BOX SCORE

Investors seeking a "snapshot" of individual underwriters may consider the so-called IPO box score featured in

Table 7-1 Top 25 Technology IPO Underwriters of 1999*

FULL TO BOOK (EQUAL IF JOINT)

Managers	Proceeds (mils)	Rank	Market Share	Number of Issues
Morgan Stanley Dean Witter & Co.	4,754.8	1	15.2	34
The Goldman Sachs Group, Inc	4,297.4	2	13.7	34
Credit Suisse First Boston	3,846.6	3	12.3	45
Donaldson, Lufkin & Jenrette, Inc.	2,341.6	4	7.5	28
Fleet Boston Corp	2,289.2	5	7.3	39
JP Morgan & Co Inc.	2,103.1	6	6.7	4
Merrill Lynch & Co Inc.	2,088.3	7	6.7	17
Lehman Brothers	1,579.7	8	5.0	19
Deutsche Bank AG	1,562.8	9	5.0	22
Bear Stearns	1,403.1	10	4.5	19
Salomon Smith Barney	1,249.6	11	4.0	11
Chase Manhattan Corp	1,145.7	12	3.7	20
Warburg Dillon Read	351.0	13	1.1	4
Prudential Securities Inc.	291.2	14	.9	7
Banc of America Securities LLC.	269.2	15	.9	4

Table 7-1 Top 25 Technology IPO Underwriters of 1999* (*Continued*)

FULL TO BOOK (EQUAL IF JOINT)

Managers	Proceeds (mils)	Rank	Market Share	Number of Issues
CIBC World Markets	262.4	16	.8	5
Dain Rauscher Corp	244.0	17	.8	4
Thomas Weisel Partners LLC.	211.2	18	.7	4
Gerard, Klauer, Mattison & Co.	140.2	19	.5	2
Societe Generale	112.5	20	.4	2
US Bancorp	109.8	21	.4	3
W.R. Hambrecht & Company	98.3	22	.3	2
ING Barings	95.5	23	.3	2
Cruttenden Roth Inc	68.0	24	.2	2
Allen & Co.	49.5	25	.2	1
Top 25 Totals	30,964.6	—	98.7	334
Industry Totals	31,360.6	—	100.0	329

* Includes communications, computer equipment, electronics, biotechnology (excluding medical devices) companies with IPOs of at least $15 million (US proceeds); excludes ADRs, ADSs, and unit offerings.

Source: Thomson Financial Securities Data.

Table 7-2 as a useful tool. The chart lists the number of IPOs, excluding closed-end funds, priced in the 1990s and examines where specific managers fall with respect to price performance. For example, in total, 1596, or about 30 percent, of all IPOs completed in the past decade ended 1999 trading above their offer price. On the other hand, 1281 issues, or about 24 percent, were changing hands lower than the initial offer price. Most surprising, and perhaps revealing, is that fact that 1600 IPOs ended the 1990s with no available price, either because the company was no longer traded or because it had halted operations. That number exceeds those currently traded IPOs priced in the 1990s that ended the decade at a price above their initial offer price. (Note that even this does not suggest that the offering was of benefit to early investors, since many IPOs, especially in 1999, were erratic on their first day of trading, going from, for example, $14 per share to $40 or higher on the first trade and then drifting back to the mid to low $20s. Thus, compared with the offer price, the IPO was trading higher; compared with the first-day close, it might be off by as much as 50 percent.)

Among the revelations of this analysis is that certain managers outdistance others with respect to the performance of their IPOs. For example, nearly one-half of Goldman Sachs' deals ended the decade trading above their offer price, while just about one-third of Salomon Smith Barney's IPOs managed a showing that high. In contrast, less than 20 percent of Credit Suisse's IPOs in the past decade met a similar fate in the aftermarket. (In some cases—for instance, Alex. Brown & Co.—there was no active price quote on the IPOs the firm completed in the 1990s.) As regards investment banks with the highest proportion of past-decade IPOs trading below their offer price, both Salomon Smith Barney and DLJ ended the decade with about 28 percent of their deals "under water." Nevertheless,

Table 7-2   IPO Boxscore*

		Deals in the 1990s		
Firm	**No. of IPOs**	**Trading Under Offer Price**	**Acquired or Merged**	**Units**
Morgan Stanley	326	68	15	3
Goldman, Sachs	325	67	13	7
Salomon Smith Barney	300	83	17	9
Deutsche Bank (Alex. Brown)	279	66	15	6
Merrill Lynch	272	59	15	5
Lehman Brothers	202	34	14	3
FleetBoston	202	39	8	2
DLJ	195	55	8	3
Credit Suisse	193	51	8	2
Banc of Americas	183	44	6	1
Top Ten	2477	566	119	41
Industry Total	5374	1281	221	69

*Prices as of December 31, 1999.
Source: Thomson Financial Securities Data.

		Deals in the 1990s	
Price n/a	Other	Gained 1 to 99% from Offer Price	Gained 100% or More from Offer Price
0	88	12	44
1	63	16	60
1	93	2	40
2	95	0	30
4	80	8	51
2	60	5	31
1	50	8	27
1	48	3	23
1	35	3	22
0	70	2	25
13	682	59	353
539	1600	68	623

about 32 percent of Salomon Smith Barney deals and over 39 percent of DLJ book-managed IPOs in the 1990s ended 1999 above their offer price. In addition, Salomon Smith Barney IPOs were more likely to be acquired or merged, as no fewer than 26 of the companies it brought public in the 1990s, or almost 9 percent, ended up as M&As.

Broker Brief: As many professions become specialized, so, too, have underwriters. Some focus on technology issues, others on financial or retailing. For investors, a key point to understand is that a firm underwriting a particular industry for the first time may encounter some stumbling blocks. On the other hand, experience and longevity in a specific sector may bring knowledge and insight that may translate into a successful offering.

8

BUY DIRECT; BUY SMALL; IF THE FRONT DOOR IS CLOSED...FIND ANOTHER ENTRY

Groucho Marx once said that he wouldn't want to belong to any club that would have him as a member. With IPOs, the average investor feels just the opposite as he or she clamors to be allowed to place at least one chip in the game, but is often turned away. As noted earlier, frustrations frequently arise as investors seek shares in an IPO, but are informed that a deal is oversubscribed or that the brokerage firm they are doing business with did not receive a sufficient allocation to meet investor demand. Much of any offering is first distributed to institutional investors, mutual funds, and

VENTURE-CAPITAL FIRMS. IT HAS EVEN BEEN REPORTED THAT SOME LEGAL ADVISORS WISH TO BE COMPENSATED, NOT IN CASH, BUT IN PREMARKET IPO SHARES FOR THEIR SERVICES. FOR EXAMPLE, LEADING TECHNOLOGY LAW FIRM WILSON SONSINI GOODRICH & ROSATI ENJOYED A WINDFALL AS THE VALUE OF THE FIRM'S INVESTMENT PARTNERSHIPS AND AN EQUITY POOL, FORMED BY PRESENT AND PAST MEMBERS OF THE FIRM, SOARED ALMOST $26 MILLION, BASED UPON THE FACT THAT THE COMPANY OWNED MORE THAN 100,000 SHARES IN THE BEST PERFORMING SINGLE-DAY IPO GAINER VA LINUX. EVEN THOSE E-BROKERS WHICH PORTRAY THEMSELVES AS PIONEERS IN "DEMOCRATIZING" THE IPO MARKET CONCEDE THAT THEY CANNOT MEET THE STRONG DEMAND FOR MANY OFFERINGS, AS THEY OFTEN ARE ALLOCATED ONLY A SMALL PERCENTAGE OF ANY GIVEN OFFERING. BASIC ARITHMETIC SHOWS THAT YOU CAN'T SATISFY A CLIENT BASE OF 100,000 OR MORE IF YOU ARE CONSISTENTLY ALLOCATED FEWER SHARES THAN CUSTOMERS.

In such an environment, some investors recognize that, rather than scrambling among the mobs for entrée into a deal, perhaps it would be better if a deal sought *them* out. Specifically, the past few years have seen an increase in the number of companies seeking to raise capital by issuing IPOs directly to investors. The prime mover of this development has, of course, been the Internet, by means of which investors can search various Web sites and seek out deals by size, industry, or region. Furthermore, investors can put their cash into private placements, venture-capital funds, or similar vehicles, all with the expectation that some component will go the IPO route. The various methods, each with its own particular risks and rewards, include direct public offerings (DPOs), community bank or thrift conversions from mutual ownership to public ownership, and corporate spin-offs, among other alternatives. The size and scope, as well as the performance, of such offerings approach both ends of the spectrum: Some deals that were offered at more than a fistful of dollars now change hands at pennies, while others that were sold at seemingly rock-bottom prices were soon acquired at substantial premiums.

DIRECT STOCK OFFERINGS

Companies that offer public issues of common stock directly to the investing public, without the services of an underwriter, do so through a Small Corporate Offering Registration, commonly referred to as an SCOR, under Form U-7. Such offerings have been in existence for several years, most notably as Rule 506 offerings, which impose no limit on the amount of money that can be raised, Regulation A offerings, which allow an issuer to raise up to $1 million, and Regulation D offerings, which permit up to $5 million to be raised by a company. Yet, it was the introduction of the Internet and e-commerce that made such deals visible and transferable. Until recently, start-up companies contemplating DPOs often relied on a closed-knit network of attorneys or accountants to market such offerings through the SEC's Small Corporate Offering Registration method. The offerings issued under Rule 506 could be sold to 35 "sophisticated" investors, who would then market the deal to individuals with a high net worth, classified as accredited investors, who could afford to take the risk in such investments and who sought diversification in their portfolios. Such individuals would be required to have a net worth of at least $1 million or an annual income of at least $200,000.

But with the Internet, barriers that once existed have fallen. Speedy communications and the ease with which information is electronically distributed have made it possible not only for promoters of DPOs to reach a larger audience, but also for investors to create a quasi-trading market for these shares. The latter issue is perhaps most critical for the proliferation of DPOs, since, in many cases, these shares do not trade on any established equity market and are extremely illiquid. Thus, the shares someone buys at $5 each from an underwriter may often have only a single bidder, if any at all, willing to pay $4 per share. Although some regional exchanges, such as the Boston Stock Exchange and the Pacific Stock Exchange, and, to a greater extent, the over-the-counter bulletin board, have a handful of DPOs trading on their respective bourses, for the most part, these offerings often leave investors frustrated both with respect to attempting to trade them and with respect to determining the actual price at which the shares are valued.

Among those companies which actively promote DPOs, as listed in Table 8-1, are the Direct Stock Market (www.dsm.com), whose principals also created SCORnet, INVBank, and Virtual Wall Street. Also, investors may consider IPOnet, which is operated by the brokerage firm of W. J. Gallagher, as a source of DPOs, as well as Virtual Wall Street, which completed a Regulation A public offering, raising nearly $3.5 million in 1998. Among the many locations on the Internet that promote such offerings are www.beststock.com, www.ipo.net, and www.fairshare.com.

Another company offering DPOs combined with the Dutch auction concept is MainStreetIPO.com. For a $100,000 fee, this firm offers access to its Web site so that one can launch an IPO. What's unusual about this effort to disseminate IPOs to the public is that the company is not a broker–dealer and offers neither equity research nor aftermarket support of the IPO. Rather, it simply acts as a platform on which firms can promote their own deals and seeks to determine the minimum amount an issuer is seeking to raise. At this time, MainStreetIPO.com claims to have several companies interested in selling their IPOs on its site. Whether this venture will be a boom or a bust is still to be determined.

While the attraction of having ready access to an IPO through such offerings is appealing to many, there still exist numerous pitfalls. Uppermost is the quality of the companies offering such deals. At a time when investment banks are raising capital in the IPO markets at record levels, it

Table 8-1 Direct Public Offerings Information

Firm	Web site	Phone
Direct Stock Market	www.dsm.com	310–395–5213
Elysian Group	www.elysiangroup.com	800–994–6588
Equity Analytics	www.equityanalytics.com	516–696–9784
PrestigeIPO	www.prestigeipo.com	800–223–9861
Rule 506	www.rule506.com	213–614–1990
Virtual Wall Street	www.virtualwallstreet.com	888–344–9377

would seem that a wide net has been cast in seeking candidates for IPOs. Yet companies issuing DPOs are, in some eyes, viewed as orphans of Wall Street that cannot find a home with any bank and must fend for themselves. While that quality may be admirable, from an investment perspective the truth is that most of these issues fail to find sponsorship in the financial community and are often ignored by major institutional and professional investors. In an article published in the *National Law Journal*, Constance Bagley,[76] senior lecturer in law and management at the Stanford Graduate School of Business, and Robert J. Tomkinson argue that, while in theory on-line offerings should boost the supply of capital to developing companies, they are likely to face the difficulty of overcoming regulatory hurdles and investor concerns regarding liquidity. With respect to their legality, the key issues concern the distribution of information in the offering documents and what may or not be addressed at pre-IPO road shows. Furthermore, as mentioned earlier, as companies opt for interactive or electronic presentations, they must figure out to what standard the presentation should be held. As regards liquidity, if investors are left holding the bag when it comes time to sell their holdings should they be unable to find a ready buyer for their shares, then it would seem likely that the supply of such offerings would dry up in light of dwindling demand.

PRIVATE EQUITY OWNERSHIP

It seems as if anyone can be a venture capitalist. From Fortune 500 companies to large accounting firms to graduate school students, all are armed with the desire and intent to secure financing for the next hot concept and jettison it onto the public market.

On the other side of the coin, there is an almost insatiable demand for IPOs such that individual investors more than ever are clamoring for ways to enter into the new-issue playing field. In doing so, they often toss out the door a fundamental financial analysis of cash flow, debt load, and earnings, as the prospect for a ticket to the latest IPO festival far outstrips other concerns. Correspondingly, there has emerged a variety of so-called private equity firms in all shapes and sizes only too willing to take one's capital for the opportunity to invest in the "next big pre-IPO" company. For those with the means, the choices are abundant. Yet, there are pitfalls, especially when the opportunity presented is too good to be true. In fact, while some choices are attractive, many others are outright dangerous.

Generally, investors thinking about private equity funds as a possible backdoor into IPOs should, at the very least, subscribe to some basic tenets. First, they should know with whom they are dealing. All too often, the appearance of a slick Web page or a lengthy research report seduces investors into a false sense of security. The investor should also use the tools supplied by the Internet to his or her advantage. Finally, one should research the background of the principals associated with an investment to determine whether any penalties have been imposed by such trade organizations as the National Association of Security Dealers, state regulators, or even the SEC. Various Web sites allow individuals to access background checks on stockbrokers to determine whether any sanctions have been imposed on them. Likewise, *The Wall Street Journal* publishes a weekly list of individuals in the securities industry who have incurred penalties, along with a description of the conduct that triggered the action.

Among some prudent steps are the following: Never volunteer information to a telemarketer or cold caller, especially credit card information or your Social Security number. Investigate any past deals with which the individual has been associated to determine whether the person's track record lives up to his or her claims. Never invest more than you can lose. Once you are satisfied with the integrity of the principals, it's then worthwhile to consider the potential risks and returns of the deal. In light of the lofty promises, investors should consider some benchmark returns. For example, the Vanguard Group's S&P 500 Index fund has generated average annual returns of 27.5 percent for the past three years for the period ending December 31, 1999, and nearly 29 percent for the five-year period ending on the same date. Claims offering a "100 percent guaranteed return on your investment" should always prompt individuals to counter by asking how much capital the individual on the other end of the phone or writing the letter has invested in the supposedly "guaranteed" investment. Obviously, if the answer is "Nothing," then the investor should walk away. And even if the soliciting party volunteers a figure, don't accept it as gospel truth. Ask for records, recommendations, and endorsements from unbiased and impartial third parties. Remember, it's your money.

While the price of admission is not rock bottom to many investors (most minimum investments are $25,000), that price nonetheless represents a crack in the door for those who need the qualifications to invest in such opportunities. For example, investors at Charles Schwab with a minimum of $1 million in assets, a number that will be greatly increased, given Schwab's pending $2.6 billion acquisition of the "old-money" bank holding company U.S. Trust Company, will be given access to private equity opportunities from San Francisco–based OffRoad Capital (www.offroadcapital.com), a firm that arranges and markets private equity financings and "angel investing" to developing companies. Typically, "angel investors" are business owners with net worth in excess of $1 million who make early-stage private equity investments in emerging or developing companies or technologies. One of that firm's notable achievements was the successful placing, and subsequent active trading on a private electronic network, of Patchlink.com., an Arizona-based software services company. OffRoad arranged for a $5.6 million convertible preferred-stock offering for the company. Previously, the company had orchestrated $5.9 million in financing for Quantum3D. The objective of OffRoad is to arrange the placement of capital and then "cash out" in perhaps five years, either through an IPO offering by its client or with the sale of the company to a third party.

Another pair of firms in the process of creating a venture-capital fund open to a broader range of individuals is the combination of Draper Fisher Jurvetson and www.mevc.com. The partnership is seeking regulatory approval to permit individuals whose net worth is between $50,000 and $150,000 to invest in amounts as low as $5000. Interested investors may also investigate California-based Charter Ventures (www.charterventures.com), which claims that since 1982 more than two dozen of its financially backed companies have gone public. And one more source of potential IPOs for investors is New York–based Angeltips.com (www.angeltips.com), a firm that seeks to connect entrepreneurs with early-stage financing from well-heeled individuals. Investors pay $1000 annually for access to company business plans and the ability to participate in private-placement offerings. Qualified individuals must meet the standards of Rule 501 of Regulation D, which calls for investors to have a net worth of at least $1 million and an individual income of $200,000 in each of the two most recent years or $300,000 of joint income with a spouse. Businesses pay $250 to list their plans on the site. Among the companies with which Angeltips.com has developed a strategic alliance are Exodus Communications, a provider of Internet solutions, and Rising Tiger Fund, L.P., a limited partnership established to invest in Korean technology companies.

From the perspective of the company, this way of raising funds has merit because it permits access to low-cost capital without the risk of giving up control of the company. In the case of Patchlink, it was reported that the company was approached by a venture-capital firm that offered a $4 million investment in return for a controlling interest in the firm. By contrast, the OffRoad deal allowed the company to raise funds without loss of control. On the other hand, some critics of the approach claim that companies would prefer to receive venture funding in a single chunk, rather than having to solicit it piecemeal in $10,000 to $25,000 to $50,000 amounts. Nonetheless, for both the entrepreneur and the investor, such operations present a varied approach to both raising capital and building portfolios. Parties interested in private equity firms either as a means of gaining access to future IPOs or simply to understand the financing process may resort to various Web sites for additional information. Recommended are the Global Entrepreneurial Institute (www.gcase.org), privateequity.com, a clearinghouse for on-line information located at www.privateequity.com, and the home page of Massachusetts Institute of Technology's Sloan School of Management, www.mitsloan.mit.edu.

MUTUAL CONVERSIONS AND COMMUNITY BANK OFFERINGS

According to SNL Securites, tens of thousands of individuals across the nation have deposited perhaps as little as $1 in scores of small banks or savings and loan associations. These individuals were not motivated by fear of any Y2K meltdown, nor were they simply mimicking comedian W. C. Field's approach of having multiple accounts nationwide so as to have cash available for him if he were ever in some far-off town. Rather, these depositors were simply placing a bet that one day those privately held businesses will announce plans to launch an IPO whereby deposit holders are given a priority over individuals without funds on deposit.

Such are the steps that have been taken to participate in what some investment pros consider to be one the surest ways for capital to appreciate in the IPO market. As an advocate of investing in things you know, famed money manager Peter Lynch, past manager of Fidelity's Magellan Fund, has been a strong proponent of purchasing shares of savings and loan associations or community banks that are converting from so-called mutually owned status (i.e., ownership rests in the deposit holders of the institution, rather than in public shareholders who own common stock). The reason for these conversions are many, although, in general, one of the primary purposes is to let the financial institution have access to publicly traded, and thus easily valued, shares in order to transact mergers of its own. Over the past decade, SNL Securities, a Charlottesville, Virginia–based firm that tracks mutual conversions and the commercial banking and thrift industries in general, has received no fewer than 700 such offerings. Among the company's past conversions is a 1995 offering by Springfield (Massachusetts) Institute for Savings (subsequently transformed into SSI Savings). In the time following the offering, the price of a share of SSI stock rose from $8 to the mid-$20s, until, in July 1998, SNL accepted a merger offer of $25.44 per share from People's Heritage Financial of Portland, Maine. Some other of the firm's notable conversions are two Brooklyn, New York–based thrifts: GreenPoint Financial Corp., which conducted an $804.7 million plan in 1994, and Independence

Community Bank, which raised $704 million from its March 1998 conversion.

Yet, the main attraction that many S&L and community bank conversions possess is not the fact that individual investors may have a better opportunity in actually seeing their order filled, nor is it that such deals are generally done without commissions being foisted on purchasers. Rather, the key advantage in such offerings is that they are nearly universally sold at a "discount" to their underlying assets, so that once trading commences, these shares enjoy a significant jump to the upside. Indeed, SNL Securities claims that, on average, a mutual conversion is offered at a significant discount to the pro forma book value of the company. For example, the GreenPoint Financial offering was priced at less than 60 percent of the thrift's book value. Similarly, Staten Island (New York) Bancorp, a December 1997 conversion that raised over $515 million, was priced at less than 85 percent of book value.

In a published study by James Wilcox and Zane Williams[77] of the Haas School of Business at the University of California at Berkeley, the thesis was presented that returns on thrift conversions can be predictable, based upon such factors as the preconversion assets of the thrift, the quality of the loan, and insider ownership, among other things. The authors put forth the proposition that the magnitude of the so-called first-day pop is correlated with the level of nonperforming assets: Those firms with fewer nonperforming assets perform better in the aftermarket than those with greater numbers of such assets. However, it was determined that loan growth was not a factor in deciding whether to embark upon a conversion plan. Hence, it was not how fast the thrift was growing that affected its performance with regard to IPO prices, but rather, as long as the firm refrained from lending to poor-quality borrowers, its price performance would be good.

Should bank and thrift IPO investing be up your alley, it is advisable to follow the recommendations of Douglas Hughes, publisher of *The Small Bank Newsletter*,[78] and the Web site www.banknewsletter.com. According to Hughes, there are five guidelines for investing in small-bank stocks. First, one should inspect the quality of the assets of the institution. Second, one should ask, Does the thrift or bank possess any special franchise value? That is, does it cater to a special clientele or offer any specialized service? Third, if the institution has been actively acquiring banks or thrifts, one should determine whether any mergers were overpaid. Fourth, one should investigate any hidden assets not reflected in the firm's books or any assets that are undervalued relative to their book value. These assets may be real property or even the firm's on-line banking operations. Finally, one should look for banks and thrifts that are growing their earnings by a minimum of 15 percent per annum. Investors interested in seeking out those institutions which are candidates for mutual conversion are urged to view www.bankinvestor.com.

Besides seeking out mutual conversions of thrifts and community banks, investors should be aware that several large insurance companies also have gone public by converting from mutual ownership to publicly traded common stock. Recently, John Hancock Financial Services, Sun Life Assurance, and Metropolitan Life Insurance, among other insurance firms, filed plans to go public in 2000. In these cases, it is the policyholder and not the depositor who has the inside track in purchasing shares at the initial offer price. Although insurance stocks as a group suffered a double-digit loss in 1999 compared with the S&P 500's gain of 19 percent, these stocks may have an added benefit, given the fact that congressional approval for insurance companies, banks, and brokerages to cross-merge may result in historic unions in the financial services sector.

SPIN-OFFS

In the 1960s and 1970s, forming a conglomerate was a popular business strategy. The belief was that if a corporation had a variety of diverse businesses under its wing, it could withstand any cyclical downtrend in one sector while, theoretically, enjoying a boom in another. Such companies as Gulf & Western and Textron were perhaps the poster children for conglomerates as they took under their wing a number of disparate businesses, including book publishing, real estate, oil services and a host of others, in the belief that more was better. However by the early 1980s, a different business philosophy took hold, arguing that, for companies to be efficient and profitable, much had to be streamlined and focused. Furthermore, as businesses grew increasingly competitive, it made less and less strategic sense for them to operate in such a diverse fashion. Thus was set off a flurry of moves by companies to cast their unwanted or unneeded divisions or subsidiaries over to management or shareholders. The result was a showering of spin-offs to shareholders as companies went about what has been described by some as an "antimerger" wave in which corporate America's unwanted or unpopular businesses were cast out to fend for themselves. As indicated in Figure 8-1, the pace has remained strong, with a record $13 billion in IPO spin-offs completed by U.S. companies in 1999.[79]

The list of companies issuing spin-offs reads like a Who's Who of American capitalism. From General Motors' recent spin-off of its Delphi Automotive Parts section, beverage company Pepsi, Inc.'s issuance of shares in its restaurant operations to shareholders, and AT&T's 1996 decision to spin off its Bell Laboratories group, renamed Lucent Technologies, and its NCR Corp. unit, which AT&T had recently acquired in 1991, each provided shareholders, employees, and managers with distinct opportunities.

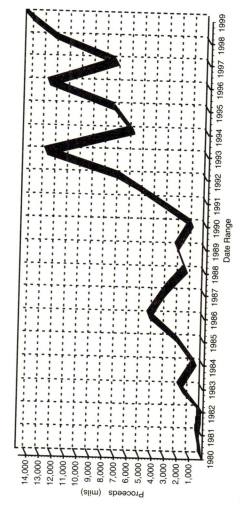

Figure 8-1 IPO Spinoff Volume

Indeed, the range of companies and industries participating in spin-off activity is extensive. For Wall Street, such offerings represent a windfall: Not only do some of the largest spin-offs completed place among the top IPO offerings of all time, but they also account for some of the most profitable deals for investment banks, based upon underwriting fees. Of the top 20 IPOs of all time, 9 were spin-offs. Moreover, the top 10 largest spin-offs accounted for more than $887 million in gross spreads, or underwriting fees, with Morgan Stanley acting as book manager on 4 of those deals. And the charges rarely end there. Once the spin-off is completed, it's not uncommon for the newly public company to use its equity as consideration in mergers and acquisitions. For example, in the case of Lucent Technologies, in the short time it has been freed from the control of AT&T, it has announced no fewer than 35 individual M&A transactions, exceeding $33 billion in value, in which it was the acquiring firm.

For those hoping to garner shares in such companies, the process often is straightforward. Firms often announce ahead of time that they are planning to spin off a particular unit whereby shareholders may opt to purchase shares in the parent company so as to participate in the spin-off. Alternatively, firms may decide to offer shares in the unit directly to the public and forgo any distribution to their shareholders. The decision is left entirely up to the parent's board of directors. For example, when Sears, Roebuck spun off its Dean Witter Reynolds brokerage division in July 1993 and its Allstate Insurance division in July 1995, shareholders respectively received a 0.39031 share of Dean Witter for each share of Sears held and a 0.91 common share of Allstate Insurance for each share of Sears held.

Still, the track record for spin-offs is split. An analysis published in *Forbes*[80] which relied upon information provided by Thomson Financial Securities Data indicated that investors would be better off with a mutual fund that tracks the S&P

500 index than holding a position in both the parent and the spin-off company. In that article, various spin-off companies and their parents were examined for performance; the analysis revealed that, while the stock prices of a handful of companies soared, most deteriorated. This result conflicts with a 1997 study conducted by the *Spinoff Report*,[81] a newsletter that focuses on spin-off activity, which argued that the gains realized by spin-offs outpaced that of the S&P 500. In an analysis by the investment bank JP Morgan of the performance of spin-offs and a related technique called "carve-out" (wherein the parent company distributes a portion of a subsidiary to investors through a public offering while still keeping a portion for itself), the results showed that those spin-offs which were directly issued to shareholders outpaced the S&P 500 in the first year and a half of trading by just over 1 percent. On the other hand, a report conducted by the consulting firm of McKinsey & Co. studying various spin-offs showed that those issues which were directly distributed to shareholders gained about 27 percent in their first 24 months of trading.

The key for investors is not simply to jump into any company announcing or rumored to be conducting a spin-off distribution. Rather, as is the case with any investment decision, it is important to investigate whether the industry the spin-off is in is one that is experiencing strong earnings growth or contraction and fierce competition. Consider, for example, railroad owner Santa Fe Pacific's move to shed its oil and gas operations to shareholders. In December 1990, shareholders of the company received one share in Santa Fe Resources for every 3.3 shares of Santa Fe Pacific they owned. By the following year, Santa Fe Resources could not even provide its shareholders with a modest return, as its stock price had declined by 14 percent from its offer price of $17. In the year after that, following acquisitions of its own, Santa Fe Resources merged with Snyder

Oil in May 1999 in a transaction valued at $637 million. The bottom line was that the newly formed company, Santa Fe Snyder, was trading at less than $9, or nearly 50 percent off its initial price, by early 2000. Likewise, The Sports Authority, which formerly was wholly owned by discount retailer Kmart Corp., was spun off in November 1994. Since then, it dropped some 80 percent in value. In contrast, spin-offs with ties to the telecommunications, electronics, or other technology-related sectors appear to offer greater potential to shareholders. For instance, it has been well documented that Lucent Technologies, spun off from AT&T in 1996, ranks among the best performing spin-offs of all time. And there are other technology stock transfers that have enriched shareholders. For example, semiconductor maker TIBCO Software was spun off from its parent Reuters in July 1999 and since then has gained over 1000 percent, placing it as one of the top 10 spin-off performers of the 1990s. Of note also is the fact that, of the more than 540 spin-offs completed in the 1990s, no fewer than 120, or about 22 percent, were technology related. Furthermore, of the 20 top-performing spin-off IPOs throughout the 1990s, more than half were from a technology-related sector. Among these firms were Lycos, Inc., which was spun off from CMGI in April 1996, Cognizant Technology Solutions, which debuted in June 1998 after being an unit of Dun & Bradstreet, and Internet service provider Satyam Infoway, which started trading as a freestanding public stock in October 1999 after being a division of Satyam Computer Systems.

On the other side of the coin, of the 20 worst performing spin-offs in the past decade, not a single one can be classified as belonging to the information technology sector, although several are from medical equipment or technology parents. Among the worst performing spin-offs that came forth in the 1990s were airline operator Tower Air, home builder Diamond Home Services, sewing machine manufacturer Singer, finance company ContiFinancial, and medical equipment wholesaler Phoenix Shannon, PLC. Each of these issues has dropped over 90 percent in value from its offer date. In total, about one-quarter of the spin-offs finalized in the 1990s ended the decade trading under their offer price. Many of these issues were from cyclical industries, such as metals, from commodity-based sectors, such as oil and gas, or from a competitive retailing and brand-sensitive segment, such as sporting goods and footwear.

In this regard, it is important for investors to keep a focus on the parent company. If the parent has not generated substantial returns for its shareholders, there is a strong probability that any corporate offspring may flounder. Furthermore, if a particular industry sector is not appropriate for your investment objective, then it would be advisable to steer clear of such companies in selecting issues for your portfolio. Thus, if your objective is growth and income, it may be unwise to burden yourself with non-dividend-paying issues in the expectation that one may spring a spin-off in the immediate future. Likewise, an investor interested in aggressive growth would not be advised to purchase shares in an electric utility that has declared a spin-off of a particular division. As in any financial decision, the choice should be tailored to the investor's immediate and long-term goals.

Finally, with respect to spin-offs, no discussion would be complete without mentioning "business incubators," firms that nurture and develop start-up companies. For investors, the most interesting companies are those publicly traded investment firms which regularly distribute shares in the companies they finance to their shareholders, either directly or through rights programs whereby those shareholders are given preference over outsiders. Perhaps the most popular of these firms are Safeguard Scientific and CMGI, Inc., which finance and own stakes in developing companies. Based in

Wayne, Pennsylvania, Safeguard[82] was formed in the early 1950s by Pete Musser and has a long history of financially backing tech-related companies, including such firms as Novell, Inc. According to published reports, a $10,000 investment in the rights offerings and IPOs that Safeguard orchestrated in 1992 was worth over $200,000 by the end of 1999. In that year, the company completed three IPOs that raised about $327 million. Among those offerings were a $23 million deal by US Interactive and a $126 million IPO by PacWest Telecom. However, what put the company on the map recently was its investment in another so-called incubator, Internet Capital Group. Safeguard had acquired a 14 percent interest in Internet Capital for less than $30 million. For Safeguard shareholders, the terms of the ICG transaction went as follows: Holders of 100 shares or more of Safeguard stock were offered shares in Internet Capital Group at a price of $12 each on a 1-to-10 basis. Thus, a Safeguard stockholder of 130 shares would have been able to purchase 13 shares of Internet Capital Group at $12 each. Within several months of the deal's completion, an individual who participated in the rights offering on such terms would have seen a $156 investment grow to over $4000 as the Internet Capital Group's equity ended the year at $170 after a December 1999 two-for-one stock split. Such so-called directed share participation programs are a part of Safeguard's stated policy of increasing shareholder value by both strengthening Safeguard's value and affording Safeguard shareholders the opportunity to participate in the company's IPOs.

By the end of 1999, Safeguard's stake in Internet Capital Group was being valued by the public at over $2 billion. In essence, Safeguard placed itself in the unique position of being an incubator to an incubator. Among the firms Internet Capital Group's investment supported were VerticalNet and Breakaway Solutions. Also, the company has backed Universal Access, Inc., which is planning a February 2000 IPO, and Emerge Interactive, an on-line auction firm that serves the cattle industry. Other past financings by Safeguard include a $6 million investment in on-line wine retailer WineAccess, a $15.7 million investment in communications service provider AirNet Communications, and nearly $35 million in wireless communications company Whisper Communications. Furthermore, in the space of about three months, the company completed two separate $1 billion fundings for its @Venture Technology Fund. A November 1999 funding was designed to finance and support business-to-business Internet companies, while a January 2000 $1 billion fund was designed to finance Web infrastructure companies.

For CMGI,[83] 1999 was an exceptional year. Not only did the company's stock soar over 130 percent, but its number of acquisitions nearly doubled from 1998's level. Among the firm's notable transactions were its $490 million bid for E-mail advertiser Yesmail.com and a $649 million purchase of Web advertising manager FlyCast Communications. But its landmark deal was a $2.3 billion acquisition of Internet search engine AltaVista from Compaq Computer. Besides ranking as one of the firm's showcase acquisitions, the deal provided CMGI with another hidden benefit. Under the Investment Act of 1940, a company that holds in excess of 40 percent of its assets in "nonownership" (i.e., investments) must be declared a mutual fund and thus operate under a more rigorous set of guidelines. The AltaVista deal effectively permitted CMGI to circumvent that legislation. In addition, the firm can boast of several holdings that it subsequently spun off and that now individually have market capitalizations in excess of $1 billion. Among these companies are Critical Path and Engage Technologies.

According to such respected analysts as Merrill Lynch's Henry Blodget, CMGI acts as a proxy for the performance of

Internet IPOs in particular and the Internet sector in general. Furthermore, while the company's public holdings are in the business-to-consumer sector of the Internet, most of its recent investments have been in the business-to-business field. Among the firms it has backed and that subsequently went public are Lycos (NASDAQ-LCOS), GeoCities, Silknet (NASDAQ-SILK), and Mothernature.com (NASDAQ-MTHR).

Other publicly traded incubators are multibillion-dollar investment firm Softbank, which trades in Japan, (OTC-SFBTF) and has financed such firms as TheStreet.com and Launch Media, and had announced plans to spend up to $100 million in South Korean technology companies. Softbank also owns shares in numerous American companies, such as a 69 percent stake in technology media company Ziff-Davis, Inc. (NYSE-ZD), and recently opened a Boston-based "netbatsu," or growing spot for early-stage companies. Of note as well are Pasadena, California–based Acacia Research (NASDAQ-ACRI; www.acaciaresearch.com), whose portfolio companies include Soundview Technologies, Greenwich Information Technologies,LLC, and Soundbreak.com, White Plains; New York–based Winfield Capital (OTC-WCAP), which has backed PNVNet, Inc., a communications company serving the trucking industry; and Net Value Holdings, a firm that has funded companies such as Asia CD and AssetExchange.com.

In addition, investors seeking a backdoor entrance into the IPO market may consider several other publicly traded venture companies. For example, New York–based THCG, Inc. (NASDAQ-THCG; www.thcg.com) calls itself an "Internet business creation firm" and holds positions in numerous private placements, as well as stakes in such public issues as Interleaf (NASDAQ-LEAF) and Etravnet.com (OTC-ETVT). Also based in New York City is Harris & Harris Group (NASDAQ-HHGP; www.hhgp.com), which operates as a publicly traded venture fund under the Investment Company Act of 1940. Another New York–based company, headquartered in what is oft referred to as Silicon Alley, the East Coast counterpart to California's Silicon Valley, is Rare Medium (NASDAQ-RRRR; www.raremedium.com),which holds positions in nearly two dozen private technology companies. The company, whose primary business is as an interactive agency and design firm, took the unconventional route of going public in 1998 by way of a "reverse merger" when it took over an air-conditioning firm called ICC Technologies and then spun off that company to management. Rare Medium provides cash, advice, and services to developing companies, including iFace.com and LifeUniverse.com, for an equity stake in their business. The company also raised more than $80 million to fund its venture-capital activities.

Investors looking for opportunities elsewhere may consider Minnesota-based Virtual Fund (NASDAQ-VFND; www.virtualfund.com), which classifies itself as an "Internet venture resources and investment company" that backs development-stage businesses. Also, San Francisco's Point West Capital (NASDAQ-PWCC) has financially backed companies that subsequently went public through its Frontier Hill Management subsidiary, while Anglo-American investment company London Pacific (NYSE-LDP) has backed and holds positions in such companies as Continuous Software (NASDAQ-CNSW) and Packeteer (NASDAQ-PKTR).

Another, perhaps less conventional and more indirect, approach to investing in IPOs, at least in a small degree, is through publicly traded commercial banks such as Chase Manhattan (NYSE-CMB) or FleetBoston (NYSE-FBF). The latter is the by-product of the 1999 merger between Bank of Boston and Fleet Financial. According to the National Venture Capital Association, the amount commercial banks have invested in venture-capital activities has increased from about $1.5 billion in 1996 to more than $4 billion in 1999, with Chase Manhattan, through its venture-capital unit Chase Capital Partners, accounting for a large share. Moreover, whereas profits from venture-capital activity were about 6 percent of operating income in 1994, by 1998 the figure reached 12 percent. Gains associated with Chase's venture-capital activities during 1999 totaled over $2.5 billion, up from less than $1 billion in 1998. In addition, the private equity division of FleetBoston reportedly has a $2.5 billion portfolio that helped it bankroll Silknet Software, Allaire, and Internet Capital Group, among other companies. FleetBoston has more than $1 billion in unrealized capital gains and reported $494 million in realized gains in 1999 from its venture-capital activities, up nearly 30 percent from the previous year's figure.

Besides such publicly traded companies, many private, university, and government-funded entities fund new businesses before they go the IPO route. A case in point is the Evanston, Illinois–based Technology Incubation Center's early backing of on-line grocery store Peapod, which went public in July 1997 at $16 in a $64 million deal. Perhaps as an example of how things can go wrong in the IPO world, Peapod's chairman resigned in March 2000, whereupon the stock tumbled to under $3, over 80 percent less than its offer price. Similarly, government entities such as the New Jersey Commission on Science and Technology have awarded grants to past IPOs. An awardee was Mikron Instrument Co. (NASDAQ-MIKR), which received assistance in the development of new technologies. Another notable Internet incubator is privately held (though planning a public offering) Sunnyvale, California–based idealab! (www.idealab.com). Founded in 1996 by William Gross, labeled by some as the most successful and influential Internet executive in Southern California, the company has been the driving force in financing such firms as jobs.com, eve.com, PetSmart.com, and weddingchannel.com, among others. Several of its funded companies have gone public, including on-line retailer eToys

(NASDAQ-ETYS), ticket merchant Tickets.com, NetZero (NADSAQ-NZRO), and GoTo.com (NASDAQ-GOTO), each having a market value greater than $1 billion. Recently, the company opened offices in New York City and Boston to advance its efforts on the East Coast.

CONVERTIBLE BONDS

Buy a bond and get an IPO? Buy a tech company security, and receive a dividend check? In the case of convertible bonds both of these statements are true! Although such offerings are primarily for institutional investors, the concept has merit for retail investors, considering that several technology companies which have issued IPOs in the past few years have reentered the capital markets by means of convertible bonds. According to reports published by Merrill Lynch, convertible bonds issued by technology companies returned more than two-thirds of the overall gain of tech issues in the five-year period from 1995 to 1999. Yet, while investors may give up some growth on the upside, they often receive a modest interest payment—on average, about 5 percent—as well as not having to experience sharp price declines. Thus, investors may be able to participate for part of the ride up, and should things head south, the descent is not likely to be as steep.

First, here is a quick primer on investing in convertibles: Simply stated, convertibles are bonds that "convert," or are exchangeable or transferable, into the common stock of the issuing company. When analyzing convertibles, investors must examine the bond's coupon as well as its "conversion ratio." The coupon relates to how much income the bond will generate, such that, in the case of a hypothetical company called E-widget Corp. issuing a convertible bond with a 5 percent coupon, bondholders will receive biannual payments of $250. (Note that bonds are typically denominated in face values of $1000 increments.) The conversion ratio tells investors how many shares of stock they will receive. In the example of E-widget, some arithmetic is necessary. If the hypothetical stock were trading at $50 per share at the time the convertible was being priced, and if the stock were offering a 20 percent premium (referred to as the conversion premium), then when the bond matured, investors could transfer their bonds into shares valued at $60 ($50 × 1.20). Upon the bond's maturity, the investors would receive 16.7 shares.

Of the more than 4200 nonfinancial companies based in the United States that completed IPOs in the 1990s, no fewer than 260 issued convertible debt securities. Nearly half of the issuing companies, including America Online (AOL), Amazon.com, and Internet Capital Group, were tech related. For investors, several issues may be of interest. Two that readily come to mind are AOL's $2.3 billion zero-coupon debenture, initially priced at $1.25 billion and maturing in December 2019, which was sold at a deep discount at about $551 for each $1000 in face value, and DoubleClick's 4.75 percent convertible subordinated notes due in 2006. The latter is viewed by some analysts as an equity surrogate. In the case of the AOL bond, the issue is convertible into 5.83 shares of AOL common with a conversion price pegged at $94.49. Also of note is CNET Corp.'s $101.7 million convertible preferred issues, which cannot be called until February 2004 and which is exchangeable into shares on NBCi, the vehicle for the National Broadcasting Company's Internet properties. Of interest, too, is Excite @Home's $500 million deal scheduled to mature in December 2006 and Exodus Communications' $400 million issuance of convertible notes that mature in July 2008. And on-line broker E*TRADE raised $500 million from a convertible in a deal that was priced in early 2000. In determining the value of such bonds, investors need to look at the so-called conversion premium. In the case of the AOL bond, the issue is convertible into 5.83 shares of AOL common, since the bond's conversion price is pegged at $94.49.

DIRECT STOCK PURCHASE PLANS: DRIPs

Many companies permit individuals to purchase shares in the firm's common stock directly. For as little as $25 or $50 per transaction, investors may be able to buy stock without a broker and thus be able to accumulate shares, over time, that otherwise they would not be able to afford with a single purchase. Such programs, commonly called direct stock purchase plans or dividend reinvestment plans (DRIPs), are a source of both company goodwill and easy access to equities for small investors. With respect to IPOs, while it is uncommon to find a brand-new issue commencing a DRIP, nonetheless several issues that have started such plans have gone public in the past few years, giving investors an opportunity to participate in a new issue.

Among recent IPOs that have launched a DRIP are Lucent Technologies, which was a 1996 spin-off from AT&T, Conoco, a 1998 IPO spun off from DuPont, and retail drugstore chain CVS, a 1996 spin-off from Rhode Island–based Melville Corp. Note that such programs do not let investors "name their own price"; rather, purchases are typically handled one a month at a set price by the company. Investors looking for additional information on direct stock purchase plans should consult the Web site www.netstockdirect.com.

IPO OWNERSHIP...WHO OWNS WHAT

Call it spreading the wealth. A recent examination of institutional owners of relatively new high-flying IPOs reveals that, for the most part, no single firm can lay claim to having a lock on top deals. According to data mined by Thomson Financial Securities Data's ShareWorld, owners of such top-performing issues as Internet Capital Group (NASDAQ-ICGE), Commerce One (NASD CMRC), and PurchasePro.com (NASDAQ-PPRO) are a diverse lot ranging from business incubator Safeguard Scientific, to office supply retailer Office Depot, to an investment arm of the Rockefeller family. Moreover, aside from the vast range of owners of these offerings, their overall number is impressive. On the other hand, perhaps proving that fortune has many friends while failure is an orphan, those IPOs which have notoriously underperformed since their debut have had little in the way of brand-name owners.

Consider, for example, the following situation: B2B holding company Internet Capital Group ended 1999 up more than 2000 percent from its debut in August of that year. The company includes among its shareholders Pennsylvania-based venture-capital firm Safeguard Scientific, which owns almost a 13 percent stake, Comcast Corp., owner of 9.8 percent, and FleetBankBoston, which controls some 2.7 percent of the firm's outstanding shares. In addition, company CEO Walter W. Buckley III owns about 4.8 percent of the firm's shares, while ICG officials Kenneth Fox and Douglas Alexander, respectively, own 4.5 percent and 2.5 percent. Overall, insiders control about 92 percent of the shares, while 8 percent is owned by institutions.

The bottom line is that, whereas individual investors may have trouble getting into the hottest IPO, plenty of institutions find easy entrance. In that regard, the opportunity for those seeking a piece of the IPO pie is perhaps to latch onto those who already have taken stakes in such deals, be it through companies owning other companies or simply by allocating funds to those managers who have a track record of ownership in those kinds of deals.

Closing Comments: Investors should realize that just because they are closed out on a specific IPO does not mean that they cannot participate in the sector through a variety of means, from bank and thrift conversion plans to direct stock offerings or indirect ownership, either through individual stocks that have stakes in IPOs or, as will be discussed in the next chapter, mutual funds.

9

THE MUTUAL FUND ALTERNATIVE... AND A FEW GOOD STOCKS

As the IPO market has exploded in the 1990s, so, too, has the mutual fund industry taken significant leaps in both size and scope. According to the Investment Company Institute, a Washington, D.C.–based trade group for the industry, assets controlled by mutual funds have risen from less than $1 billion in 1990 to more than $6.5 trillion at the close of the decade. Thus, for some investors, rather than performing the research, exploration, and, finally, selection of an individual IPO, an optimal alternative is to let someone else perform those tasks in the form of a mutual fund

MANAGER. ON THE DOWNSIDE, INVESTORS SHOULD NOT THINK THAT ALL FUND MANAGERS ACT ALIKE. FOR WHILE ONE MAY BE IN LOVE WITH TECH STOCKS, ANOTHER MAY FEEL THAT THEY ARE OVERVALUED. HENCE, RESULTS MAY VARY WIDELY. FURTHERMORE, OF LATE MUTUAL FUND EXPENSES HAVE BEEN ON THE RISE, WITH THE AVERAGE EXPENSE RATIO FOR AN EQUITY FUND INCREASING FROM 1.45 PERCENT A DECADE AGO TO 1.55 PERCENT TODAY, DUE IN PART TO HIGHER PORTFOLIO TURNOVER BY SOME FUNDS AND IN PART TO GREATER MARKETING EXPENSES TO ATTRACT INVESTORS' DOLLARS. WHILE THE INCREASE MAY APPEAR MODEST, IT NONETHELESS PLAYS AN IMPORTANT ROLE IN DETERMINING THE INTERMEDIATE TO LONG-TERM PERFORMANCE OF A MUTUAL FUND AND THUS THE ABILITY OF SOME FUNDS TO MARKET THEM-SELVES AS BETTER PERFORMERS THAN OTHERS. ASIDE FROM MARKETING EXPENSES, TRADING COSTS MAY AFFECT THE PERFORMANCE OF A MUTUAL FUND, ESPECIALLY WHEN IT COMES TO IPOS. SINCE, IN MANY CASES, THERE ARE FEWER SHARES AVAILABLE TO BUY OR SELL, FUNDS THAT HAVE A LARGE NUMBER OF IPOS IN THEIR PORTFOLIO ARE LIKELY TO INCUR HIGHER TRAD-ING COSTS.

Still, given that many fast-growing IPOs now trade in excess of $100 per share, thereby requiring more than $10,000 on the part of individual investors to buy a 100-share lot, mutual funds provide a ready alternative not only for participation in the IPO market in particular, but also for easy stock diversification in general. In addition, mutual funds affiliated with a so-called fund family, as is the case with Fidelity, Vanguard, Janus, or MFS funds, allow investors the convenience of switching into other types of funds, as well as into money market accounts if market conditions change.

First, here is a quick overview of mutual funds:[84] Simply stated, a mutual fund is an assortment of securities purchased by a group of investors, but controlled by professional managers. A mutual fund may own stocks, bonds, cash, or some combination of all three. Mutual funds are designed for various investment objectives, from the preservation of capital, for which money market funds may be suitable, to growth, which may put index funds as the top choice, to aggressive growth, which may be composed of small-cap emerging-market companies. Some mutual funds (called load funds) carry sales charges, while others (labeled no-load funds) do not, and there are even funds that do not access a fee when one buys into them, but that do when one sells them. (These funds are termed back-load funds.)

MUTUAL FUNDS WITH A LARGE IPO EXPOSURE

Listed in this section are some notable mutual funds with above-average IPO holdings. Given that most IPOs of late have been in the technology and small-cap sectors, it is not surprising that many mutual funds in those sectors would have a high proportion of IPOs. Additionally, Table 9-1 lists some mutual funds with significant IPO holdings.

IPO Plus Aftermarket Fund (IPOSX)

If you're looking for a simple way to participate in the IPO market, perhaps there is no better one than investing in the IPO Plus Aftermarket Fund. This mutual fund was conceived by Renaissance Capital Growth, a Greenwich, Connecticut–based equity research and money management firm and was launched in December 1997, prior to the IPO frenzy that occurred in 1999. The fund's managers, including Kathleen Smith, employ a research-oriented approach to equity selection and portfolio management and place at least 65 percent of the fund's assets, about $58 million at the end of 1999, in IPOs. Among the factors considered in selecting

Table 9-1 Mutual Funds with Large IPO Holdings

Fund	Ticker	Minimum Investment Individual	Minimum Investment IRA	Assets ($mil)	Percentage of Assets in IPOs	Sales Charge	Phone Number	Largest Holding	Average Annual Performance 1 Year	3 Years	5 Years	Average Holding P/E	Price/Book	Morningstar Rating
Westcore Small Cap	WTSMX	$1,000	$250	23.8	48	0%	1-800-392-2673	Interwoven	211.6	83.3	n/a	43.2	16.9	not rated
Amerindo Technology	ATCHX	$2,500	$1,000	616.6	54	0%	1-888-832-4386	Ariba	78.2	n/a	n/a	60	22.5	*****
Atlas Emerging Growth	ATEAX	$2,500	$250	20.2	39	0%	1-800-433-2852	Bindview Development	208.6	54.3	n/a	39.5	13.6	not rated
Pilgrim 1 Smal Cap Opportunities	NSPAX	$2,500	$250	135.4	32	5.75%	1-800-334-3444	Triquint Semiconductor	151.6	73.6	n/a	52.7	16.9	*****
WWW Internet Fund	WWIFX	$2,000	$2,000	107.1	32	0%	1-888-263-2204	Security First	149.3	n/a	n/a	53.4	18.3	*****
Monument Telecommunications	MFTAX	$1,000	n/a	3.4	32	4.75%	1-888-520-8637	Net2Phone	307	n/a	n/a	60	19.5	not rated
Homestate Year 2000	HSYTX	$500	$500	18.6	31	2.90%	1-800-232-0224	Sterling Software	302.1	79.3	n/a	49.8	18.3	not rated
PBHG Technology & Telecommunications	PBTCX	$2,500	$2,000	2230	31	0%	1-800-433-0051	InfoSpace.com	249.1	71.7	54.4	57.4	24.1	*****
1st America Technology	FATAX	$1,000	$250	74.2	31	5.25%	1-800-637-2548	Nokia	178.2	n/a	54.4	57.6	20.3	*****
Berger Mid Cap Technology	BEMGX	$2,000	$2,000	95.1	31	0%	1-800-551-5849	Sapient	159.4	n/a	n/a	51.6	17.9	not rated
IPO Plus Fund	IPOSX	$2,500	$500	66.1	30	0%	1-888-476-3863	E*Trade	159.4	n/a	n/a	38.8	14	not rated

stocks is the degree of research coverage a particular company has within the investment community; the fund favors those issues with limited coverage. Also, the fund seeks out those IPOs with a limited float, limited public ownership, and limited operating history. Foreign issues that are not generally known in the United States are considered for selection. As regards what means the fund uses to wedge precious offerings from underwriters, according to fund manager Smith in a *Forbes* article,[85] the answer is to "beg."

About 45 percent of the fund's assets are in technology issues, with on-line broker E*TRADE, which has gained over 900 percent since its August 1996 offering, the fund's top holding, followed by Equant, a European network service provider whose IPO has risen over 290 percent since its July 1998 debut, and United Pan European. For the one-year period ending December 31, 1999, the fund gained 71.6 percent, compared with a 19 percent gain by the S&P 500. While some investors may be turned off by the fund's 2.5 percent expense ratio, among the highest in the industry, others will consider it a small price to pay to participate in the IPO game.

Hambrecht & Quist's IPO & Emerging Company Fund

Investors had a small window of opportunity to purchase shares in Hambrecht & Quist's IPO & Emerging Company Fund. After debuting the fund in the summer of 1999, H&Q management publicly stated that it was their intention to close the door on the fund for new investors once assets reached the $300 million mark. At the time, it was expected that it would have taken perhaps a couple of years before that level would be reached. In fact, David Krimm, president of H&Q's Fund Management, publicly stated that he was hoping the fund would reach $100 million in assets by the summer of 2000. However, to say demand was strong would be an understatement: Before the end of 1999, the fund's assets exceeded $330 million, with Charles Schwab customers alone accounting for much of that amount, based upon a preferential selling arrangement with H&Q.

Neuberger Berman Millennium Fund

Unlike other small-cap mutual funds, the Neuberger Berman Millennium Fund aims primarily at service, rather than technology, stocks. About one-sixth of it's the fund's assets are in past IPOs. Its main holdings include SFX Broadcasting, which completed its IPO in September 1993 in a $52.5 million offering managed by Kidder Peabody. Also among its core holdings is CSK Autogroup, an auto supply retailer servicing the western United States. CSK Autogroup went public in March 1998 at $27 in a deal managed by Morgan Stanley Dean Witter. In less than two years, the company's stock was trading below its offer price, suggesting that fund managers were hoping for a reversal to catch hold. The fund's mandate is to hold up to 65 percent of its assets, which total approximately $66 million, in small-cap stocks, primarily those with a market capitalization of under $1.5 billion. Also, the company may hold up to 20 percent in foreign company stocks. Among the primary factors fund managers look at in determining which issues to buy are the financial strength and the competitive nature of the company, the strength of the company's brand, the prospects for future earnings growth, and the management and valuation of the stock relative to other companies in the same industry. Management has had two years of experience at the fund.

PBHG New Opportunities

Sometimes things get too good. A case in point is Pilgrim Baxter's New Opportunities Fund, which shut its doors to investors in 1999, in part to prevent a surge of capital *into* the fund! (Many funds close new accounts that become too unwieldy and disrupt their own performance.) In 1999 the fund ranked as the top-performing mutual fund, with a gain of 166.1 percent. Much of this increase can be tied to the number of IPOs in the fund's portfolio. Among the top holdings in PBNOX are Gemstar International, which went public in October 1995, Juniper Networks, a June 1999 IPO managed by Goldman Sachs, and PMC Sierra, a technology company that became public at $16 in April 1991. More than 80 percent of the fund's $228 million in assets are in technology issues.

Dreyfus Founders Discovery Fund

Another mutual fund whose portfolio is composed of some seasoned IPOs is the Founders Discovery Fund, marketed by the Dreyfus organization. The fund invests up to 65 percent of its assets in small-cap issues, focusing on stocks with a market capitalization of between $10 and $500 million. Included in its portfolio are several companies that debuted as IPOs in the past few years, perhaps most notably Digital Microwave, a manufacturer of telecommunications products, which went public in a 1987 offering led by Goldman Sachs. The fund is the third-leading mutual fund investor in that particular stock. Another key holding is Sawtek, which some investors tagged a Qualcomm look-alike, a reference to the high-flying communications company whose stock gained nearly 2000 percent in 1999. At the close of 1999 the fund's largest holding was Cree Research, which accounts for about 3 percent of its total assets. Although *Business Week*'s Mutual Fund Scoreboard gave the fund only a C− rating, it tallied an 87 percent after-tax return in 1999. The fund's expense ratio that year was 1.55, and its turnover rate was 121 percent. At the start of 2000, the fund's managers had three years of experience. According to a report written by Christine Benz, associate editor at the mutual fund reporting service Morningstar (www.morningstar.com), about 14 percent of the fund's assets are held in IPOs.

Putnam OTC Emerging Growth Fund

Owned by insurance company Marsh and McLennan, the Putnam family of mutual funds offers a diverse group of investment choices. One fund of interest to IPO investors is the Putnam OTC Emerging Growth Fund, managed by Steven Kirson and Michael Mufson since June 1998. With more than $11 billion in assets, the fund, which focuses on small-cap stocks, posted average annual returns of nearly 44 percent for the three-year period ending January 21, 2000. In contrast, a typical small-cap fund yielded under a 28 percent average annual return over the same period. Since their mandate is to invest in early-stage companies, it's no surprise that the fund managers are apt to select recent IPOs for their portfolio. At the end of 1999, the fund's top holding was in Metromedia Fiber Networks, which accounted for about 6 percent of its assets. Also among the fund's holdings that year was Breakaway Solutions (NASDAQ-BWAY), a developer of Web sites and Internet solutions priced at $14 per share and brought public in October 1999 by Morgan Stanley Dean Witter in a $42 million offering. Another issue the fund scored large gains with was Silknet Software (NASDAQ-SILK), which it purchased at $15 a share and which ended

1999 at $165.75. Soon thereafter, in February 2000, Silknet received a $4.2 billion takeover offer, or about $258 per share, from Kana Communications. The fund has an expense ratio of 0.98 percent and a turnover rate of 140 percent. The managers have four years of experience with the fund.

Among other mutual funds with significant holdings in some past IPOs are Amerindo Technology, with a better than 25 percent portion of its more than $400 million in assets allocated to shares of Yahoo!, Kemper Technology Fund, which has a 4 percent stake of its $2.6 billion in assets in Lucent Technologies, and Munder Netnet, whose $2.1 billion portfolio has a 5 percent position in Infospace.com. In addition, RS Emerging Growth fund's $2.6 billion in assets includes a 2 percent portion of Network Solutions. Futhermore those investors who are seeking small-cap mutual funds, which typically hold several IPOs and are led by managers with 10 or more years of experience, indicating that the fund has operated through several market cycles, may consider the following entries: Wasatch Growth Fund, with a management with 14 years of experience and a 5-year average annual return, ending in 1999, of 20.4 percent; Standish Funds Small Cap Equity, whose manager has 10 years on the job and which has delivered average annual returns of 26.2 percent; and the Fasciano Fund, with a 13-year experienced management that has directed the fund to a 5-year average annual return of 18.1 percent.

Besides putting their money into open-ended mutual funds, investors seeking to participate in the IPO market may consider several closed-end mutual funds that invest in emerging-growth companies and IPOs. The primary difference between an open-ended and a closed-end fund is that the latter issues a fixed number of shares while the former's outstanding shares vary with the inflow and outflow of funds. Furthermore, closed-end funds typically trade on a securities exchange, while open-ended funds are sold primarily in the over-the-counter markets. Finally, and perhaps most significant, is pricing. The pricing of closed-end funds is dependent on the buy and sell orders for the individual shares. Thus, in most cases, the shares of these funds often change hands at prices less than the underlying value of their portfolio.[86]

Closed-end funds typically focus on certain geographic regions or certain sectors of the economy. For example, country-specific funds, such as the Japan Fund and the Taiwan Fund, invest just in the stocks of those countries, and funds such as the H&Q Healthcare Fund, obviously, invest in the health care sector. With respect to IPO investing, several closed-end funds with a focus on small-cap stocks may be most appropriate. Among those closed-end funds which may be considered as an IPO alternative is Renaissance Capital Group's (www.rencapital.com) Capital Growth and Income Fund III (NASDAQ- RENN). The firm, which might mistakenly be thought to be affiliated with Greenwich, Connecticut–based Renaissance Capital, is actually a Dallas, Texas–headquartered money management firm. The fund invests primarily in private placements of emerging-growth companies, as well as convertible debt and the convertible preferred equity of such companies. According to published reports, the fund registered a gain of about 53 percent during the period between January and October 1999, compared with less than an 11 percent gain by the S&P 500 and less than a 2 percent gain for the Russell 2000 index. Among the fund's largest holdings are equity in privately held eOriginal, a Baltimore-based company developing paperless transactions, and a stake in Jakks Pacific.[87]

Even such firms as Dell Computer, chipmaker Intel, and Apple Computer, all one-time IPOs, may indirectly be viewed as plays on the IPO market. The rationale for doing so is that such firms possess investment portfolios composed of private equity investments in technology companies, which, when they eventually go public, translates into a large windfall for the investing company. For example, Intel owns some 3 million shares of Linux company Red Hat at an estimated investment cost of $2.6 million. At the end of 1999, that stake was valued at nearly $700 million. All in all, Intel reportedly has an investment portfolio of some 300 companies valued at over $8 billion at the end of 1999, including $300 million in financings on 100 deals in 1997 and another $830 million for 130 individual deals made in 1998. During 1999, it was reported that Intel had invested some $1.2 billion in more than 240 start-up enterprises. In 1998 one of its core holdings, Inktomi, went public. Furthermore, Intel's IPO holdings indirectly played a part in an advance in the Dow Jones Industrial Average in early January 2000. Specifically, the company, which was added to the Dow in mid-1999, saw its stock price spike when the firm reported fourth-quarter 1999 earnings of $0.69 per share, beating Wall Street's expectations of $0.63. But upon investigation, it was found that not much of that gain was due to more efficient control of costs and higher revenues, although they did play some part. Rather, profits from Intel's investment portfolio, laden with IPOs and Internet offerings, more than doubled to $508 million, compared with a year-earlier gain of $280 million. Thus, in the absence of that windfall, Intel's quarterly earnings would have been flat for the period, and likely the Dow Jones would have not reached a then-record high of 11,722 by mid-January 2000.

Similarly, Apple Computer parlayed a $12.5 million investment in Akamai Technologies into more than $1 billion when the Massachusetts-based company's stock soared upon its IPO in late 1999. (Incidentally, Akamai got into the IPO game itself by investing $5 million in a Seattle-based company named Loudeye Technologies, which eventually went public during the spring of 2000, gaining more than 150 percent on its first day of trading.) Thus, it's no surprise that Apple is now reporting strong earnings growth, and its own stock likewise reached all-time highs in early 2000. As regards software powerhouse Microsoft, the company does not disclose financial information regarding its investments. Nonetheless, one company it did finance, VeriSign, went public in 1998. Dell Computer also scored several gains from investing in companies that subsequently went public, including Netforma.com, a January 2000 offering that more than tripled on its first day of trading. Finally, even IPOs have come to the aid of other IPOs, at least when it comes to publishing their earnings. New York–based Internet advertising network 24/7 Media (NASDAQ-TFSM) reported its first-ever quarterly profit in the first quarter of 2000, achieved through the company's having sold 150,000 shares of its stake in Internet service provider China.com (NASDAQ-CHINA), which was part of a partnership between the advertising network and the portal company, for a reported $11 million. After that transaction, 24/7 Media still owned 3 million shares, or about 7.3 percent, of the Hong Kong–based portal.

IPO Observation: Mutual funds offer small investors a convenient and low-cost entry into IPOs. However, as is the case with any investment decision, an informed consumer of financial products will likely post better returns than one who rushes into perceived "sure things." Remember, not all mutual funds are alike, as their managers, expenses, and returns differ significantly.

10

WHEN IS IT TIME TO SELL?

I F YOU WERE A LUCKY INVESTOR ABLE TO PURCHASE SHARES IN SOME OF THE PAST DECADE'S HOTTEST IPOS, AN APPROPRIATE QUESTION WOULD BE "WHEN IS ITS APPROPRIATE TO CASH IN THE CHIPS?" OFTEN, A VARIETY OF GENERALITIES AND BANAL BROMIDES ARE VOICED BY FINANCIAL PLANNERS AND THE LIKE WHEN INVESTORS ASK WHETHER THEY SHOULD SELL OR HOLD. TWO SUCH PLATITUDES ARE "LET YOUR PROFITS RUN" AND "CUT YOUR LOSSES." OTHERS SAY THAT ONE MAY LOVE ONE'S SPOUSE, LOVE ONE'S CHILDREN, AND EVEN LOVE ONE'S PET, BUT ONE SHOULD NEVER LOVE A STOCK.

If only it were that simple! While another worn adage that no tree grows to the sky is often cited to mean that no stock can keep on growing, the truth often lies somewhere in between. One consideration is that, from the perspective of financial history, time is short. That is, consider the fact that Microsoft went public in 1986. Relatively speaking, it took less than two decades to transform Bill Gates from just a Harvard dropout to the world's richest human being. Likewise, for *Time's* 1999 Person of the Year, Jeff Bezos, founder of Amazon.com, just three years have passed from the company's initial public offering to his transformation into another forty-something billionaire. In that space of time, the Princeton graduate has gone on to become one of that university's wealthiest alumni. That being said, it stands to reason, in some cases, that the soundest decision is to buy and hold. Yet, many investors have a difficult time attaining such discipline. Lackluster earnings, poor consumer response, declining Web traffic, and other factors have played havoc with investors' mental state, causing a premature rush to the exit.

To answer the question, "When is it appropriate to sell a downward-trending stock?" the general rule would be that it is advisable to sell an investment once it fails to do what it was purchased for. Thus, if an income-oriented investor purchased a portfolio of public utilities for a regular stream of dividends, and one of those issues encountered regulatory or financial difficulties, as occurred with Connecticut's Northeast Utilities or New York's LILCO, so that the utility is forced to trim or even eliminate the payout, then that issue would be a prime candidate for being tossed out. Similarly, if an investor who was interested in growth selected an issue for its record of above-average increases in earnings and consistent double-digit profit growth, and that issue suddenly, because of either changing market condition or managerial error, could no longer could deliver those stellar results, then the issue would rightfully be a candidate for elimination. Investors in IPOs may apply the same approach. Thus, given the fact that many IPOs have gone to market of late with investors expecting that extraordinary earnings are just around the corner, any sign of retreat may not have been expected and may be taken to be an omen of things to come.

WARNING SIGNS

Just as a good detective can dig through a pile of rubble to unearth clues to a crime, so must investors don their inspector caps and take magnifying glass in hand to sift through financial reports and corporate announcements in order to find out how a company is truly operating. Footnotes must be closely examined for irregularities, including charges and changes in accounting procedures. Statements by management that the company's prospects are strong, despite a falling stock price, must be questioned. If a company delays reporting its quarterly earnings or, even worse, adjust its previously reported earnings due to a financial error, investors may soon find the exits crammed as many seek to sell the stock.

Signs of caution include whether the company's management has exaggerated its credentials or made material misstatements with respect to such issues as contracts or revenues. Furthermore, if management previously was associated with an IPO that either faltered or operated under a cloud, it would be not unreasonable to stay clear of such a deal. Given the fact that there are hundreds of IPOs coming to market each year, as well as several thousand with just a few years of operating history, it would be prudent to avoid any company with even the hint of misconduct or wrongdoing. In a world that some may believe is losing its cultural standards, perhaps investors can start their own moral crusade by not investing in those companies which give even the inkling of an appearance of impropriety.

Another clear-cut sign of whether to hold onto a particular IPO or to sell is whether there have been any equity analyst downgrades or upgrades on the offering. Because such decisions often have a great impact on the underlying stock as institutions either scramble to buy or commence unloading shares, depending upon the particular call, investors would be well advised to heed those decisions.[88] A search of Yahoo! Finance pages includes a section highlighting such analyst recommendations. Investors may refer to Thomson Investors Network to determine whether the consensus estimates of Wall Street's analysts, as surveyed by First Call, a Boston-based firm that tracks earnings estimates, are on the rise or falling. Moreover, companies themselves are apt to announce potential shortfalls in earnings, in order to prevent a mass exit to the doors once the bad news is out. For investors, an ability to determine whether such developments are one-time occurrences or the harbinger of a more ominous situation would aid in determining whether to sell or hold. On the one hand, a sale may trigger a tax liability. On the other, holding an issue may squander precious capital as the stock heads lower. One clue may be whether competitors are encountering the same warnings about shortfalls in earnings. If they are, then the resulting erosion of profits may be an industry-wide factor and thus could be short lived or halted once industry conditions change for the better. IPOs whose products are commodity driven, such as products relating to oil production, mining, or even DRAM chipmaking, are prime candidates in this regard. Conversely, if a company suffers a shortfall in earnings while its competitors are posting healthy gains, then an investor may be justified in dumping the stock, since the trouble may be company-specific and not industrywide.

Layoffs, reductions in staff, and plain old firings often send a warning shot that things at the company are not going as planned. When it was announced by Amazon.com in late January 2000 that the company was, for the first time ever, reducing its workforce by dismissing 150 employees, the stock dropped nearly 8 percent. On the other hand, signs of a tight labor market, like that which occurred in the 1999–2000 period, are likely to adversely affect such labor-intensive industries as restaurants and retailing, whereby higher wages would result in lower margins. Furthermore, the threat of imposing a so-called Internet tax on fledging e-commerce companies would dampen their prospects and thus likely send prices lower.

Also of note are alert services, which trigger sell or buy signals for stocks that violate a 50-day or 200-day moving average. One free site that offers such information is www.oxysoft.com. Another valuable source in determining whether an IPO should be sold is the business newspaper *Investor's Business Daily* (IBD), which presents analytical methods for such determinations. The publication is a wealth of information with regard to technical analysis; its charts and proprietary indicators for a stock's relative strength and earnings momentum are well documented as successful tools for many investors. Key here is the publication's SmartSelect Corporate Ratings, which include an earnings-per-share (EPS) rating and a relative-strength rating. The former measures a company's long- and short-term earnings growth rates relative to those of other companies in the IBD universe on a percentile scale of 1 to 99, with 99 being the highest. In the publication's analysis of the "greatest stock market winners," a typical issue had an EPS rating of 93 before making its run up. IBD's relative-strength rating allows investors to determine which stocks have the best price performance. A stock with a rating of 90 outperformed 90 percent of all other equities in the preceding one-year period.

Another indicator that an IPO, or, for that matter, any stock, should be sold is when large investors such as mutual funds or pension plans begin unloading shares. If a stock rises sharply in volume, yet its price is drifting lower, that may very well be a combination that spells a prolonged downturn. Furthermore, if the dip in the stock price comes in conjunction with a violation of the issue's 50- to 100-day moving average, then the issue may be headed sharply lower. Individuals need to exercise discipline with respect to holding an IPO that is trending lower, because every move down requires a greater advance to return to one's original position. For example, if a stock selling at $40 were to fall by 25 percent to $30, it would require a 33 percent bounce back to return to where the stock started out. Likewise, an IPO trading at $75 that suffered a 33 percent decline to $50, not uncommon in recent times, would have to appreciate by 50 percent to get back to where it left off.

Buy or Hold Guidelines: Investors should recognize that IPOs generally are more volatile than other types of equity investments. For example, beta, a variable that indicates a stock's movement in conjunction with the overall market, is considerably higher for IPOs than non-IPOs. In the case of General Electric, beta is 1.21, indicating that GE's stock moves 21 percent more than the overall market does on the upside. By contrast, eBay's beta is 1.60. Thus, the on-line auctioneer's stock is 60 percent more volatile then the over-all market. With that in mind, IPO investors should find that a typical new issue will just as likely decline 20 percent, 30 percent, or more and soon recover, and even double in value, in a matter of a few weeks, only to give back most of that gain in a single day if bad news is revealed. Overall, IPO investors more often than not find themselves on a roller-coaster ride. The trick is to exit at the top and not after a steep descent.

FLIPPER: A GREAT MAMMAL...A NOT SO GREAT STRATEGY

There's no denying that, for many, instant gratification is a way of life. Whether in personal relationships, career pursuits, or financial matters, if positive results aren't forth-coming, those individuals are apt to move on. Perhaps that's one reason some investors are reluctant to have a long-term perspective. Furthermore, according to some market observers, the booming IPO market, along with rock-bottom commissions, has put the long-term investor on the list of endangered financial species. A study conducted by the New York–based investment research firm of Sanford Bernstein indicated that investors are holding onto stocks for less and less time. The firm concluded that a typical NASDAQ stock is owned by investors for about five months before it is sold. Among the top 50 most actively traded issues on NASDAQ, the average holding time is just three weeks, compared with a near-two-year holding period previously reported for such securities.

Fueling this rapid turnover is a variety of factors, the foremost being cheap commission rates. Once, investors would have to think long and hard before buying and selling a particular stock, given that such a "round-trip" trade cost upwards of $200. Now, with commissions as low as $4.95 and in some cases free, it's not uncommon for investors to be trading on an hourly basis. Another factor is increased volatility, as high-priced shares often gyrate several points a day. As an example for volatility a stock may open at $48, reach $52 by noon, slip to $47.25 later, and end the session at $49.125. All along the way, investors, both individual and institutional, are picking their entry and exit points for a quick gain. Finally, and perhaps most effectual, has been the actions of mutual fund managers. A casual observation of any mutual fund prospectus or annual report will reveal that it is not uncommon for a manager to turn over his or her portfolio once, twice, and even three times in a single year. However, the prize for either the most impatient man-ager or the most eager trader would likely go to such a fund as the Ark Small Cap Equities Fund, which had a turnover rate of nearly 700 percent, or the Phoenix-Seneca Strategic Theme Fund, with a better than 530 percent turnover rate. Hence, with some managers constantly buying in and out of stocks in pursuit of an additional fractional gain to booster their overall return, it's no surprise that such action has spread to individual investors.

Among investors who are prone to trade their portfolios aggressively is the "flipper"—one who purchases an IPO, only to "flip it," or quickly sell it, once it soars on the opening day or soon thereafter in order to lock in quick gains. To the underwriter, flipping IPOs is viewed as an intolerable act that must not go unpunished. The reason is simply that flipping costs money, but more precisely, that, if left unchecked, it will cause instability in the price of the stock, which will lead to lower prices, which in turn will lead to more selling, which puts the firm's capital at risk, which...well, you get the picture by now. In fact, the simple reason some firms are adamant against investors selling back IPOs is that those firms just don't want the risk of holding the IPO in case it falls in value. If investors were flipping IPOs back to the underwriter on a large scale, the latter would soon find itself in the position of having a large inventory of a particular stock that may very well fall in value. In such a situation, the underwriter may sell shares from its own account to a market maker in the stock, which would likely cause more pressure on the stock and result in lower prices and even more selling by investors, leading to still lower prices. As a way to halt such activity, investment banks simply prohibit investors from selling the IPO for a specific number of days.

Several years earlier, the antiflipping policies of investment bankers were more uniform. Across the board, many underwriters held fast to the same standards. However, as earning commissions has become more competitive and IPO underwriting increasingly centered on a handful of investment banks, cracks have appeared in the antiflipping prohibitions of some brokers. For example, whereas Wit Capital has implemented a six-month antiflipping ban in some instances, Schwab's embargo is 30 days and Fidelity Investments is just 15. At one time, Charles Schwab prevented an investor from buying a new stock offering for six months if he or she flipped an IPO. Now that period has been cut back to three months. On the other hand, E*TRADE uses the following language on its Web site: "[O]ne of the most important goals of the underwriting syndicate is to try to ensure a degree of price stability for new issues. For that reason E*TRADE would prefer that customers hold their allocated shares for at least 30 days. E*TRADE will not in any way impede the sale of shares within this time, but customers with a record of short holding periods may be excluded from future offerings."

Furthermore, just as some investors perceive a double standard with respect to IPO allocations, so, too, do they find that institutional investors can flip IPOs with immunity while an individual who commits a minor transgression is dealt with harshly, being banned from buying any IPOs for several months. Evidence of the latter double standard came to light when *The Wall Street Journal* reported that not only were episodes of institutional flipping of IPOs not being discouraged or penalized, but they were actually viewed in a positive light, since, in the dynamic IPO environment of late, underwriters of a hot IPO could immediately resell a flipped deal for an even higher price than what it was sold back at. Furthermore, whereas once underwriters were reluctant to take back an IPO for fear that its price might tumble in the aftermath of selling, now they are more than happy to buy back a deal, because it is quite likely that the shares will continue moving to higher ground.

Selling Signs: It has been said that the first step to recovery from an addiction is to admit one's problem. By extension, the first step for some investors in salvaging their portfolios is to concede that a particular choice of stock was wrong. Often, selling a stock is difficult because it becomes an extremely emotional act, with the investor having to acknowledge that his or her selection was wrong. The nature of many individuals is perhaps to deny their error and put the blame elsewhere. Some individuals may say, "I made the right choice, but those rotten chat room rumors drove my stock's price down." Others may blame a particular Wall Street analyst for his or her negative comments in a stock's dive. Still others proclaim their faith and wait for miracles to occur, all the while contending that a company's prospects will recover in the next quarter, or the quarter after that in the following year. The truth is that once the stock fails to do what you purchased it for, it's grounds for divorce.

11

BEHIND EVERY TRADE LURKS THE TAXMAN

IT'S BEEN CALLED THE PRICE WE PAY FOR LIVING IN A FREE SOCIETY. OTHERS LABEL IT A SCOURGE AND AN IMPEDIMENT TO OUR LIBERTIES. BUT ONE UNAVOIDABLE FACT WHEN IT COMES NOT ONLY TO INVESTING IN IPOS, BUT ALSO TO ENGAGING IN NEARLY ANY FINANCIAL TRANSACTION, IS THAT A TAX CONSEQUENCE IS INVOLVED. IN FACT, TAXES ASSOCIATED WITH SECURITIES TRANSACTIONS HAVE PRODUCED A WINDFALL FOR THE COFFERS OF THE FEDERAL GOVERNMENT: IT HAS BEEN ESTIMATED THAT SOME $25 BILLION IN TAXES WERE PAID BY INVESTORS FROM STOCK TRANSACTIONS IN THE FISCAL YEAR ENDING OCTOBER 31, 1999. FOR INVESTORS, THOUGH, TAXES ARE FREQUENTLY A COMPLICATED AND BURDENSOME MATTER. CONGRESS OFTEN TINKERS WITH THE TAX CODE, PROVIDING INCENTIVES FOR ONE GROUP AND PENALTIES FOR ANOTHER. FURTHERMORE, WHILE THE CAPITAL-GAINS TAX WAS MODESTLY CUT TO 20 PERCENT FROM 28 PERCENT EFFECTIVE JULY 28,

Still, the most troublesome aspects of taxes and IPOs is how to classify the taxpayer. The Internal Revenue Service categorizes those who buy, sell, or hold stock into three groups: investors, traders, and dealers. Each is defined and treated in a distinct matter as follows:

Investors Generally speaking, an investor is someone who purchases a financial instrument with the expectation of a capital gain or dividend income. An investor must regularly report to the IRS transactions resulting in gains or losses on his or her investments.

Traders What distinguishes a trader from an investor is whether the activities of the individual "rise to the level as to be considered in a trade or business." Sound simple? Actually it is, since what someone does as a trader is rather clear-cut and distinct from the activity of a simple investor. For example, a trader will conduct many trades on a daily basis, to the exclusion of any other professional employment activity. So a person who completes five or six trades in a day and perhaps 100 in a year would likely be considered an investor, in today's turbocharged financial world. But one who completes a dozen or more trades per day every day of the week and who trades 1000 or more times per year would certainly be classified as a trader.

Unlike investors, who can claim only a portion of their expenses as itemized deductions, since they must first cross a threshold of 2 percent of their adjusted gross income, a trader may claim all of his or her expenses as business costs and thereby receive the full benefit for them as deductions. In the eyes of the IRS, a trader is self-employed and therefore may deduct all investing expenses on Schedule C. Moreover, these write-offs may be used to reduce the trader's adjusted gross income, which in turn may permit that individual to deduct all of his or her personal exemptions. Furthermore, unlike investors, whose interest from margin accounts may be considered an investment expense, traders may deduct such amounts as a cost of doing business. On the downside is the fact that the deduction of losses in a single year is limited to $3000. Thus, even if the trader had suffered a particularly bad trade, there are limits to the amount he or she may deduct.

Dealers The trader's trades are made not for any long-term objective, but rather to "skim the market" for short-term gains. Hence, if an individual accumulates nearly all short-term gains, then it is likely that he or she would be classified by the IRS as a trader. But what if some of the person's trades are done for the long-term while others are for the short term? Then, according to tax professionals, a trader may also have taxable gains, which may be classified as investment gains, and an investor may have a portion of his or her gains subject to taxation under traders' regulations. However, such cases are subject to interpretation by the agency, if any, the person works for and by tax officials from the IRS.

CAPITAL GAINS

It may seem like ancient history to some, but up until the early 1980s the capital-gains tax rate was as high as 49 percent. With the passage of President Ronald Reagan's tax cuts in 1982, however, the tax was trimmed to 20 percent, only to be hiked to 28 percent in 1987 and again to 33 percent in 1988. In 1997, the Clinton administration's tax bill raised individual tax rates for upper-income taxpayers and cut the capital-gains tax from 28 percent to 20 percent and then to 18 percent in 2000. Since 1978, there have been seven changes in the capital-gains tax rate that have been correlated negatively with the issuance of IPOs. Specifically, in the five years in which the capital-gains rate was cut, three of them saw a gain in IPO volume. On the other hand, in the two most recent years in which the capital-gains rate was raised, 1987 and 1988, IPO volume declined.[89]

As a backdrop to understanding capital gains, investors should know the basic method of calculating taxes associated with the sale of equities. Simply stated, a tax loss or gain is determined by comparing the proceeds from the stock, less commissions, with the original tax basis. However, if you're selling only a portion of a particular holding—say, 19 common shares of America Online that you have been accumulating for the past few years—then some other calculations are required. One step is called the specific ID approach and allows investors to indicate which shares they are selling. For sellers of highly appreciated IPOs, this approach works better than the others, since one's tax liability is reduced by selling the highest-cost shares first (although if the shares are held for one year or less, then they are treated as ordinary income and may be taxed as much as 39.6 percent). If one is selling losing IPOs, it is advisable to sell those held for a shorter period, since such losses may be used to offset short-term gains, which may be taxed at the higher ordinary income rate.

For IPO owners, and especially those holding large capital gains, there are certain basic rules and dates to be aware of. First, investments sold after July 28, 1997, that have been owned for more than one year but less than 18 months are still taxed at the old maximum rate of 28 percent. Effective January 1, 2001, an 18 percent capital-gains tax rate kicks in for investments held more than five years by certain investors. Therefore, those investors who purchased IPOs which went public prior to 1996 may consider taking advantage of that rate. However, not everyone qualifies for such treatment: If the investor is in a tax bracket above 15 percent, defined as including single taxpayers with a taxable income above $24,650 or married taxpayers filing jointly with a total income above $41,200, then the five-year holding period applies only to investments acquired after December 31, 2000. Thus, the gains associated with many hot IPOs from the 1990s are ineligible for the lower rate, unless the taxpayer can lower his or her taxable income to below the foregoing levels. However, beginning in 2002, taxpayers in the 15 percent bracket will see their rate cut to 8 percent on gains from assets held longer than five years, while those in upper-income brackets are scheduled to see their rate fall to 18 percent in 2006 for those assets purchased after December 31, 2000, and held for five years or longer.

SHELTERING GAINS

In the search for ways to trim one's tax liability with respect to gains achieved through the appreciation of financial assets, investors are provided with several tools: offsetting gains with losses, adjusting the holding period, and donating assets, among other measures.

Those with close family ties may opt to give their assets to their children or grandchildren, rather than selling those assets, in order to provide them with cash for college, marriage, or other of life's events. Donors may give a single individual up to $10,000 in assets each year, free of estate and gift taxes. Thus, a married couple with three children may give $60,000 annually in appreciated assets to their children, whereupon, assuming that the children are in a lower tax bracket, less tax will be paid than if those shares are sold. (Note that gifts above $10,000 in a single year are taxable to the donor.) Beginning in 1999, such tax-free gift limits are to be indexed to inflation. Once the children assume ownership of the asset, a few rules come into play. First, the children essentially stand in the shoes of the donor parent for the purpose of calculating the cost basis of the transfer. Thus, if Julia Jones receives 100 shares of a stock trading at $20 each at the date of the gift, but that was purchased by a parent at $15 each at the time of the company's IPO, then Julia's capital gain would be equal to the difference between the sale price and $15. If the market were to tumble and the shares began trading at $10 each, then the capital loss would be the difference between the $10 sale price and $20, the price at the time Julia received the stock as a gift. Recipients of gifted assets should determine whether the donor had already paid a gift tax prior to completing the transfer. If so, the recipient may adjust the cost basis higher by an amount equal to the gift tax paid on the stock.

A corollary issue is dealing with assets received from an inheritance and the corresponding tax liability. The first rule is to determine the date of the benefactor's death. The cost basis of the asset is then its market value on the date of death. Yahoo! Finance pages have a convenient tool for looking up a stock's daily historic pricing. (See the "Profile" section of a company under the heading "Historic Prices" on the Yahoo! page.) Thus, if your Uncle Harry left you shares of Amazon.com in his last will and testament, and he passed away on January 10, 2000, if you find that the company's price range on that day was between a high of $72.69 and a low of $65.56, then the cost basis of the asset would be the average of those two prices, or $69.13.

However, the executor of the decedent's estate has the authority to select an alternative valuation date, which can be either six months after the date of death or the date the assets were distributed to the beneficiary if earlier than six months after the death date. The reason for such an option is that if the value of the asset were to decline in the six-month period postmortem, the estate tax liability could be limited. The amount that may be passed to an heir's estate tax free is scheduled to be raised from $625,000 in 1998 to $1 million in 2006. Presently, estate taxes stand at a staggering 55 percent on any amount above $3 million. A simple solution for those with estates valued at that level may be to purchase life insurance and relinquish ownership in it by placing the policy in a trust, to cover any liabilities. The important factor is to surrender control of the policy; otherwise it will be counted as being within the decedent's estate.

Investors should also be aware that, besides the federal government looking to grab a slice of someone's estate, some states impose their own gift and estate taxes. However, unlike state income taxes, which are piled on top of one's federal income tax burden, many state gift and estate taxes are not levied on top of federal liabilities: Rather, there is a credit of up to 16 percent of the asset's value on states' gift and estate taxes such that the federal taxes are effectively reduced dollar for dollar. This means that, as a whole, the combined federal and state estate tax liability may not exceed what the federal tax would have been if there were no state tax. Financial planners view such a situation as tantamount to a so-called sponge tax, since it absorbs the federal tax credit and gives states a free ride in taxing their citizens. Still, several states have estate taxes that exceed the federal tax limit and thus create an added burden on the residents of those states. Finally, in planning their estates, investors of IPOs should take into account the fact that several states, including Connecticut, Louisiana, North Carolina, and Tennessee, impose gift taxes.

Taxing IPOs: In seeking to take control of one's tax liability with respect to IPOs, investors should be aware of several basic considerations. First, they must determine whether they are traders, investors, or dealers in the eyes of the IRS.

Second, they must calculate how long they held onto the investment. Third—and this sometimes is overlooked by some—if they purchased a stock on margin and incurred interest charges, that amount can possibly be deducted as an expense. Finally, they must heed the "wash rule" in order to avoid delays in taking losses. The "wash rule" is defined as the IRS rule prohibiting a taxpayer from claiming a loss on the sale of an investment if that same investment was purchased within 30 days before or after the sale date.

12

IPOs IN YOUR PORTFOLIO

Are IPOs for everyone? While it's difficult for some investors to sit on the sidelines while others are raking in enormous gains, the fact is that some investors are best advised to stay clear of such offerings for several reasons. First, IPOs are incredibly volatile: By nearly every measure, IPOs demonstrate greater price swings than non-IPOs. Consider the fact that some IPOs that came to market in 1999 and quickly doubled in value on their first day of trading ended the year below their original offer price. In like manner, while more than 100 IPOs completed in 1999 doubled in value on their first day of trading, a similar number of deals priced that year are now showing losses in investors' portfolios. In light of the record-setting gains many IPOs posted in 1999, a good number of investors prospered while other remained out of the market, convinced that the prices of many technology deals, as presented in Table 12-1, were wildly overextended and that the stocks were poised for a fall.

Table 12-1   Top 25 Technology IPO Performers*

Issuer	Business Description	High-Tech Industry	Ticker Symbol	Issue Date	Proceeds Amount in This Market ($ mil)
Commerce One, Inc., Inc.	Dvlp ecommrce solutions	Internet Services & Software Communication/ Network Software	CMRC	7/1/99	69.3
Purchasepro.com, Inc.	Pvd Internet commerce svcs	Internet Services & Software	PPRO	9/13/99	48.0
VerticalNet, Inc.	Oprts Web sites for utility cos	Networking Systems (LAN,WAN)	VERT	2/10/99	56.0
Brocade Comm Sys, Inc.	Mnfr data comm software equip	Data Commun (Exclude networking)	BRCD	5/24/99	61.8
Vignette Corp	Develop Internet mgmt software	Internet Services & Software Communication/ Network Software	VIGN	2/18/99	76.0
Liberate Technologies	Dvlp Internet software	Communication/ Network Software Internet Services & Software	LBRT	7/27/99	100.0
Redback Networks, Inc.	Dvlp Internet access products	Networking Systems (LAN,WAN)	RBAK	5/17/99	57.5
Ariba, Inc.	Pvd business solutions via Int	Communication/ Network Software Internet Services & Software	ARBA	6/22/99	115.0
Red Hat, Inc.	Develop open source software	Networking Systems (LAN,WAN) Internet Services & Software	RHAT	8/11/99	84.0
Vitria Technology, Inc.	Dvlps enterprs sftwr	Internet Services & Software	VITR	9/16/99	48.0
Phone.com, Inc.	Dvlp communica- tions software	Internet Services & Software Communication/ Network Software	PHCM	6/10/99	64.0
E.piphany, Inc.	Dvlp Internet software	Internet Services & Software Communication/ Network Software	EPNY	9/21/99	66.4
Kana Communi- cations, Inc.	Provide Prepack- aged Software	Internet Services & Software Applications Software (Business)	KANA	9/21/99	49.5

Offer Price	Offer Price Adjusted for Splits	Stock Price at 12/31/99	Pct Change in Stock Price to 12/31/99	Original Low Filing Price	Original High Filing Price	Book Manager(s)
21.00	7.00	196.50	2,707.14	13.00	15.00	CS First Boston
12.00	5.33	137.50	2,478.13	11.00	13.00	Prudential Securities , Inc.
16.00	8.00	164.00	1,950.00	8.00	10.00	Lehman Brothers
19.00	9.50	177.00	1,763.16	8.00	10.00	Morgan Stanley Dean Witter
19.00	9.50	163.00	1,615.79	12.00	14.00	Morgan Stanley Dean Witter
16.00	16.00	257.00	1,506.25	11.00	13.00	CS First Boston
23.00	11.50	177.50	1,443.48	12.00	14.00	Morgan Stanley Dean Witter
23.00	11.50	177.38	1,442.39	16.00	18.00	Morgan Stanley Dean Witter
14.00	7.00	211.25	1,408.93	10.00	12.00	Goldman Sachs & Co
16.00	16.00	234.00	1,362.50	10.00	12.00	CS First Boston
16.00	8.00	115.94	1,349.23	10.00	12.00	CS First Boston
16.00	16.00	223.13	1,294.53	9.00	11.00	CS First Boston
15.00	15.00	205.00	1,266.67	11.00	13.00	Goldman Sachs & Co

Table 12-1 Top 25 Technology IPO Performers* (*Continued*)

Issuer	Business Description	High-Tech Industry	Ticker Symbol	Issue Date	Proceeds Amount in This Market ($ mil)
Akamai Technologies, Inc.	provide web site services	Internet Services & Software	AKAM	10/28/99	234.0
Foundry Networks, Inc.	Dvlps network switches	Workstations	FDRY	9/27/99	125.0
F5 Networks, Inc.	Dvlp specific software	Communication/ Network Software	FFIV	6/4/99	30.0
Silknet Software, Inc.	Dvlps internet sftwr	Internet Services & Software Networking Systems (LAN,WAN) Communication/ Network Software	SILK	5/5/99	45.0
Art Technology Group, Inc.	Develop computer software	Other Computer Systems	ARTG	7/20/99	60.0
Agile Software Corp	Dvlp,whl content mgmt software	Applications Software (Business	AGIL	8/19/99	63.0
Braun Consulting, Inc.	Delive eSolutions	Other Computer Related Svcs Internet Services & Software	BRNC	8/10/99	28.0
TIBCO Software, Inc.	Develop Internet software	Communication/ Network Software Internet Services & Software	TIBX	7/13/99	109.5
Juniper Networks	Mfr switchs for intrnt pvdrs	Modems	JNPR	6/24/99	163.2
Proxicom, Inc.	Pvd computer systems dvlp svcs	Other Computer Systems Operating Systems Networking Systems (LAN,WAN) Workstations Other Computer Related Svcs	PXCM	4/19/99	58.5
Digital Island, Inc.	Internet Service Provider	Internet Services & Software Communication/ Software Network	ISLD	6/29/99	60.0
MyPoints.com, Inc.	Pvd Internet-based mktg svcs	Internet Services & Software	MYPT	8/19/99	40.0

*Includes communications, computer equipment, electronics, biotechnology (excluding medical devices) companies with IPOs of at least $15 million (U.S. proceeds); excludes ADRs, ADSs, and unit offerings.
  Source: Thomson Financial Securities Data.

Offer Price	Offer Price Adjusted for Splits	Stock Price at 12/31/99	Pct Change in Stock Price to 12/31/99	Original Low Filing Price	Original High Filing Price	Book Manager(s)
26.00	26.00	327.63	1,160.10	16.00	18.00	Morgan Stanley Dean Witter
25.00	12.50	301.69	1,106.75	14.00	16.00	Deutsche Banc Alex Brown
10.00	10.00	114.00	1,040.00	10.00	12.00	Hambrecht & Quist
15.00	15.00	165.75	1,005.00	10.00	12.00	CS First Boston
12.00	12.00	128.13	967.71	10.00	12.00	Hambrecht & Quist
21.00	21.00	217.25	934.52	15.00	17.00	Morgan Stanley Dean Witter
7.00	7.00	71.50	921.43	10.00	12.00	Donaldson, Lufkin & Jenrette
15.00	15.00	153.00	920.00	9.00	11.00	Goldman Sachs & Co
34.00	34.00	340.00	900.00	21.00	23.00	Goldman Sachs & Co
13.00	13.00	124.31	856.25	10.00	12.00	BT Alex. Brown
10.00	10.00	95.13	851.25	10.00	12.00	Bear Stearns
8.00	8.00	74.00	825.00	10.00	12.00	BancBoston Robertson Stephens

Yet, for all the skepticism some investors may have towards IPOs, an examination of the developments in such fields as finance, commerce, and media must lead even the most jaded to recognize that some recent entrants onto the business landscape are making history. Perhaps no clearer illustration of this phenomenon can be found than America Online's record-setting $181 billion merger with "old-line" media giant Time Warner, announced in January 2000. Founded in 1923, Time had a long and distinguished record in journalism. By contrast, AOL wasn't even a public company until March 1992. Yet, in the changing and fast-paced world of technology and publishing, such terms as "e-commerce," "broadband content delivery," and "integrated cable systems" became part of the day-to-day jargon (remember when it was just sales and earnings that mattered), and AOL managed to assemble the resources (read high stock price) and capital (access to willing and believing bankers) to pull off the biggest M&A deal in history. What actually fueled the deal was AOL's stock price, which had risen over 63,000 percent from the time the company went public on March 19, 1992, through March 2000, compared with Time Warner's gain of less than 600 percent from the time AOL first went public to the time the deal was announced. In that regard, many market observers commented that it would just be a matter a time before another high-flying IPO of recent vintage would aggressively enter into the M&A field to further its business by means of an octane-charged stock valuation.

At the other end of the spectrum, some notable companies have gone public in the past few years, only to see their stock price remain flat or stumble despite solid finances and a history of earnings growth and customer loyalty. And in contradistinction to the near-universal love affair many investors have had with technology stocks, some investors are taking a second look at neglected companies that could turn out to be hidden gems. Some of these firms, such as drugstore chain Duane Reade or pet store PetSmart, are in the traditional retailing sector, while others are in manufacturing or real estate. These IPOs may be suitable for those investors waiting patiently for a turnaround and who lack the temperament necessary to withstand the incredible volatility associated with many high-tech IPOs. To that end, it would seem reasonable for even the most risk-averse investors to include some recent IPOs in their portfolio. Featured next are some selected IPOs that fall into certain categories. Although they are presented only to illustrate where some IPOs may be classified, and are not meant as a recommendation or endorsement of the companies, their stories should aid in making investment decisions.

...TO INFINITY AND BEYOND!

There seems to be no shortage of IPOs that have shown explosive price appreciation even after an incredible first-day pop. Such offerings as Internet Capital Group, Red Hat, and Commerce One, completed in 1999, continue to be bid higher by investors. Likewise, one-time IPOs such as Oracle Systems, Microsoft, and Sun Microsystems, each of which went public in the 1980s, continue to attract new investors and reward those who have held onto their shares for the long term. Investors with a tolerance for wide price swings may consider these issues as core holdings in a portfolio structured for aggressive growth. Similarly, Yahoo! and CMGI are other candidates that, in a short time after having completed their own IPOs, have earned investor support.

Investors willing to get on board for may what may very well be a bumpy, though exciting, ride may consider the following IPOs as candidates for aggressive growth portfolios: DoubleClick (NASDAQ-DCLK) is a Silicon Alley–based advertising network that has seen its revenues climb from $258 million in 1999 to an estimated $459 million in 2000 and is expected to reach the $721 million mark by 2001, according to a report published by the investment firm Stephens, Inc. Another New York–based company of merit is RCN (NASDAQ-RCNC), an Internet and cable infrastructure firm that provides high-speed Internet access via cable modem. In 1999, the firm acquired two Internet service providers and received more than $1 billion in capital from ex-Microsoft, now Vulcan Ventures, executive Paul Allen.

Another interesting company is JDS Uniphase (NASDAQ-JDSU), a San Jose–based developer of telecommunications equipment for optical networks. The company was formed in January 1999 when JDS Fitel, a majority-owned unit of Furukawa Electric Co., Ltd., announced a merger with Uniphase Corp. in a $3.1 billion transaction. Subsequently, the newly formed company continued its pursuit of growth by an aggressive acquisition campaign that included 10 acquisitions totaling over $58 billion. The deals began when the Canadian securities firm CIBC Wood Gundy acquired a 4 percent stake in the company for $125 million the following month. In September 1999, JDS Uniphase acquired AFC Technologies for an undisclosed amount, a deal that was followed by two further acquisitions in October. The first was the purchase of all of the outstanding stock of New Jersey–based optical detector supplier Epitaxx, a unit of Nippon Sheet Glass, for $400 million; the second was the purchase of Massachusetts technology company Ramar Corp. Then, in early November 1999, JDS Uniphase agreed to acquire Optical Coating Laboratory for $2.77 billion, after which the company ended the month with the planned $97 million acquisition of SIFAM, Ltd., a U.K.-headquartered fiber-optics firm. Not one to end the year quietly, the firm closed 1999 with the acquisition of Oprel Technologies for an undisclosed amount.

But the deal that put JDS Uniphase on the map was its proposed $15.4 billion acquisition of E-TEK Dynamics, a manufacturer of telecommunications equipment and a majority-owned-unit of Summit Partners, L.P. The flurry of deals helped JDS Uniphase transform itself into a firm with a $62 billion market capitalization. While the stock gained over 840 percent in 1999, aided in part by two 2-for-1 stock splits, industry analysts anticipate that earnings will grow from 1999's actual report of $0.37 per share to $1.10 in 2001, as revenues are expected to climb from $588 million to over $2.2 billion.

FOREIGN ISSUES

With all the opportunities that exist among domestic companies, why would an investor consider buying shares in a foreign company? As noted in an earlier chapter, the performance of a typical foreign-issued IPO lags that of its domestic counterpart. Yet, interest in foreign IPOs persists. Perhaps the reason can be found in McDonald's restaurants' increasing focus on overseas sales as the driving force for its business in the 21st century: Market economies are in their infancy in many East European and Asian nations wherein a new middle class with the power to buy goods and services is just being created. In addition, in the aftermath of the 1998 global currency crisis, many foreign equities saw their values slashed in half or worse. Now those issues have stabilized and are poised for recovery. Many of them are issues within the technology and telecommunications sectors. For example, investors may consider Mexican cellular communications company Nuevo Grupo Iusacell SA, an August 1999 IPO managed by JP Morgan, Dutch Internet service provider VersaTel Telecom BV, a July 1999 offering handled by Lehman Brothers, and French telecommunications equipment manufacturer Wavecom Sa, a $37 million offering led by CS First Boston. Also, individuals anticipating greater economic growth in Europe may consider Dutch telecommunications giant Royal KPN (NYSE-KPN). Together with Qwest Communications in a joint venture called KPNQwest, Royal KPN is deploying a fiber-optic network connecting 40 European cities. Work already has been completed in London, Paris, and Amsterdam.

Investors looking for bargains within foreign IPOs may consider Telstra Corp., Ltd., an Australian cellular communications company that, despite much fanfare concerning its 1997 debut, ended 1999 about 40 percent off its ADR offering price of $47.50. Those individuals looking for ideas beyond technology and perhaps not so geographically distant may view Canadian real-estate firm Cadillac Fairview as a suitable issue, both in terms of the recovery of the Canadian economy and as an adventure in real estate per se. The November 1997 deal, managed jointly by Goldman Sachs and CIBC-Oppenheimer, raised $217 million in the United States, but is essentially trading flat from its offer price. Another Canadian issue worth a second look is insurance company Manulife Financial. The firm raised over $544 million in the United States, one of the largest amounts ever by a Canadian IPO, but has hardly budged from its $12.20 offer price. In Latin America, several foreign technology issues, including America Online Latin America and Yupi.com, may spark investor appeal.

For speculative investors, one interesting IPO play is one that seeks to capitalize on both the IPO market itself and the expansion of technology and Internet-related companies in Europe. In this regard, TFG Venture Capital (OTC-TFGGF), a financial holding company, stands to see strong appreciation, according to some analysts, because of an effective management team and its track record of acquiring stakes in new high-tech companies through early-stage financings. Given that German venture-capital activity (says the European Venture Capital Association) accounts for about 15 percent of all European VC activity, and because Germany ranks second in the European market, it stands to reason that there is ample opportunity for TFG to discover, finance, and eventually profit from emerging-growth companies in that country. Furthermore, according to industry reports, while in 1997 just 4 percent of German companies that received venture-capital financing went public, in the following year the figure quadrupled. Among TFG-backed companies that went public are Vectron, Eckert & Ziegler, and Comroad.

DOUBLE DOWN

After doubling on their first day of trading, what do some IPOs do for an encore? In the case of some more than two dozen issues, the answer is to head lower. On first appearance, investors may want to have nothing to do with an issue that cannot hold on to its early gains. Such issues as Value America and iVillage, which gained over 100 percent on their first day of trading, only to end 1999 under their offer price, may be hard pressed to win over new investors, given that many of their early backers are likely to be suffering a loss. And while these companies may still generate some speculative appeal as management seeks to turn the company around to regain its early glory, some investors may not have the patience to wait for such a recovery.

On the other hand, those IPOs which initially soared in value, only to have pulled back in price, but not so far as to go below their initial offer price, may present investors with some gems. Among names to consider are Perot Systems, which priced at $16 and gained over 170 percent on its first day of trading, only to settle back into the mid-$20 range, and Drugstore.com, which, despite the fact that Amazon.com owns 26 percent of the company, still lags behind other health-related Web sites in generating traffic and has seen its stock ease back from an initial-day gain of nearly 180 percent. Similarly, many health care and medical-related e-commerce IPOs, with the exception of Healtheon, which merged with WebMD, have not delivered sparkling returns as of yet. Among these issues are Healthcentral.com., drkoop.com, and Mothernature.com, each of which is off substantially from its offer price. Indeed, drkoop.com was almost put on financial life support when auditors questioned whether it had the resources to continue operating.

IT'S IN THE NAME

Although to some it appears to be a recent phenomenon, branding and product identification has been around for many years. Whether it was Fels Naptha soap in the 1920s, Nehi soda in the 1940s, Bounty paper towels in the 1970s, or Amazon.com in the 1990s, consumers have long reserved a special spot for particular products and staples. So, too, in the stock market and, by extension, the IPO sector, many companies have had strong and loyal customers who support the company's services and products, as well as its stock.

Among IPOs of the past few years that have demonstrated strong customer support and consumer recognition are such companies as freight carrier United Parcel Service (NYSE-UPS), specialty coffee retailer Starbucks (NASDAW-SBUX), and e-auction house eBay (NASDAQ-EBAY). Also worth considering is on-line book retailer barnesandnoble.com (NASDAQ-BNBN), which at one point in its history could brag of having the largest Internet IPO, over $450 million, and one of the most widely distributed offerings with 25 million shares. The company, which is partially owned by both Bertlesmann AG and Barnes & Noble, has yet to turn a profit, but has showed revenue growth and ranks as the fifth-leading e-commerce site in terms of viewer traffic, according to Media Metrix. Moreover, with its shares beaten down in early 2000 as some e-commerce firms fell into disfavor, the issue may represent a turnaround.

As regards another Internet company being partially bankrolled by one of the investment community's most recognizable names, one need go further than consider Bluefly (NASDAQ-BFLY), an e-commerce firm that focuses on discount brand-name clothing. Last year, the company received a $10 million investment from the Soros Private Equity group, a unit of famed financier George Soros's global network. Today, Bluefly is building both traffic and customer loyalty. Also of merit is medical and health-care content provider Medscape (NASDAQ-MSCP), which has developed several notable transactions, including a move whereby broadcaster CBS launched MedScape's consumer Web site, www.healthwatch.com.

FUTURE IPOS

Contrary to what one may think, there is a stable of private companies that are viewed by industry insiders as likely IPOs in the near future. Typically, such companies have received a series of financings from venture-capital or private-equity investors and are poised to launch their own IPOs. The publication *The Red Herring* frequently lists several privately held companies that are expected to launch an IPO in the near future. For example, in the March 2000 issue, such companies as B2B industrial steel e-commerce site E-Steel (www.e-steel.com), which received private-equity financings from such firms as Goldman Sachs and Kleiner Perkins, and Vstream (www.vstream.com), a Colorado-based developer of e-mail voice-messaging software and hardware, which includes Excite@Home and GE Equity among its backers, were touted as potential IPOs.

Also a likely IPO candidate may be Wavesplitter Technologies, a California-based developer of fiber-optic networking technology that has received financing from Lucent Technologies, Goldman Sachs, and others. In addition, firms that are recipients of late-stage venture financing could be poised to launch their IPOs in the upcoming months. For example, NaviMedix, a Boston-based firm that offers B2B e-commerce services to the health-care community, has over $5 million from such firms as Hearst Communications and GE Capital. Likewise, ClearCommerce Communications, a Texas-based firm that produces software used in processing on-line orders, secured $30 million in financing from Hewlett-Packard in early 2000.

Investing Notes: For investors, the IPO market presents opportunities in many shapes and forms. For those seeking exceptional earnings growth, there are issues such as JDS Uniphase or Doubleclick. Individuals who are interested in potential turnarounds may consider barnesandnoble.com. And those who want to stay clear of high-tech issues may want such firms as wood products company Trex, Inc., and junior apparel retailer Charlotte Russe Holding, whose stores include "Rampage," in their portfolios. In sum, the IPO market provides choices for a variety of investment styles and preferences.

Conclusion

Often in early winter, eager skaters will don their blades and race out on a newly frozen pond only to discover the ice below is thin and threatening. What was believed to be solid and supporting is now seen as thin and unsubstantial once the first signs of a crack appear. Immediately, enthusiasm gives way to fear and a mad scramble enfolds as the once daring race to the safety of the sidelines. However, the conditions that existed at that moment often would change as a new wind blows in and skaters can return to glide and slide.

So it is at times with the IPO market. Investors at times will jump into a highly publicized offering at a price far above what a reasonable and prudent person would pay. Other times they will buy a stock without any clear knowledge of what the underlying company does or what its prospects are. Should prices begin to soften or if there is crack in the deal's support, many investors often will flee for safety by dumping their once coveted holding and curse the day they brought it.

Yet if one lesson can be learned from the preceding pages, it is that investors, armed with knowledge, often can successfully invest in IPOs through a variety of ways. By focusing on a particular underwriter, avoiding an underperforming sector, or knowing that highly priced securities are not guaranteed to climb to still higher value, investors in the long run will likely be rewarded. In closing, the IPO market is certainly an exciting and often enriching investment opportunity. It is my hope that this book played a small role in helping individuals understand the process and how to profit from it.

Chapter 1

1. The performance figures for pre-1990 IPOs were calculated from Thomson Financial Securities Data's New Issue databases.
2. IBM's and Ford Motor's early stock history can be found on the respective Web sites of those companies in the investor information section.
3. Arthur Levitt's comments at Columbia University Law School were delivered at an Investor's Town Hall meeting on December 9, 1999. Levitt, the 25th chairman of the agency, was responsible for the creation of the Office of Investor Education and Assistance. Related information may be found at the agency Web site, www.sec.gov.
4. One of first reports of Roger Lipton's critique of Boston Chicken appeared in the June 12, 1995, issue of *Business Week* in Gene Marical's column.
5. Highlights of theglobe.com's financial background and related data were derived from the firm's annual reports.
6. Accounts of eBay's IPO were from published news articles at the time of the offering.
7. The *Silicon Alley Reporter* is a New York–based monthly covering the Internet industry in New York City. Its parent company is Rising Tide Studio and is run by Jason McCabe Calacanis.
8. Information obtained from TFSD.
9. Information obtained from TFSD.
10. Information about Worldwide Wrestling Federation derived from company prospectus.
11. The full text of the Securities Act of 1933 and 1934, as well as the rules promulgated under these statues, plus the proposed and final rules, may be found on various Web sites. One that offers a convenient directory is located at www.bx.com/finance/sec/html.
12. Information obtained from TFSD.
13. Information obtained from TFSD.

Chapter 2

14. Most covers of "red herrings" are standardized. An example is whether a company is a multibillion enterprise or a small development concern, each will essentially follow the same format regarding its prospectus.

15. Individuals may refer to several on-line sources for quick access to filings and related documents. Among these sources are www.edgar.com and www.multex.com.

16. Information obtained from Breakaway Solutions' prospectus dated October 5, 1999.

17. Regarding executives' backgrounds, current technology makes it increasingly difficult for one to disguise past episodes that may be injurious to one's career. Likewise, when executives switch positions, sometimes eyebrows are raised when their past is revealed. For example, *Barron's* reported that the founder of onegrocer.com, a $264 million IPO underwritten by blue-chip Wall Street firm Morgan Stanley Dean Witter, had previously been employed by a company whose shares were traded on the Vancouver Stock Exchange.

18. According to a CS First Boston press release dated July 1, 1998, Quattrone, Boutros, and Brady were instrumental in several notable IPOs, convertible offerings, and M&A transactions. Among the companies the three have advised are Amazon.com, Netscape, E*TRADE, and CNET. Within two weeks of their hiring, CS First Boston announced that over 100 investment bankers, equity research analysts, and sales professionals moved to the firm.

19. Of course, there are other "name" analysts whose commentary has a significant impact on the IPOs their respective firms underwrite. Among such individuals are Mary Meeker of Morgan Stanley and Jonathan Cohen of Wit Capital.

20. Investors wishing to contact the SEC directly may phone 1-800-SEC-0330.

Chapter 3

21. Delayed IPOs occur with greater frequency than those of postponed deals. Since many IPOs often file with only a tentative date as to when the issue will actually be completed, it's not uncommon for companies to push ahead their "expected date" by several days or weeks. In contrast, a postponed deal is a deal in which both issuer and underwriter agree to take the offering off the registration calendar.

22. The hike in the average number of shares being issued in any given deal has been used as ammunition in the argument that underwriters are intentionally holding back on the number of shares in order to boost prices. In fact, after a 10-year drought between 1988 and 1997, when the number of domestic IPOs with a global share offering (more than 25 million shares) never exceeded 8, an uptick in such deals brought 12 to market in 1998 and another 14 in 1999.

23. Rising prices and increasing numbers of shares often present a dilemma for both the issuer and the underwriter, since, if the deal is too hot, some investors may be priced out of the offering and thus may find themselves unable to participate, whereupon new buyers would have to be found.

24. A broad and expansive literature exists on IPO underpricing. Among the recommended sources are works by Laura Field of Pennsylvania State University.

25. Dr. Kathleen Weiss Hanley is associate professor of finance at the University of Maryland at College Park, School of Business and Management. Among her published works are "The Underpricing of IPOs and the Partial Adjustment Phenomenon," *Journal of Financial Economics*, February 1995, pp. 239–257.

26. A comprehensive review of proposed rules, as well as currently enforceable rules, regarding road shows may be reviewed at the SEC's Web site, www.sec.gov.

27. Scott Ehrens, an equity analyst at Bear Stearns & Co., initiated coverage of Freemarkets on December 10, 1999, in a 25-page report with a 12-month target price of $300. The company had just completed its IPO the previous day in a deal managed by Goldman Sachs and Morgan Stanley Dean Witter. Although the stock price climbed above $350 before the end of 1999, within three months it was changing hands at less than $200 a share, or about 30 percent less than its first-day close.

28. Technology issues and privacy matters are critical topics for regulators, as is evidenced by the remarks, comments, and speeches of many SEC commissioners.

29. Commissioner Laura S. Unger has commented extensively on the topics of technology, on-line IPO distribution, and road shows. Among her published remarks are a speech before the Ninth Annual New England Securities Law Conference on June 11, 1999, and remarks before the San Diego Securities Institute on January 27, 2000.

30. While it has not yet been attempted, at least on a widespread basis, it may be interesting to see if a two-tiered lockup agreement would be

proposed and upheld in the courts if challenged. In this case, venture-capital firms may be permitted to exit at one definite point, employees at another, and management at a third.

31. Michael McBain and David Krause in the *Journal of Business Venturing,* 1989.

32. Search through Thomson Financial Securities Data's New Issues database.

33. Analysis through Thomson Financial's database.

Chapter 4

34. In September 1998, John Steffens, head of Merrill Lynch's private equity group (i.e., the retail brokerage arm), remarked, "The do-it-yourself model of investing, centered on Internet trading, should be regarded as a serious threat to Americans' financial lives." The Motley Fool, a popular financial Web site, responded that on-line trading is bad for Merrill, since the company would likely lose millions of dollars in revenues as some of its 8.4 million retail clients moved some of their assets to lower cost firms.

35. One of the more excessive signs of the era before on-line trading was Merrill Lynch's charge of $4.95 for handling and mailing a customer's trade confirmation. Hence, Wall Street's largest full-service broker was levying a fee just for mailing statements that was nearly equal to, if not more than, what some deep-discount brokers were charging for actual trades.

36. Despite the proliferation of on-line trading, the recruitment of brokers (i.e., financial consultants, or, in reality, sales personnel) is still strong. Now, instead of merely offering brokerage activity, firms are seeking to portray themselves as comprehensive in nature, offering financial services from estate planning and tax consultation to mortgages and related matters.

37. "Sale of IPO Stocks for Fast Profit Marks Turnaround," *The Wall Street Journal*, February 3, 2000, p. C1, by Randy Smith.

38. "Underwriter Reputation, Initial Returns, and the Long-Run Performance of IPO Stocks," by Richard B. Carter, Frederick H. Dark, and Ajai K. Singh, associate professors of finance, College of Business, Iowa State University, *Journal of Finance*, Vol. 53, February 1998.

39. 7 percent gross spreads, which are composed of management fees, underwriting fees, and selling concessions, from IPOs in 1999 exceeded $3 billion.

40. When Netscape went public in August 1995, Hambrecht & Quist reported that it was receiving more than 1000 calls per day from

investors seeking to buy shares of the deal. While it is likely that some retail investors managed to crack their way inside, the more representative investor was the likes of NBC News anchor Tom Brokaw, who reportedly was able to purchase 1000 shares at the offering price. More recently, IPO compensation for celebrity endorsements of e-commerce sites raised eyebrows when it was reported that William Shatner received options to purchase 100,000 shares of Priceline.com for his appearance as a Priceline spokesman.

41. Wit Capital's senior executives owned a significant stake in the company's common shares. For example, in early 2000, reports showed that Robert Lessin controlled 6.4 percent of the firm's shares, valued at some $75 million, while founder Andrew Klein had a 6 percent stake valued at about $71 million.

42. Reports on CNET: "Efforts to Open IPOs to Individuals Stall," Dawn Kawameto, March 10, 2000.

43. E*OFFERING CEO search is now moot as E*OFFERING entered into an agreement with E*TRADE and WitSound/View Corp. whereby E*OFFERING is transferring its retail accounts to E*TRADE. Shareholders of E*TRADE approved the transaction in October 2000.

44. Schwab limits with respect to IPO allocations were reported in *The Wall Street Journal*'s "Deals & Deal Makers" section.

Chapter 5

45. For purposes of this *Inside IPOs*, IPO proceeds are considered to be just the portion of the deal sold in U.S. capital markets. However, a significant number of IPOs sell part of their deal to foreign markets. For example, UPS' $5.47 billion deal, when generally reported in the U.S. press, often excludes the more than $1 billion sold abroad to European, Asian, and other investors. In total, of the nearly $69 billion worth of IPOs sold in the United States during 1999, another $30 billion in issuance from those deals was sold abroad.

46. Another aspect that suggests a heightened interest in foreign investing relates to the demographic shift of global investors during the 1990s, similar to that of their U.S. counterparts. In this regard, rising incomes, higher educational achievements, and more entrants into the workforce have boosted the fortunes of many equities trading overseas.

47. Worldwide, there are probably several dozen local stock exchanges, from the Budapest Stock Exchange to one operating in Zanzibar. The issue of liquidity for IPOs in various emerging markets is of significantly greater concern than it is for more developed markets.

48. It is generally conceded that recent IPO activity has been marked by significantly more companies with shorter track records, compared with companies that went public 10 or even 5 years earlier. One additional factor investors should consider is the experience of management. Specifically, since many recent IPOs have their original founders at the helm, none of whom have experienced a downturn or recession in today's bullish cycle, the commercial mettle of these firms may yet be tested.

49. Another issue related to listings is the expense associated with the privilege of being able to have one's shares on a listed exchange. For example, Packaging Corp. of America paid a filing fee of $466,100 to have the shares from its $555 million offering trade on the New York Stock Exchange. Alternatively, Tel1European Holdings, which completed it $493 million IPO in early 2000, was charged just $35,000 to have its shares trade through NASDAQ.

50. Response from inquiry by NYSE's communications group.

51. Tim Loughran and Jay R. Ritter, "The Operating Performance of Firms Conducting Seasoned Equity Offerings," *Contemporary Finance Digest*, Spring 1998, Vol. 2, No. 1.

52. It is likely that the large number of IPOs now trading at over $100 per share may be a factor in the growth of so-called penny stocks. Nearly 10 percent of all IPOs completed between January 1999 and March 2000 were trading above $100 per share. In contrast, of the 447 IPOs completed between January 1998 and March 1999, only 10, or 2 percent, were trading at $100 or more at the end of the first quarter of 1999.

53. Typically, venture capital financing involves funding at various "stages" wherein there are usually five levels of activity. The stages are the "other stage," "early stage," "expansion stage," "later stage," and, finally, "buyout or acquisition stage."

54. William L. Magginson and Kathleen A. Weiss, "Venture Capitalist Certification in Initial Public Offerings," *Journal of Finance*, Vol. 46 No. 3, July 1991, pp. 879–903.

55. Information regarding the Baker Communication Fund, which operates as a private buyout firm, was derived from Thomson's VenturExpert. On the basis of the latest reports, the fund's size is in excess of $400 million. Besides its investment in Akamai Technologies, among its other notable investments are Advanced Switching Communications and Sequoia Software. The fund's phone number is 212-848-2000.

56. Akamai Technologies represents the largest individual holding for MIT's $509 million investment portfolio. At the end of 1999, no less than 32 percent of the institution's equity holdings were in this single

stock. The next largest of MIT's individual holdings was its $88 million holding in Analog Devices. That amount represented about a 17 percent share of the institution's portfolio.

57. Burton G. Malkiel, "Tracking Stocks Are Likely to Derail," *The Wall Street Journal*, February 14, 2000, p. A42.

Chapter 6

58. Insurance company IPOs were in the headlines in early 2000 as John Hancock Financial Services completed a $1.5 billion offering and Metropolitan Life announced its intention to scale back its proposed IPO from a preliminary $5 billion to an anticipated $2 billion.

59. Incidentally, both Netscape and UUNET Technologies were subsequently acquired. Netscape was taken over by America Online in November 1998 in a $4.1 billion transaction, while UUNET was purchased by MFS Communications (which became MCI Worldcom through several additional acquisitions) in April 1996 for $2.1 billion.

60. One factor affecting some retailers has been the shift by consumers away from specialty stores to midmarket discounters such as Kohl's or Target Stores. Perhaps the most notable development here is the fact that Toys 'R' Us, once the nation's largest toy retailer, now ranks second to Wal-Mart.

61. One of the classic IPO roller-coaster stories is that of Oxford Healthcare. The Connecticut-based HMO debuted at $15 per share in August 1991 and in the next few years became a high flyer, reaching as high as $77.88 in October 1997. But rising expenses and lower earnings drove the stock down to the single digits in the summer of 1998, although it recovered to the mid-teens by early 2000. Still, from the time Oxford first began trading, the stock has risen some 680 percent.

62. ENI, formerly known as Enel Società per Azioni, is one of Italy's largest electric utilities. The offering, which sold $1.1 billion in the United States and another $15.3 billion, ranked as the largest Italian offering in U.S. capital markets and the second largest IPO worldwide.

Chapter 7

63. Over the past few years, the number of individual book managers who have handled at least one IPO has contracted. The information is based upon the fact that in the mid-1990s more than 150 managers worked on IPOs, compared with fewer than 100 in 1999.

64. The data relating to proceeds for an individual book manager include those issues which were previously handled by firms that may have been acquired by a particular book manager. For example, totals for Deutsche Bank include the IPOs completed by Alex. Brown & Sons, which the former acquired.

65. Autex, a division of Thomson Financial, tracks block trade activity. Further information on the company may be obtained on its home page, located at www.tfautex.com.

66. Acquisitions have played a key part in the strategy of many underwriters. Among notable deals are BankAmerica's $470 million purchase of Robertson Stephens in June 1997, Fleet Financial's $1.5 billion takeover of Quick & Reilly in September 1997, and PaineWebber's October 1994 acquisition of KidderPeabody for $670 million.

67. Goldman Sachs is located at 85 Broad Street, New York, NY 10004. The company's home page is located at www.gs.com. The company is publicly traded on the New York Stock Exchange under the ticker symbol "GS."

68. Merrill Lynch's address is World Financial Center, New York, NY 10281. Merrill's home page may be found at www.ml.com. The shares trade on the NYSE under the symbol "MER."

69. Morgan Stanley Dean Witter is located at 1585 Broadway, New York, NY 10036, and its home page is found at www.msdw.com. The company is publicly traded under the ticker symbol "MWD."

70. Salomon Smith Barney is a unit of Citicorp that trades on the NYSE under the symbol "C." The firm is headquartered at 388 Greenwich Street, New York, NY 10013. The company's Web site is found at www.smithbarney.com.

71. JP Morgan is located at 60 Wall Street, New York, NY 10260. The company's common shares are traded on the NYSE under the ticker symbol "JPM," and the firm's home page is www.jpmorgan.com.

72. Donaldson, Lufkin & Jenrette's headquarters is located at 277 Park Avenue, New York, NY. The company shares trade on the NYSE under "DLJ," and the firm's home page is www.dlj.com.

73. Lehman Brothers' headquarters is found at Three World Financial Center, New York, NY 10285. The company trades under the symbol "LEH" on the NYSE, and the firm's home page is www.lehman.com.

74. Credit Suisse First Boston's headquarters is at 11 Madison Avenue, New York, NY 10010. The firm's home page is www.csfb.com. The company is not publicly traded in the United States.

75. Bear Stearns' headquarters at this time is located at 245 Park Avenue, New York, NY 10167. The stock trades on the NYSE under the ticker "BSC," and the firm's Web site is www.bearstearns.com.

Chapter 8

76. Constance Bagley and Robert Tomkinson, "Internet Is Seeing Its Share of Securities Offerings," *National Law Journal*, February 2, 1998.

77. Wilcox and Williams's work was a finance working paper written at the University of California, Berkeley, RPF-283, entitled "Predicting Excess Returns with Public and Insider Information: The Case of Thrift Conversions," September 1998.

78. Information on the *Small Bank Newsletter* may be obtained at 1-888-814-7575.

79. 3Com's spin-off of its Palm unit was one of the more highly anticipated offerings in the past several years. The transaction was a two-stage procedure whereby 3Com sold shares in its subsidiary to the investing public in early 2000 and then distributed another portion to 3Com shareholders later that year.

80. John R. Hayes, "Pepsi's Panacea: The Track Record on Split-ups," *Forbes*, October 10, 1997.

81. Information about the *Spinoff Report* may be found at www.spinoff-stocks.com or by contacting the company directly at spinoffs@mindspring.com or by mail at 730 24th Street, Suite 703, Washington, DC 20037. The company is affiliated with the company Incubator.

82. Safeguard Scientific is located at 800 The Safeguard Building, 435 Devon Park Drive, Wayne, PA 19087. The firm's phone number is 610-293-0600. Total revenues for the company for the year ending December 31, 1999, rose 29 percent to $2.95 billion, with net income increasing 12 percent to $123 million. Insiders own 21 percent of the outstanding shares, while institutions account for 31 percent.

83. CMGI's headquarters is at 100 Brickstone Square, Andover, MA 01810. The company's phone number is 978-684-3600. Insiders control 30 percent of outstanding common shares, while institutions own 30 percent of CMGI's shares.

Chapter 9

84. Readers seeking further information on specific mutual funds may consult a variety of information providers. Morningstar is an excellent source of performance statistics, information on managerial tenure, and related data on the mutual fund sector. The company's Web site is www.morningstar.com. Also, many business and financial publications, such as *Barron's,* publish quarterly mutual fund surveys with in-depth analysis of the mutual fund industry.

85. Kathy Smith comments in *Forbes*.com, January 24, 2000.

86. The fact that many closed-end funds trade at a discount to their net asset value is perhaps a clear sign that, for investors seeking short- to-intermediate-term gains, open-ended mutual funds are clearly preferred.

87. Renaissance Capital Growth's performance figures were derived from Yahoo!'s Finance page.

Chapter 10

88.. It has long been a contentious point in the financial community that there are few outright sell recommendations among Wall Street analysts. Even if a company's stock were to nosedive, more often than not it would be common for an analyst to couch his or her opinion by revising a "buy:" opinion to "long-term accumulate" or "hold," but rarely "sell."

Chapter 11

89. Capital-gains tax rates around the world vary dramatically. For example, in such nations as Belgium, Germany, Singapore, and South Korea, as well as in Hong Kong, there is no capital-gains tax. At the other end of the scale, France's capital-gains tax rate is 18.1 percent, Canada's rate is 23.8 percent, and in Italy the amount levied is 25 percent. The highest rate for assets held for more than one year, according to the American Council for Capital Formation, is the United States' present 28 percent rate.

INDEX